CHICANOS AND NATIVE AMERICANS

CHICANOS
AND
NATIVE AMERICANS

The Territorial Minorities

Rudolph O. de la Garza
Z. Anthony Kruszewski
The University of Texas at El Paso

Tomás A. Arciniega
California State University, San Diego

A SPECTRUM BOOK

Prentice-Hall, Inc., *Englewood Cliffs, New Jersey*

Library of Congress Cataloging in Publication Data

DE LA GARZA, RUDOLPH O   comp.
    Chicanos and native Americans: the territorial
minorities.

    Some of the chapters are revisions of papers
presented at the Workshop on Southwest Ethnic Groups:
Sociopolitical Environment and Education at the
University of Texas at El Paso, July 27–29, 1972.
    Includes bibliographical references.
    1. Mexican Americans—Addresses, essays, lectures.
2. Indians of North America—Addresses, essays, lec-
tures.   I. Kruszewski, Z. Anthony, joint comp.
II. Arciniega, Tomás A., joint comp.   III. Workshop
on Southwest Ethnic Groups: Sociopolitical Environment
and Education, University of Texas at El Paso, 1972.
IV. Title.
E184.M5D39   1973   301.45′16′872073   73–10396
ISBN   0-13-129791-0
ISBN   0-13-129783-X (pbk.)

Excerpt from T. C. McLuhan, *Touch the Earth: A Self-Portrait of Indian Existence*
(copyright © 1971 by T. C. McLuhan) used by permission of E. P. Dutton & Co., Inc.
(Outerbridge & Lazard, Inc.).

"New Way, Old Way," by David Martin Nez, used by permission of the author,
former student The Institute of American Indian Arts, Santa Fe, New Mexico, a
Bureau of Indian Affairs School.

The use of the hyphen in the word "Mexican American" has been determined
by the publisher as follows: when used as a noun there is no hyphen; when
used as an adjective, there is a hyphen.

Dedication

To those who came before us and gallantly fought for freedom, justice, and dignity, and to those who without regard to hardships and obstacles are implementing and guarding these freedoms.

Dedication

Acknowledgment

This book resulted from the Workshop on Southwest Ethnic Groups: Sociopolitical Environment and Education at The University of Texas at El Paso, July 27–29, 1972. Some of the chapters included here are revisions of papers presented at this workshop, and others were commissioned for the volume. This workshop was sponsored by The Cross-Cultural Southwest Ethnic Study Center at The University of Texas at El Paso, which is funded by The Spencer Foundation of Chicago and co-directed by Professor Jacob Ornstein of the Departments of Modern Languages and Linguistic Studies and Professor Z. Anthony Kruszewski of the Department of Political Science at the University of Texas at El Paso. Grants from the Gulf Oil Education Fund and the Office of the Vice President for Academic Affairs of the University of Texas at El Paso directly supported the workshop. The Center is devoted to cross-cultural and interdisciplinary ethnic research in the humanities, social sciences, and education.

The editors would like to acknowledge the help of The Cross-Cultural Southwest Ethnic Study Center for the clerical and financial support granted in preparation of this book, but first and foremost express their gratitude to its Senior Secretary, Sarah E. Boyer, and Librarian, Shirley C. Coit, for their editorial help and devoted effort in coordinating various phases involved in preparation of this manuscript and organization of the workshop from which it originated. Both tasks required countless hours of their swift and expert attention and initiative.

Biographical Notes on the Editors

Rudolph O. de la Garza. Ph.D., University of Arizona. Assistant Professor of Political Science at The University of Texas at El Paso. Dr. de la Garza's interests lie in comparative and minority politics. He has published on Mexican legislative behavior and is currently researching Chicano political behavior. He has participated in numerous conferences on Chicanos and is a consultant to a special program to prepare teachers of Mexican-American students. He has served two years as Student Affairs Officer in the U. S. Information Agency in Cochabamba, Bolivia. Dr. de la Garza is a member of the Board of Advisors and Research Associate of The Cross-Cultural Southwest Ethnic Study Center.

Z. Anthony Kruszewski. Ph.D., The University of Chicago. Professor of Political Science and Co-Director of the Cross-Cultural Southwest Ethnic Study Center at the University of El Paso. His interests lie in the general field of cross-national political institutions and behavior and the specialized fields of social and economic stratification, political development and modernization, and ethnic politics. Dr. Kruszewski's research activities have included communication research at The University of Chicago, Human Relations Area Files research on area monographs, and socioeconomic research as a visiting scholar in the Center of Sociology and History of Culture of the Polish Academy of Sciences. His writings include books, monographs, and articles on socioeconomic and cultural change and political development. In the past academic year he has participated in two invitational conferences on "Basic Research in Race and Ethnicity" organized by the Ford Foundation.

Tomás A. Arciniega. Ph.D., University of New Mexico. Dean, School of Education, California State University, San Diego. His interests are in the field of Educational Administration. Dr. Arciniega's publications have been primarily in educational administration, international education, and Mexican-American education. He is a member of the Board of Advisors of The Cross-Cultural Southwest Ethnic Study Center and a former Special Adviser to the President of UT El Paso for Disadvantaged.

Contents

CHICANOS AND NATIVE AMERICANS

Introduction

Events of the 1950s and 60s forced many Americans to realize that for many of their fellow citizens, the "American Dream" had been a living nightmare. Sheriff Bull Conners and his dogs and fire hoses; Lester Maddox and his ax handle, the savage murders of Black and White civil rights workers; the chains, bricks, and callousness with which Mayor Daley and the citizens of Cicero greeted the Reverend Martin Luther King, Jr.; the riots in New York, Detroit, Los Angeles, and elsewhere; the murders of Martin Luther King, Jr., and of Freddie Hampton—these and other events forced all but the most extreme racists to admit that American society had failed its Black members. By 1968, 63 percent of the American public agreed that "until there is justice for minorities, there will not be law and order." Fifty-eight percent agreed that "America has discriminated against Negroes for too long."

Changes in governmental policies reflected these attitudes. Major civil rights legislation was enacted, and the Department of Justice devoted considerable time and energy to achieve compliance. Programs such as Job Corps, Model Cities, and VISTA were designed to aid the poor and provide them access to sympathetic government agencies.

It is now clear that the events of the past two decades have yielded mixed results. Major legislative and legal battles have been won, but the actual long-range results of these victories are unclear. As early as 1965, 45 percent of the American public, especially the white sector, felt that integration was being pushed too fast. Public dissatisfaction with the demands of Blacks and other groups played a major role in President Nixon's narrow victory in 1968, and the Nixon administration has responded to and fueled the public mood by virtually ignoring the needs and demands of the Black people. Given that Blacks voted against President Nixon by a 4 to 1 margin in 1972, there is little

1

reason to expect the administration's policies to change during the next four years.

An unanticipated but potentially beneficial result has been the phoenix-like rise of cultural nationalism and political militancy within the Mexican-American and Native-American communities. Native Americans for centuries and Mexican Americans for over a century have been the objects of scorn and ridicule, of prejudice and discrimination, of abuse and violence. Initially, both communities tried to fight off their white oppressors, but the invaders almost always triumphed. The protests and anger of these communities was effectively stifled for decades, and it was not until the 1960s that the Chicano and Native American once again physically protested in an organized manner the discrimination, abuse, and violence inflicted upon them by the dominant society. Impressed by the American public's initial support for Black civil rights and by the apparent concessions made to Blacks following the riots, some Native Americans and Chicanos began to emulate the Black model.

The Chicano movement began much as had the Black movement in the 1950s. The first issue attacked was one of blatant injustice, the slavelike treatment of migrant farm workers. In California, Cesar Chavez brought years of community organizing experience, a devotion to nonviolence, and a tireless spirit to the fields. He and his fellow farm workers, with the support of sympathizers nationwide, won major victories in their battle against corporate farm interests. The battle continues, however, with the result still in doubt.

Following the Black model, the Chicano movement quickly escalated to militancy and physical confrontations. In Colorado, Rodolfo "Corky" Gonzalez founded the Crusade for Justice. The Crusade provides a variety of much-needed services to Denver Chicanos, and it has also shown itself willing to defend with force if necessary the interests of the community against perceived injustices perpetrated by Denver police and other authorities. Reies Lopez Tijerina, in New Mexico, protested the loss of lands given to early Spanish settlers by the kings of Spain and guaranteed by the Treaty of Guadalupe Hidalgo, and led his followers on the now-famous Tierra Amarilla "Courthouse Raid." In Los Angeles, the Chicano Moratorium in protest against the Vietnam war resulted in confrontations with the police, mass arrests, and the death of Ruben Salazar, a Chicano news correspondent.

The violence and confrontations produced a few concrete benefits, and Chicano leaders channeled their energies toward more traditional political activities. Founded in 1970 by José Angel Gutiérrez, La Raza Unida political party had won numerous local elections and established itself as an important force in Texas politics by 1972. In the gubernatorial race of that year, La Raza Unida won over 200,000 votes from traditional Democratic voters. This impressive showing must be interpreted as a warning—either Texas Democrats will become responsive to the Mexican-American community or they will lose more and more of their Mexican-American supporters to La Raza Unida. Strongest in Texas, La Raza Unida is also active throughout the Southwest and has fielded candidates for local and state offices in Arizona, California, and Colorado. Although many older Mexican Americans refused to support the earlier tactics of the militants, they appear much more enthusiastic in their support for La Raza Unida. It is obvious that today this party has support from all sectors of the Mexican-American community.

Unlike the Mexican American, Native Americans have a long history of protesting the treatment they have received at the hands of government agencies. Originally, each tribe defended its own interests, but more recently intertribal associations have been formed out of the recognition that government policies affected all tribes adversely. Founded in 1944, The National Congress of American Indians sought to insure that "Indians themselves could freely express their views and wishes on national legislation and policy."

Nonetheless, decision makers ignored the needs and petitions of the Native American, and like the Black and Chicano, he began to defend his rights physically and resist continued injustices. In 1964, The National Indian Youth Council led hundreds in the fish-ins in Washington state that resulted in massive arrests, violence, and litigation. In California, a group of Indians took over Alcatraz and held it for over a year. In November 1972, the anger and frustration of the Native American became manifest when hundreds of Indians representing tribes from across the nation gathered in Washington D.C. to meet with government officials to discuss Indian policy. Shortly after their arrival, they took over the "Native American Embassy of Washington" —the Bureau of Indian Affairs—and vowed to remain there until the White House responded to their twenty demands. In February 1973, members of the American Indian Movement captured Wounded Knee South Dakota, the site of the 1890 massacre of hundreds of Sioux, and held the residents captive to insure that government officials would recognize the depth of their anger and deal in good faith with their demands. Indicative of the AIM's militancy was a sign on the door of the Wounded Knee trading post: "We can only die once, so let's die here together. Wounded Knee again."

As the political behavior of these two groups has changed over the last decade, the academic world has demonstrated a renewed interest in them; unfortunately, it has shown itself ill-prepared to understand the relationship of American society to the Native American and Chicano. Scholars, bound by the traditions of their academic disciplines, their vision distorted by their unarticulated biases, have been slow to recognize that Chicanos and Native Americans are not foreigners and that frameworks for understanding the relationships of immigrant groups to the American policy are incapable of explaining the relations of Native Americans and Chicanos to Anglo-American society.

Anglo-American scholars and policymakers have shown an inability to appreciate the uniqueness of the Chicano and Native-American experience. Studies of Native Americans have either romanticized them or concluded that Indian values would succumb to Anglo influences and thus the "Indian problem" would soon disappear. The Bureau of Indian Affairs has implemented policies designed to accelerate the "Americanization" of the Native American. Scholars have viewed the Chicano in the same light. They assume the Chicano to be the *pelado* described by Samuel Ramos and explain his misfortunes in terms of a "folk culture." Policymakers, especially educators, have followed a similar pattern: they too have designed remedial programs for the "culturally deprived" [sic] Chicano in the expectations that these programs would correct the "Mexican problem."

Chicanos and Native Americans have successfully, but at great human cost, resisted the efforts to Americanize them. Indeed, with few exceptions, social scientists have been amazed at the tenacity of tribalism, language, and other cultural values within these communities. Unable to understand the roots of these cultural patterns and their importance to the Chicano and Native American, academics have authored substantial amounts of literature that distort the values and behavioral patterns of these communities, and these studies have been instrumental in legitimizing racist stereotypes that are used to justify the continued oppression of these people.

An equally serious error is that scholars have ignored or denied the relationship that exists between the Chicano and Native American. The Chicano is *mestizo*—part Indian, part Spanish—and shares in the heritage of the Native American. Chicano leaders emphasize the union of the two races and thus acknowledge their common bond. That Native-American militants share this view is evidenced in the words of Mad Bear Anderson, a leader of the Alcatraz takeover: "The only people who have a right to live on Alcatraz are the Indians and the Chicanos."

In recent years Chicano, Native-American, and Anglo-American scholars have begun producing a body of literature challenging the validity of former studies and suggesting new perspectives from which to interpret the Chicano and Native-American experience in the United States. This reinterpretation suggests the impact of minority students in graduate programs. Established scholars, influenced by the negative reaction of Chicano and Native-American students to the traditional literature, began reexamining their approaches, and together minority students and concerned, responsive Anglo-American academics have generated a new approach to the study of Chicanos and Native Americans in U.S. society. Although this literature is growing rapidly, there remain many questions to be asked and answered. It is hoped that this book will suggest directions for future research even as it attempts to respond to existing questions.

This volume focuses on both Chicanos and Native Americans because the editors believe that they share a common relationship with Anglo-American society—a relationship no other ethnic or racial group shares. This is not to imply that Chicanos and Native Americans are alike in all respects; rather it is to emphasize that their experience with Anglo-American institutions differs qualitatively from the experiences of other American ethnic peoples.

The most fundamental difference is that Native Americans and Chicanos are this nation's only territorial minorities. Both were here first. Both had well-developed, viable institutions and societies before the Anglo arrived, and both have roots that go deeper than any planted by the Anglo. The Chicano and Native American did not immigrate to this nation; on the contrary, they fought to protect their lands from Anglo invaders. They were defeated, but they did not abandon their claims to the land nor did they forsake their cultural heritage. In effect, Anglo Americans imposed colonial rule upon the Native American and Chicano peoples.

The significance of this common experience is difficult to exaggerate. Although the immigrants came to the United States prepared to become part of the American way of life, Native Americans and Chicanos have fought—and continue to fight—against joining the mainstream. While immigrants pledged to become "good Americans," the United States government pledged through treaties to protect the rights of the Chicano and Native American. This is the foundation upon which Red Power and Chicano demands are made, and it is from this perspective that the Native-American and Chicano movement must be analyzed. Native Americans are claiming their lands and rights as guaranteed in numerous treaties and the Constitution. Chicanos are insisting that the letter and intent of the treaty of Guadalupe Hidalgo be honored and that their rights as citizens be respected.

Although Chicanos and Native Americans are the nation's only territorial minorities, it would be incorrect to assume that they are identical in all other respects. Culturally, they are quite distinct, even though the Chicano is part Indian. Politically, they confront different challenges. The great majority of Chicanos are urban residents and over 70 percent live in the five Southwestern states of California, Texas,

Arizona, Colorado, and New Mexico. Native-American reservations can be found from Alaska to Mississippi, but their urban colonies are growing at a rapid rate.

In sum, these are two culturally distinct groups, and they confront similar, but not identical, problems in American society. They do share a common bond, however—both were defeated by the Anglo but neither has given up claims to the lands they settled or the institutions and languages developed prior to the Anglo-American invasion. The editors believe that this common experience unites Chicanos and Native Americans, and that as territorial minorities they must be viewed separately from other ethnic or racial groups in American society.

This volume differs from others currently available in two respects. First, it is exclusively concerned with America's territorial minorities. Second, there is neither an attempt to discuss historical issues nor to cite again the depressing economic and educational statistics that describe these people. Rather it is our intent to bring together previously unpublished papers focusing on some of the major problem areas confronting the Chicano and Native American. The authors, moreover, are not uninvolved scholars who merely study minority groups. Many of them are Chicanos or Native Americans, all share a commitment to improve the position of these groups in American society, and the great majority actively participate in programs and activities designed to achieve this change.

This collection has been organized in a manner designed to indicate to the reader the interrelatedness of what are often seen as unrelated social, governmental, and educational phenomena. To this end, the concept of the political system has been utilized as the organizational framework. The readings are divided into two parts—*Political Inputs*, with a focus on the values, attitudes, and political behavior of Chicanos and Native Americans and *Political Outputs and Feedback*, which examines the outputs of the political system as they affect Native Americans and Chicanos. The core questions asked here are: How are policies made that affect these groups? What impact do these policies have on their target audiences?

The contributions herein have been restricted to recent unpublished materials in the belief that such studies will offer evidence and interpretations that will challenge existing generalizations (stereotypes?), and that this new information will provide a basis for reevaluating archaic frameworks and generalizations used to explain the place of Chicanos and Native Americans in United States society. It is our hope that these ends are served.

I. POLITICAL INPUTS: VALUES, ATTITUDES, AND POLITICAL BEHAVIOR

The Values and Attitudes of Chicanos and Native Americans

For centuries, Anglo Americans have felt it necessary to rationalize the relationship that exists between America's native peoples and the Anglo majority. As has been the case with all colonizing powers, the primary justification for conquest and continued domination has been founded on the alleged cultural superiority of the conquering white man. Whether in Algeria, India, Texas, or Arizona, the conqueror sees himself as virtuous, industrious, highly motivated, and God-fearing, and the colonized people as lazy by nature, morally degenerate, unintelligent, and inherently inferior. Given the differences between the two groups, the colonizer accepts the "white man's burden" and sets out to civilize the natives.

Chicanos and Native Americans have had their lands and rights taken from them by their Anglo-American conquerors, and have suffered the further humiliation of having this conquest justified on the basis of their own supposed cultural inferiority and decadence. Anglo Americans in the past took it as an obligation to educate Chicanos and Native Americans so that they would become motivated and hard-working, learn the meaning of democracy, and become good citizens. As Stan Steiner, Vine Deloria, Jr., Nick Vaca, Octavio Romano, and many others have shown, social scientists and educators rallied to provide "objective" studies documenting the bankrupt cultural values and innate inferiority of these groups. With this as proof, governmental agencies and the Anglo-American public were satisfied that their analysis was correct. The way to resolve the Mexican and Indian "problems" was to make them "Americans"; this has been the thrust of governmental policy, and it has been used to justify the systematic oppression of Chicanos and Native Americans and their cultures.

Scholars have recently begun to rethink these earlier interpretations, but they continue to show an insensitivity to the reality they examine and seem unable to shed the influences of their earlier biases. Herbert Hirsch documents the unwillingness or inability of social scientists to analyze the relationship of Anglo Americans to Chicanos, Native Americans, and other minorities from any but an Anglo perspective. Rather than criticize the minority group member for his cynicism as many scholars do, Professor Hirsch suggests that we indict American society for being racist and generating cynicism among large groups of citizens. Professors Brischetto and Arciniega, in later chapters, indicate that educators also share a racist stereotype view of minorities. Rather than viewing Chicano children as benefiting from their rich cultural heritage capable of making positive contributions to Anglo American society, educators instead design their programs to eliminate all traces of Chicano culture. The irony of these efforts, as shown in the chapter by Professors Wright, Salinas, and Kuvlesky, is that Chicano and Anglo children are similarly motivated, and that Chicanos consequently hold high professional ambitions. These authors warn that unless there are significant increases in opportunities for these highly motivated youth, there may be a "considerable and dramatic increase in forms of 'innovative' [i.e., militant] behavior."

Like the Chicanos, Native Americans enjoy a rich cultural heritage. They too have been forced to defend their values and practices against social science-supported pressures to mold them to the Anglo form. Professor John Haddox provides an overview of American Indian values and convincingly shows that the Native-American cultural system emphasizes justice, a sense of community, a deep religious commitment, and a sincere respect for one's fellow man in his environment. Nowhere is there evidence of the savagery ascribed to the Native American by early apologists for the government's "Indian policy." Professor Krueger's study documents the depth of the commitment to traditional values among Native Americans. Even where Anglo institutions have been imposed on them, tribal representatives continue to rely on tribal customs and employ consensual decision-making rather than majority rule when making important decisions affecting the community. Krueger warns, however, that continued penetration of tribal society by the urban culture is breaking down these commitments, and he suggests that tribal nationalism may be the only alternative for preserving Native-American culture. The willingness of Indians to defend their culture and rights is suggested in the chapter by Stauss, Chadwick, and Bahr, whose study indicates that a significant percentage of Native Americans have participated in Red Power protests, and that an even larger group is willing to participate in such activities in the future.

In summary, then, this section suggests that social scientists and educators are maintaining rather than destroying racist stereotypes of Chicanos and Native Americans. That these stereotypes have little foundation in fact is documented by several of the chapters presented here, as is the implication that there is a real potential for increased political militancy within both Chicano and Native-American communities unless there is a major positive change in the relationship between the Anglo majority and the Chicano and Native-American minorities. Above all, these chapters strongly argue that it is not cultural factors that prevent Native Americans and Chicanos from articulating their demands to the political system and from participating fully in American life—to the contrary, they have become so "Americanized" that they expect the Constitution to be upheld, and if it is not, it is likely that they will follow the example of great Americans and resort to unconventional behavior to insure that the Constitution is respected.

Herbert Hirsch

Political Scientists and Other Camarades: Academic Myth-Making and Racial Stereotypes

Introduction

. . . as might be expected, there occurs among the Mexican American a high incidence of political indifference, ignorance, timidity, and sometimes venality. V. O. Key, *Southern Politics*, p. 272.

Today the Negro's main disadvantage is the same as the Puerto Rican's and Mexican's: namely, that he is the most recent unskilled and hence relatively low-income, migrant to reach the city from a backward rural area. Edward C. Banfield, *The Unheavenly City*, p. 68.

By admitting to being Chicano, to being this new person, we lose nothing, we gain a great deal. Any Mexican American afraid to join with the Chicano cause can only be afraid for himself and afraid of the gringo. The black has faced this truth and found that he must make his way as a black or as nothing, certainly not as the white man's "nigger." We can no longer be the Anglo's "Pancho." Armando B. Rendon, *Chicano Manifesto*, p. 14.

The Chicano has begun to write his own history. The fabrication of the myth of the docile, sleepy "Pancho" under the cactus is a creation of gringo social scientists such as Edward Banfield and V. O. Key. In fact, the Chicano's history under Anglo rule has been a history of rebellion and political oppression, not a history of "indifference," "ignorance," "timidity," and "venality." From the first exploration of the Southwest to the Tierra Amarilla Courthouse incident and the emergence of Raza Unida Party, Chicanos have attempted to throw off

Herbert Hirsch, Department of Government, The University of Texas at Austin. This paper was prepared for delivery at the Workshop on Southwest Ethnic Groups: Sociopolitical Environment and Education, sponsored by The Cross-Cultural Southwest Ethnic Study Center, The University of Texas at El Paso, El Paso, Texas, July 27–29, 1972.

the Anglo yoke of oppression.[1] But the Anglo academic has not been content to misrepresent the individual and group psychology of the Chicano. He cannot even get his "facts" straight. Chicanos are not a rural people—nor are they recent migrants. Today, 80 percent of the Chicano people live in urban settings; in fact, they established cities as far back as 1718 when San Antonio was founded. Chicanos are not recent migrants to the cities of the Southwest—they founded those cities. It is no wonder, then, that the fabrications of Anglo academics have left a bitter taste in Chicano mouths. Even though political scientists have only recently discovered Chicanos, the basic thrust of their analyses remain the same.

Lured by the promise of increased government funds to sponsor research among the "culturally deprived" and armed with question-naires, cameras, and tape recorders, they have undertaken a massive invasion of ethnic communities throughout the United States and other so-called "underdeveloped" sections of the world. They come to these communities to observe and "systematically record" the way of life of these "strange" people. These observations in turn become "books by which future . . . [scholars] will be trained, so that they can come out to the reservations [barrios, hollows, or "ghettos"] years from now and verify the observations they have studied." [2] These activities then be-come the basis for competing theories of ethnic politics "testing whether this or that school can endure longest." [3] As Deloria notes, the battlefields upon which these intellectual wars are fought are the lives of the ethnic people.[4] In the Southwest, the battlefields are most often Chicano communities. Unfortunately, the only winners in these confrontations are the individual social scientists whose prestige, tenure, and monetary reward are dependent upon the acceptance by the aca-demic community of their respective "theories." The people studied usually receive nothing more than increased attention to and per-petuation of the stereotypic characteristics assigned to them by the invading academics.

The recent discovery of the Chicano by political scientists[5] has been

1. See Carey McWilliams, *North From Mexico* (New York: Greenwood Press, 1968), Armando B. Rendon, *Chicago Manifesto* (New York: Collier Books, 1971), and Nick Vaca, "The Mexican American in the Social Sciences, 1912–1970," *El Grito* (Part I, Spring 1970, pp. 3–24; Part II, Fall 1970, pp. 17–51).

2. Vine Deloria, Jr., *Custer Died for Your Sins: An Indian Manifesto* (New York: Avon, 1970), p. 84.

3. Ibid., p. 85.

4. Ibid.

5. According to Carlos Munoz, "Of all the social sciences, however, political science is perhaps the only discipline that has almost totally ignored the Chicano. . . ." Munoz, "Toward a Chicano Perspective of Political Analysis," *Aztlan*, I, No. 2 (Fall 1970), p. 18.

based, therefore, upon false and stereotypic characterizations left behind by previous generations of Anglo historians and sociologists. Because most of these authors found little previous writing on the Chicano, they usually assumed that the Chicano had done nothing to merit their interest. It followed that many of the books written carried subtitles such as *Mexican-Americans: An Awakening Minority* and *La Raza: Forgotten Americans*.[6] In fact, it was only the scholars and political authorities who had awakened. Ignoring the fact that the Chicano had been fighting for his land and dignity for many years, these scholars decided to ignore the past and rely on their own image of the Mexican.[7] This image was further proliferated in the media. Characters such as José Jimenez and Speedy Gonzales became popular, and movies such as *The Magnificent Seven* and *The Alamo* served to reinforce the stereotypes of the people of Aztlan.[8]

It is clear, therefore, that one of the major areas to be confronted in attempting to do research in ethnic communities is the legacy left by those who came before. To be sure, there are the usual problems one finds outlined in fieldwork manuals, but these pale into insignificance alongside the inadequate theory and insensitive stereotypic perceptions most researchers carry with them into the field.

Academic Theory and Racial Stereotypes

> In a hundred subtle ways, we have told people of all origins other than English that their backgrounds are somehow cheap or humorous. And the tragic thing is that this process has succeeded. Harold Howe II. "Cowboys, Indians, and American Education," address before the National Conference on Educational Opportunities for Mexican-Americans, Commodore Perry Hotel, Austin, Texas, April 25, 1968.

Social scientists are extensions of their socialization and experience. That they view ethnic communities through glasses tinted by years of middle-class academic socialization should not be surprising. Indeed, what is surprising is the unconscious nature of that view.

Recent critics of the dominant behavioral perspective agree that most social science theory rests upon epistemological assumptions re-

6. Julian Samora, ed., *La Raza: Forgotten Americans* (Notre Dame: University of Notre Dame Press, 1966); Manuel Servin, ed., *The Mexican-American: An Awakening Minority* (Beverly Hills, Cal.: Glencoe Press, 1970).

7. See McWilliams, *North From Mexico;* also Octavio Ignacio Romano-V., "The Anthropology and Sociology of the Mexican-Americans," in Octavio Ignacio Romano-V., ed., *Voices: Readings from El Grito* (Berkeley, Cal.: Quinto Sol Publications, 1971), pp. 26–39.

8. Thomas M. Martinez, "Advertising and Racism: The Case of the Mexican-American," in Romano-V, *Voices*, pp. 48–53.

garding the nature of man and his relationship to his environment.[9] General, abstract theories which ignore these assumptions and which are not designed with a particular contextual environment in mind are not necessarily generalizable to particular ethnic settings. According to Munoz:

> One can conclude that political science has not properly interpreted the reality of the Chicano experience. The social sciences as a whole have not provided us with sufficient empirical research about the structural conditions in the Chicano barrios. Consequently, the intensity of the urban problems which Chicanos are confronting have been little understood by the society at large. The principal reason for this lack of understanding is that what has been written about Chicanos has been based on a dominant Anglo perspective which has been predicated on the cultural values and norms of the dominant society.[10]

Thus, when socialization theorists speak about roles, values, beliefs, and attitudes, they often fail to identify the contextual environment involved. For example, David Easton and Jack Dennis,[11] Fred Greenstein,[12] and other scholars studying political socialization find, after examining the *content* of the political orientations of White middle-class children, that they are benevolently disposed toward political authority figures. Other scholars examining other populations—other cultures—have not been lucky enough to discover this same benevolence.[13] Examination of political socialization in south Texas yielded interesting results more similar to those found in this author's earlier

9. There is a great deal of discussion of this in the philosophy of science literature. For a recent admission by a psychologist, doubly significant because it represents a revision of his earlier work, see Richard S. Lazarus, *Personality* (Englewood Cliffs, N.J.: Prentice-Hall, 1971). Seymour L. Halleck, *The Politics of Therapy* (New York: Science House, 1971), p. 34, makes the same point regarding psychiatry; i.e., "Value systems, usually implicit rather than explicit, have always dominated the practices of the different schools of psychiatry."

10. Munoz, "Toward a Chicano Perspective," p. 21.

11. David Easton and Jack Dennis, *Children in the Political System* (New York: McGraw-Hill, 1969).

12. Fred I. Greenstein, *Children and Politics* (New Haven: Yale University Press, 1965).

13. See Dean Jaros, Herbert Hirsch, and Frederick J. Fleron, Jr., "The Malevolent Leader: Political Socialization in an American Sub-Culture," *The American Political Science Review* (June 1968), pp. 564–75; and Herbert Hirsch, *Poverty and Politicization: Political Socialization in an American Sub-Culture* (New York: The Free Press, 1971). There has been a recent increase in the number of good articles on Blacks in the United States. See, for example, the works of Edward Greenberg, "Children and Government: A Comparison Across Racial Lines," *Midwest Journal of Political Science* (May 1970), pp. 249–75, and Schley R. Lyons, "The Political Socialization of Ghetto Children: Efficacy and Cynicism," *The Journal of Politics* (May 1970), pp. 288–304.

study of Appalachian children. Compared to other cultural groups who have been asked to respond to measures of benevolence, Chicanos are much more cynical. (See Figure 1) In the Appalachian study we found that fully 48 percent of the respondents scored high on political cynicism.[14] This figure compares with the 56.6 percent of the Crystal City high school students. Compared to Lyons' sample of inner-city black students from Toledo, the Crystal City Chicanos are again the most cynical.[15]

FIGURE 1.   POLITICAL CYNICISM IN FOUR CULTURES:
GRADES 10, 11, 12

Cynicism	Inner City Blacks	Appalachian Whites	Crystal City Chicanos	National Sample
Low	26%	21%	2%	42%
Medium	50	31	42	50
High	24	48	56	8
Total %	100	100	100	100
N	380	54	108	1869
Blacks and Appalachian Whites			$D = .24, p < .01$	
Blacks and Chicanos			$D = .32, p < .001$	
Blacks and National Sample			$D = .16, p < .001$	
Appalachian Whites and Chicanos			$D = .19, p < .10$	
Appalachian Whites and National Sample			$D = .40, p < .001$	
Chicanos and National Sample			$D = .48, p < .001$	

The inner-city Black data are from Schley R. Lyons, "The Political Socialization of Ghetto Children: Efficacy and Cynicism," *The Journal of Politics* (May 1970), p. 295.

The SRC data and the Appalachian data have been previously compared in Dean Jaros, Herbert Hirsch, and Frederick J. Fleron, Jr., "The Malevolent Leader: Political Socialization in an American Sub-Culture," *The American Political Science Review* (June 1968), p. 570.

The only case in which the differences between the four cultures studied are not statistically significant involves the Appalachian whites and the Crystal City Chicanos. Figure 1 buttresses an argument that has been all but ignored by most socialization theorists, namely, that cultural differences have a tremendous impact upon the socialization process. Both the Appalachian and Crystal City samples are drawn from rural cultures that have been treated badly by the dominant political system. It is surprising that the black sample scored as low on

14. Jaros, Hirsch, and Fleron, "The Malevolent Leader," pp. 85–109.
15. Lyons, "The Political Socialization of Ghetto Children."

cynicism as it did in that it too has been subject to discrimination by the larger White society. When confronted with these findings, we were unable to find any but the most tentative and tenuous theoretical explanations in the literature—and most did not come from political scientists. For one possible explanation we went to Bronfenbrenner's argument that there are differences in the socialization processes in urban and rural contexts.[16] He suggests that rural families "lag behind" urban families because they are isolated from the "agents of change (e.g., public media, clinics, physicians, and counsellors." [17] This is not to say that such cultures do not change. Even a cursory glance at the history of these so-called "traditional" cultures reveals important adjustments to time and circumstance. One could hypothesize, however, that the rate of change is less dramatic in a rural than in an urban setting.[18] Yet Crystal City itself demonstrates the inadequacy of this theoretical explanation.

It is also possible to argue that in the last few years Blacks have seen the dominant White society make important and obvious overtures to erase its racist image. Such acts may have served to give some Blacks a feeling that government is working for them. It is also possible to argue as an adjunct hypothesis that the personalistic nature of politics in rural areas means that rural residents have more intimate personal contact with the primary political authority figures in their area. Thus, they may know them to be corrupt but also know that they are amenable to influence. They are, consequently, high in cynicism and also high in efficacy.[19]

This finding of high cynicism should not, it seems to us, be particularly startling. The usual contact the Chicanito and his parents have with the dominant system is rarely of a benevolent nature. Early in life they learn to be distrustful of anything that is controlled by Anglos. The Chicano is thus very likely to question the veracity of the declarations of White institutions. What is more, the already negative attitude of the child in early adolescence becomes intensified as he matures. This negative impression of Anglo society is the result of a variety of forces. In early childhood the family serves to socialize the child into the realities of life for a Chicano; it teaches the child to be cautious among the greedy Whites. His peers in and out of school merely reinforce this feeling. Finally, the child's experiences in a school dominated by Whites is often a final, solidifying force. He is likely to

16. Urie Bronfenbrenner, "Socialization and Social Class Through Time and Space," in Harold Proshansky and Bernard Seidenberg, eds., *Basic Studies in Social Psychology* (New York: Holt, Rinehart & Winston, 1965), p. 358.

17. Ibid., p. 356.

18. Romano-V, *Voices*, pp. 26–39.

19. Hirsch, *Poverty and Politicization*, pp. 144–49.

be ridiculed and punished by Anglo teachers and administrators for no other reasons than that he is a Chicano. This explanation does not adopt the usual political science method of explanation. Instead of asking what is wrong with the Chicanos of Crystal City because they are highly cynical, we accept as given the high cynicism and place no negative value judgment upon it. We do not blame the Chicano for being cynical. We blame the racism of the Anglo society. Moreover, we note that not only is cynicism justified, but that it has positive consequences. Here again we depart from the dominant form of explanation which usually tells us that cynicism is bad because it leads to lack of stability. We believe that lack of stability is exactly what is needed. The cynicism of the Chicano is manifested, we show, in willingness to use whatever means possible to overturn the repressive Anglo power structure. Cynicism, therefore, can be construed as a positive good for the Chicano community.

Researchers were caught totally unprepared for this kind of contradictory findings.[20] Previous theorizing based upon studies of predominantly white, middle-class children gave no hint as to what to expect when a culture is continually oppressed. For scholars to have concluded, therefore, that American children view political authority benevolently, and that those who manifest different orientations are somehow either "deviant" or "imperfectly socialized" [21] is to wrongly attribute negative characteristics to the indigenous Chicano or Appalachian White ethnic culture.

It does not, in the words of Barrera, Munoz, and Ornelas, "speak particularly well for the ability of 'impartial' social scientists to escape society's dominant myths." [22] Most social scientific research in ethnic communities has been a reflection of these dominant myths, whose political implications are basically counterrevolutionary. Thus, if one does not conform, or if one's culture is different, one is labeled as "deviant." Order is decreed as the natural way, while change, especially within ethnic communities, is viewed with a mixture of fear and

20. Greenberg, "Children and Government," p. 182.

21. That these terms are still in use among contemporary political scientists is evident. For a most conspicuous example, see Guiseppe DiPalma and Herbert McClosky, "Personality and Conformity: The Learning of Political Attitudes," *The American Political Science Review* (December 1970), pp. 1054–73. This article is filled with examples such as "Indeed, it is an argument of this paper that many people hold non-conforming attitudes not because they are led by superior sensitivity to weigh alternatives and to reject conventional views, but mainly because they have been so imperfectly socialized that they are either indifferent to many social issues or unable to recognize what the society believes [p. 1069]."

22. Mario Barrera, Carlos Munoz, and Charles Ornelas, "The Barrio as Internal Colony," in Harlan Hahn, ed., *People and Politics in Urban Society: Urban Affairs Annual Review*, 6 (1972), 12.

a desire to repress. If, however, change within ethnic culture is prescribed by the dominant culture, it is viewed from the perspective of another myth; i.e., the myth of cultural pluralism.

As perpetuated in the United States, this myth would have ethnic peoples believe that it is the "right" of all peoples to engage in political activity. In fact, cultural pluralism exists on only one level. There are, of course, numerous cultural groups residing within the territorial boundaries of this country. Yet this is not what is meant by cultural pluralism—or at least this is not what the rhetoric tells us. The melting-pot concept reigns supreme—assimilate, become Anglo, and be accepted. This, we submit, is a pattern of cultural domination that destroys ethnic identity and inculcates the most repressive of nonconscious ideologies—self-hate.[23] When one culture succeeds in socializing another to the extent that the other culture (usually an ethnic culture) believes in its own inferiority and incapacity for political action, it has succeeded in instilling a virulent form of self-racism.[24] This type of oppression involves less cost to the dominant culture than manifest oppression. Every time the dominant culture is forced to resort to arms to put down an indigenous uprising it expends certain valuable resources. It is much more efficient—i.e., involves less cost—if it can succeed in socializing large numbers of ethnic citizenry (and for that matter, dominant cultural citizenry) to believe not only that they are inferior and therefore must blindly and obediently defer to the dominant leadership, but that the members of the ethnic communities are themselves part and parcel of that dominant culture— that they are, in other words, Anglos. Thus, political activity is constrained by the Chicano's very perception of his own identity. The creation of these myths of objectivity and cultural pluralism has been aided and abetted by the social sciences. Again, Deloria's observations regarding the effect of anthropological investigation upon the Indians are relevant.

> Over the years anthropologists have succeeded in burying Indian communities so completely beneath the mass of irrelevant information that the total impact of the scholarly community on Indian people has become one of simple authority. Many Indians have come to parrot the ideas of anthropologists because it appears that the anthropologists know everything about Indian communities. Thus many ideas that pass for Indian thinking are in reality theories originally advanced by anthropologists and

23. Daryl J. Bem, *Beliefs, Attitudes and Human Affairs* (Belmont, Cal.: Brooks/Cole Publishing Co., 1970), pp. 89–99, defines a nonconscious ideology as "a set of beliefs and attitudes which . . . [a person] accepts implicitly but which remains outside his awareness because alternative conceptions of the world remain unimagined."

24. See Louis L. Knowles and Kenneth Prewitt, *Institutional Racism in America* (Englewood Cliffs, N.J.: Prentice-Hall, 1969).

echoed by Indian people in an attempt to communicate the real situation.[25]

Deloria goes on to note that "not even Indians can relate themselves" to the mythical creature created by the social scientists who redefine ethnic peoples in "terms white men will accept." [26] Simply substitute Chicano for Indian and the results are the same—the creation of a caricature!

It is, therefore, quite clear that social scientists are not prepared to deal realistically with the ethnic communities within which they attempt to carry out their studies. The "ideological background" of academics and the "ideology of research" [27] create a situation in which ethnic peoples are viewed as "objects for observation, . . . for experimentation, for manipulation, and for eventual extinction . . . [as] so many chessmen available for anyone to play with." [28] If this situation is to change, if academic social scientists are to be more than parasites feeding on ethnic communities, then the social scientist, rather than the communities they investigate, must change. Researchers must begin as empathic members of the ethnic culture within which they wish to carry out their studies.

Field Work and Socialization: Understanding Ethnic Cultures

The United States has been anything but a melting pot, because the gringo has purposely segregated, separated, and relegated the non-Anglo to an inferior and degraded status. Melting pot has meant surrender of one's past and culture to something euphemistically called American society or culture. The melting pot worked only for immigrants with a white skin who came to America. Regardless of nationality, these were willing to sacrifice a discrete identity in order to succeed and enter the polluted mainstream of American "can-doism"—can cheat, can swindle, can steal, can discriminate, can invade, can kill.

Armando B. Rendon, *Chicano Manifesto*, p. 107.

As noted earlier, most research in ethnic communities has been conducted by White middle-class academics who have no adequate basis upon which to interpret the data they have gathered. Entering the research setting with their bias intact, academics view ethnic communities as a "problem" because they are not part of the mainstream.

25. Deloria, *Custer Died for Your Sins*, p. 87.

26. Ibid., pp. 86–96.

27. Joan W. Moore, "Political and Ethical Problems in a Large-Scale Study of a Minority Population," in Gideon Sjoberg, ed., *Ethics, Politics, and Social Research* (Cambridge, Mass.: Schenkman, 1967), pp. 242–43.

28. Deloria, *Custer Died for Your Sins*, p. 86.

Therefore, when Anglo academics are confronted with questions regarding the nature of research problems within these communities they point to qualities indigenious to the particular culture. Research among Chicanos is a problem because they speak Spanish. Or, as one recent article on "Interviewing Mexican Americans" puts it:

> The biggest problem in the fieldwork was the marginal condition of the community being surveyed.[29]

Marginality in and of itself is not a problem in fieldwork. One might more accurately classify the problem as the middle-class Anglo socialization and lack of understanding on the part of the academic researcher. Hernandez is right when she states that

> While accurate, meaningful research findings do not necessitate childhood recollections of life in the barrio, it is essential to have a more than casual familiarity with, and sensitivity to, the human group being observed. This could be achieved over a prolonged period of time by a nonmember of the group.[30]

In other words, the prerequisite for the interpretation of data gathered in a community other than that within which one's own primary socialization occurred is a form of secondary socialization leading one to understand the new culture. This point is admirably addressed in a recent fieldwork manual, in which Rosalie Wax notes that

> Understanding is not an "operation" or a scientific instrument capable of generating fresh knowledge. It does not generate knowledge about a culture any more than being fluent in a language generates knowledge about it. Rather, it is a *precondition of research* in any social situation. This is more easily apprehended if we consider how understanding is acquired, namely, through socialization—either primary into one's native culture or the secondary (or resocialization) into an alien culture, or even vicarious socialization.[31]

The argument here is not that only those who are socialized within a particular culture are equipped to study it. On the contrary, secondary socialization is the necessary ingredient to prepare academic researchers to interpret data gathered within an ethnic culture. This means that the researcher must come to be accepted by that culture,

29. Donald M. Freeman, "A Note on Interviewing Mexican Americans," *Social Science Quarterly*, 49, 4 (March 1969), 913.

30. Deluvina Hernandez, *Mexican-American Challenge to a Sacred Cow*, Chicano Studies Center, Monograph No. 1, University of California, Los Angeles 1970, p. 15.

31. *Doing Fieldwork: Warnings and Advice* (Chicago: University of Chicago Press, 1971), p. 13.

not that he must deny his own identity. Rather, he must have a solid sense of his identity.

> . . . the wise and well-balanced fieldworker strives to maintain a conscious-ness and respect for *what he is* and a consciousness and respect for *what his hosts are.*
>
> Clumsy and amateurish attempts to alter or adjust his identity make him look silly, phony, and mendacious. Besides, many people will inter-pret his assurances that he is one of them as rude, presumptuous, insulting, or threatening.[32]

Acceptance and understanding are joint processes dependent upon both the researcher and the community to be observed. This should also lead to a concomitant lessening of what I call academic imperial-ism; that is, the tendency of academic researchers to exploit ethnic culture for their own ends without giving anything in return. What Deloria notes about Indian communities is applicable to Chicano communities. "We should not be objects of observation for those who do nothing to help us." [33] He proposes that each social scientist

> desiring to study a tribe should be made to apply to the tribal council for permission to do his study. He would be given such permission only if he raised as a contribution to the tribal budget an amount of money equal to the amount he proposed to spend on his study.[34]

If this proposal were followed, social scientists would become "produc-tive members" of the ethnic communities instead of what Deloria refers to as "ideological vultures." [35]

Immediate reaction will, of course, be to brand such proposals as "unrealistic." Yet it is not considered unrealistic for universities to take a percentage of "overhead" out of each grant given to an individual faculty member in return for which the university usually provides nothing more than office space which the faculty member already had anyway. Nor is it considered unrealistic for local school boards to scrutinize carefully every research proposal to be undertaken within its jurisdiction. This scrutiny assures the board that researchers are not asking "sensitive questions." In my experience, "sensitive ques-tions" may refer to anything from asking for the parent's political party identification to asking about attitudes toward the necessity for violent revolution to bring about change. If the institutions of the dominant culture have the right to scrutinize research proposals, then ethnic peoples have the same right. This assumes even greater im-

32. Ibid., p. 47.
33. Deloria, *Custer Died for Your Sins,* p. 98.
34. Ibid.
35. Ibid.

portance if we realize that social scientific knowledge is a two-edged sword. Data on such seemingly innocuous considerations as the political socialization of children may be used to design programs enabling the dominant culture to continue to control the subordinate, or it may be used by the oppressed to design programs to socialize their children to a strong sense of identity and a willingness to engage in political action to gain control over their own communities. One of our studies of Crystal City demonstrates the impact of resocialization to a sense of Chicano identity. Once we have succeeded in further identifying the process, our findings will be made known and available to Chicanos. These same findings, however, might theoretically be utilized by the dominant Anglo power structure to circumvent such programs. The ultimate use of such knowledge depends finally upon the holders of power. If you control your own community you use the knowledge to your benefit—if you do not, it will be used against you.

Social scientific knowledge is, therefore, inherently nonobjective. It is, furthermore, unrealistic for political scientists who favor, consciously or unconsciously, keeping the status quo, to protest loudly when others adopt what they perceive to be a less oppressive, more humanistic viewpoint.

In our case there was no problem with the Crystal City Chicanos. Our research team, composed of Anglo and Chicano professors and students, was basically sympathetic to the aims of the Chicano people. As such, any biases were evident and we did not attempt to hide them. We were welcomed into the research setting. All the problems we have experienced in attempting research in Texas have come from the suspicion, hostility, and ethnocentrism of the dominant Texas ethnic group—Anglos. Consequently we have not been able to conduct studies where Chicanos have not yet gained control of their own communities. The Anglo power structure apparently believes we are either investigators for HEW or the vanguard of an imagined Cuban plot to take over.[36]

The Chicano children we interviewed likewise showed no hostility.

36. Letter to the *Zavala County Sentinel*, May 20, 1971. Some excerpts from this letter are enlightening:

"Communism continues to be openly displayed and advocated among La Raza people in our school system. . . .

"Last week all junior high and high school students were given and ordered to fill out an hour-and-a-half questionnaire, and told to sign their names to it. . . .

"A questionnaire practically identical to this one was given by the militant and radical students at the University of Havana to all the school children of Cuba. From this questionnaire information, Fidel Castro was able to pick the leaders for his communist takeover of Cuba five years later.

"The question is—what will these La Raza people do in our school next?

"CITIZENS COMMITTEE TO FIGHT COMMUNISM IN CRYSTAL CITY"

Anglo children were markedly more hostile and extremely racist. For example, we received numerous questionnaires marked with obscene comments such as "Texas A & M; fuck U. T." written all over them. Anglo responses to a series of projective tests asking for an evaluation of Chicano organizations and individuals such as Cesar Chavez also revealed deep-seated hatred and violent racism. One seventh-grade Anglo male, when asked to identify "Huelga," "La Raza," "M.A.Y.O.," "Cesar Chavez," "Pachuco," and "Chicano," wrote, in large letters, "HATE" alongside each. An Anglo female, when asked to respond to a question regarding whether or not the community leadership was responsive to individuals problems, responded; "only if a Meskin complains." Other projective questions demonstrated deep-seated Anglo feelings of violence, with a continuous use of terms such as "dirty meskin," and "greaser" to refer to Chicanos. This hostility, which extends well beyond the boundaries of Crystal City, has been responsible for preventing our undertaking of longitudinal studies or investigation of Anglo communities.

In conclusion, it is time for all political scientists to become conscious of the basic assumptions underlying their research and interpretations of their data. In most cases the assumptions are clearly those of the dominant, white, middle-class culture. Research in which these underlying values remain unrecognized tend to reinforce racial and cultural stereotypes[37] and makes violence inevitable. We must begin, late as it is, to recognize the socio-racial-cultural-class differences within us, rather than attempting to cover them with myths, and build upon these to create a system which, in the words of John Schaar, moves toward a society based upon "equality of being," i.e., "which strives incessantly toward the widest possible sharing of responsibility and participation in the common life." [38] Social scientists should lead the way toward this goal rather than perpetuating academic myths and racial stereotypes.

37. Following Bem, *Beliefs, Attitudes and Human Affairs,* p. 9, I define stereotypes as "overgeneralized beliefs based on too limited a set of experiences."
38. John H. Schaar, "Equality of Opportunity and Beyond," in Roland Pennock, ed., *Equality: Nomos IX* (New York: Atherton, 1967), reprinted in Frederick M. Wirt and Willis D. Hawley, *New Dimensions of Freedom in America* (San Francisco: Chandler, 1969), p. 283.

Robert Brischetto / Tomás Arciniega

Examining the Examiners:
A Look at Educators' Perspectives
on the Chicano Student

Introduction

The issue of changing educational systems to meet more adequately the needs of minority students is one aspect of a more encompassing problem—the failure of U.S. society to face squarely the issue of equalizing opportunities for Blacks, Chicanos, and Indian Americans. Thus the problem of changing for the better what schools are doing to and doing with Chicano students becomes translated into an urgent need to achieve structural changes in the interrelated national, regional, and community subsystems of society.

The complexity and magnitude of that task will require careful and systematic appraisal of the educational terrain. The authors have been involved in one of several major incipient efforts that attempt such a systematic appraisal. This paper is designed to present the conceptual basis for the research effort in which we are engaged on our campus.

Toward a Systematic Analysis of Educational Approaches

One of the occupational hazards of being a disadvantaged minority group member in a post-industrial society is that one is subjected to a wide variety of tests, measures, and social research. The "disadvantaged pupil" is no exception to this rule. More than anyone else, he has been studied and restudied and tested and retested by social scientists,

Robert Brischetto, Department of Sociology, Our Lady of the Lake College, and Tomás Arciniega, Dean, School of Education, California State University, San Diego. This paper was presented at the annual meeting of the Rocky Mountain Social Science Association, Salt Lake City, Utah, April 27–29, 1972. This paper was part of a research project on the school systems of the Southwest, The Southwestern Schools Study, co-directed by the authors of this paper.

educators, and psychometrists. The sad truth of the matter is that all this studying and testing has not basically changed the position of the disadvantaged pupil in American society, and in some cases it has hurt more than helped. In spite of all the obstacles, some of these same "disadvantaged pupils" have gone on to get graduate degrees and are now critically examining the literature about them. Romano suggests that the situation is a unique one in the annals of American social science. "It is unique because a population heretofore studied is now studying the studiers." [1]

In this paper we shift the focus of research from the Chicano students, who have been subjected to so much scrutiny, to their educators, educational administrators, and educational policymakers who we feel should be the subject of more study. We hope to arrive at a classificatory scheme which identifies the different views that educators[2] have of the Chicano students and their culture. We will look further at the approaches to education that seem to follow from these views. Finally, we will examine the implications of these views for the formulation of public educational policy toward the Mexican American.

A basic assumption in our analysis is that the educator's evaluation of the *life styles*[3] that the Chicano student brings with him to school is a crucial factor in determining ultimately the educational program adopted for educating that student. Two basic controversies can be identified in the educational and social science literature on Chicano student life styles. The first concerns whether the consequences of Chicano life styles are seen as primarily functional or dysfunctional for the Chicano student. Or, to put it differently, the Mexican-American students' affiliation with his subculture and group can be viewed as having chiefly a positive or a negative[4] effect relative to the educational goals set for most students by the school. The second controversy

1. Octavio Romano-V, "Social Science, Objectivity and the Chicanos," *El Grito,* 4 (Fall 1970), 4–16.

2. "Educators" is used in this paper to refer not only to classroom teachers but to all those involved in the public educational system. These would include, for our purposes, teachers, noninstructional staff, administrators, policymakers, and academicians in the educational system.

3. "Life styles" are used throughout this paper in a very broad sense to include behavior, norms, values, beliefs, and other cultural characteristics of a group.

4. In theory, the distinction between positive and negative consequences of Chicano student life styles need not involve a value judgment. If the distinction is based strictly on *objective* consequences without reference to a set of values, then supposedly there is no value judgment made. We are not so naive, however, as to suggest that this distinction does not involve very much ideological consideration. Indeed, one of the aims of this paper is to remove the mask of a "value-free" social science and identify the ideological assumptions underlying the social science and educational literature.

centers on whether the chief causes of the Chicano student's life styles are seen as internal or external to his ethnic group. Factors *internal* to the group may be either genetic or cultural characteristics; *external* factors are those social and economic circumstances which are imposed on the group members by virtue of group "class" or "caste" position.

Typology of Educators' Views of the Chicano Student [5]

By juxtaposing the distinction between internal and external determinants of Chicano student life styles with the dichotomy between their positive and negative consequences, a fourfold scheme is obtained for classifying educators' perspectives on the Chicano student. (See Figure 2) Behind each view is a philosophical position value-laden with a set of assumptions about "what ought to be." Thus, each view implicates a different approach to the education of the Chicano student and different educational programs follow logically from these various approaches. The educational approaches flowing from these four views are outlined in Figure 3.

Before an attempt is made to elaborate the various approaches to the education of the Chicano student, a few comments are in order concerning the nature of typologies. Typologies tend to oversimplify and dichotomize where distinctions in reality are not so clear-cut. A more valid picture might be given if the two dimensions were treated as continua along which educators might be located in their views of Chicano student life styles. Furthermore, typologies seldom produce complete classifications. It should be recognized that life styles have multiple determinants and multiple consequences. Chicano life styles are influenced both by forces from within such as the family and group culture and by external forces such as the restraints of the educational and economic systems. Likewise, the consequences of Chicano life styles may be seen as both functional for survival in a lower-class milieu and dysfunctional for achievement in the wider society. Hence, it may be that the most realistic view of Chicano life styles is a mixed view which considers both internal and external causes and positive and negative consequences. Recognizing these limitations, our scheme

5. The conceptual scheme presented here is adapted from a model developed by Robert R. Brischetto ("Social Scientists' Views of Minority Group Life Styles: A Classification of Perspectives on Blacks and Chicanos," paper presented at annual meeting of the Southwestern and Social Science Association, Dallas, Texas, 1971) in his research on social scientists' perspectives on minority group life styles. This basic scheme has been elaborated by Tomás A. Arciniega ("Toward a Philosophy of Education for the Chicano: Implications for School Organizations," paper presented at the November 1971 Office of Education/Teacher Corps Conference) and Thomas P. Carter (*Mexican Americans in School: A History of Educational Neglect* [Englewood Cliffs, N.J.: College Entrance Examination Board, 1970]).

FIGURE 2. CLASSIFICATION OF EDUCATORS' VIEWS OF CHICANO STUDENT LIFE STYLES ACCORDING TO THEIR PERCEIVED CAUSES AND CONSEQUENCES

CONSEQUENCES OF CHICANO STUDENT LIFE STYLES SEEN AS CHIEFLY:

		Positive	Negative
CAUSES OF CHICANO STUDENT LIFE STYLES ARE CHIEFLY:	Internal	1. Chicano student life styles constitute a distinct *culture* which provides a *satisfying* way of life. Chicano students seen as "NOBLE POOR"	2. Chicano student life styles constitute a distinct *subculture* which perpetuates *deficiencies* along generational lines. Chicano students seen as "PATHOLOGICAL"
	External	3. Chicano student life styles are *functional adaptations* to *external restraints* imposed by the larger society. Chicano students seen as "COPERS"	4. Chicano student life styles are *dysfunctional* responses to *external* restraints imposed by the larger society. Chicano students seen as "THE OPPRESSED"

Source: adapted from Robert R. Brischetto, "Social Scientists' Views of Minority Life Styles: A Classification of Perspectives on Blacks and Chicanos," paper presented at Annual Meeting of The Southwestern and Social Science Association, Dallas, Texas, 1971.

should be seen as an oversimplified attempt to identify extreme positions which can serve as guidelines for evaluating various approaches and for shaping alternatives. The purpose of the typology is to stimulate serious discussion and thought regarding conceptual alternatives to the education of Mexican Americans.

Cell 1: Chicanos as "Noble Poor"

Conceptual View

Those who ascribe to this view contend that Chicano life styles constitute a distinct culture which provides a satisfying way of life for its members. Chicanos are seen as having a culture that is superior in many ways and must be preserved. This view is found in the writings of cultural relativists who point out the inherent value of minority group life styles.

Many Chicano writers themselves have made a concerted effort recently to shift the predominant emphasis on "cultural deprivation" toward a positive view of Chicano culture and group life. The positive

FIGURE 3. CLASSIFICATION OF APPROACHES TO THE EDUCATION OF CHICANOS
ACCORDING TO THE PERCEIVED DETERMINANTS AND CONSEQUENCES
OF CHICANO STUDENT LIFE STYLES

CONSEQUENCES OF CHICANO STUDENT LIFE STYLES SEEN AS CHIEFLY:

		Positive	*Negative*
CAUSES OF CHICANO LIFE STYLES ARE SEEN AS CHIEFLY:	*Internal*	1. Educational system which views Chicano students as "NOBLE POOR" *Goals:* Promotion, enhancement, and glorification of Mexican and Chicano culture and life styles. *Means:* Separatist strategies designed to secure community control of education. Only Chicanos can shape valid educational programs for Chicanos. Separate schools with Spanish as the primary language.	2. Educational system which views Chicano students as "PATHOLOGICAL" *Goals:* Elimination of the cultural deficiencies brought from home and peer group by the Chicano student and inculcation of middle-class values of the majority culture. *Means:* Compensatory education designed to overcome cultural deprivation.
	External	3. Education system which views Chicano students as "COPERS" *Goals:* The development of a society based on cultural pluralism. The educational system should be restructured to provide programs which: (1) provide the basic knowledge, skills, and political awareness to adequately (2) promote constant institutional changes designed to improve the opportunity structure. *Means:* Bilingual/bicultural education for all students which recognizes the functional aspects of both cultures and equips students to deal with the societal institutions while working to change them.	4. Educational system which views Chicano students as "THE OPPRESSED" *Goals:* Complete restructuring of the educational system along with the political and economic system to equalize wealth and power in society. *Means:* Development of programs which reinstate the worth of the Chicano culture and overcome their condition of internal colonialism. Education must be organized to liberate Chicanos from their oppressed conditions. Basic changes in the economic and political systems must also be made because these affect the educational system.

Source: adapted from Tomás A. Arciniega, "Toward a Philosophy of Education for the Chicano: Implications for School Organizations," paper presented at the November 1971 Office of Education/Teachers Corps Conference.

aspects of Chicano life styles have often been made to look particularly attractive when contrasted with the negative aspects of the dominant Anglo culture. Nathan Murillo, for example, describes the sociocultural values of Chicano family members as the result of personality styles which contrast sharply with certain deficient Anglo life styles. Anglos "live in a future-time orientation" whereas Chicanos "are not likely to be as locked into the clock" but instead "experience life more completely as it occurs." [6]

This positive view of Chicano life styles is also found in certain aspects of the movement toward cultural nationalism. In the first Chicano Liberation Conference held in Denver in 1969, a position paper was issued entitled "El Plan Espiritual de Aztlan" which articulates well this position: "Our cultural values of life, family, and home will serve as powerful weapons to defeat the Gringo dollar-value system and encourage the process of love and brotherhood." [7]

Educational Approach

The type of educational approach that follows from this view is based on the goals of promoting Chicano and Mexicano cultural traditions. Spanish is the primary language in this type of school system. Non-Spanish speakers are provided with Spanish as a Second Language program to help them overcome their deficiency. Educational programs are geared to emphasize the cultural and historical contributions of the Chicano in U.S. society. Neighborhood schools would be shored up and segregation sanctioned as long as it involved true community control of schools. Alternative school systems funded, staffed, and controlled by Chicanos for Chicanos would be an acceptable alternative to the present public school system under this approach. Colegio Jacinto Trevino, a graduate school for Chicanos in Mercedes, Texas, is an example of such an alternative.

Cell 2: The Chicano Student as "Pathological"

Conceptual View

According to this perspective, Chicano life styles are seen as "pathological" in that they handicap the student's learning process. The source of this handicap may be viewed as genetic or cultural. Vaca, in his very extensive review of the social science literature on the Mexican American, refers to these two pejorative models as *biological*

6. "The Mexican-American Family," unpublished paper delivered at Stanford University, 1970, pp. 7–8.
7. Anonymous, "El Plan Espiritual de Aztlan," paper presented at The Chicano Youth Liberation Conference, Denver, Colorado, March 30, 1969.

determinism and *cultural determinism*.[8] The biological determinism model has been replaced by the cultural determinism model which is now the predominant perspective in the social science literature. Chicano students' poor performance in school and on IQ tests, instead of being attributed to the innate biological inferiority of their group, is now seen as the result of cultural characteristics learned at home and among peers. Nowhere is the "pathological" view of Chicano culture more apparent than in the literature dealing with the Chicano family. Celia Heller's work on *Mexican American Youth* is typical of this literature depicting deficient socialization in the Chicano home environment.

> The kind of socialization the Mexican-American children receive at home is not conducive to the development of the capacities needed for advancement in a dynamic industrialized society. This type of upbringing creates stumbling blocks to future advancement by stressing values that hinder mobility—family ties, honor, masculinity, and living in the present—and by neglecting the values that are conducive to it—achievement, independence, and deferred gratification.[9]

In similar fashion, social scientists have conveniently dichotomized Chicano and Anglo value systems. Saunders, Edmonson, Ulibarri, Madsen, and Zintz, to mention only a few, have all suggested that it is the traditional value system of the Mexican American that is the chief impediment to academic achievement.[10]

Educational Approach

The task of the school, viewed from this perspective, is to eliminate the cultural deficiencies that the Chicano pupil brings from home. The overriding concern of public education is to assist Chicanos and other minority group members to learn and incorporate, through education, the middle-class values of the dominant group. Compensatory education programs become the major vehicles for effecting changes

8. Nick C. Vaca, "The Mexican American in the Social Sciences, 1912–1970," Part I, 1912–1935, *El Grito*, 3 (Summer 1970), 3–24.

9. Celia S. Heller, *Mexican-American Youth: Forgotten Youth at the Crossroads* (New York: Random House, 1966), pp. 34–35.

10. Lyle Saunders, *Cultural Differences and Medical Care: The Case of the Spanish-Speaking People of the Southwest* (New York: Russell Sage Foundation, 1954); Munro S. Edmonson, *Los Manitos: A Study of Institutional Values* (New Orleans: Middle American Research Institute, Tulane University, 1957); Horacio Ulibarri, "Teacher Awareness of Socio-Cultural Differences in Multicultural Classrooms," *Sociology and Social Research*, 45 (October 1960), 49–55; William Madsen, *The Mexican Americans of South Texas* (New York: Holt, Rinehart & Winston, 1964); and Miles V. Zintz, *Education Across Cultures*, 2nd ed. (Dubuque, Iowa: Kendall/Hunt Publishing Company, 1969).

in the minority student. Bilingual education and English as a Second Language program would be offered to assist the Chicano student to learn and use English, which is the primary language of the school and the dominant society. Other compensatory education programs such as early childhood education, basic skills development, parent education, remedial reading, and so forth would likewise need to be offered to help the child overcome the negative effects of his low economic status, home, family, and cultural background.

These first two cells have represented views of a Chicano subculture with internal mechanisms maintaining certain characteristic life styles, viewed positively from one perspective and negatively from the other. The next two cells are reserved for those views of Chicano life styles as primarily responses to conditions imposed by virtue of this minority group's position in the larger society. Chicanos as a minority group generally occupy a subordinate *class* position vis-à-vis the dominant group. They are further stigmatized by the larger society because of certain ascribed characteristics and thus may be said in a broad sense to share a common *caste* position. Cells 3 and 4 view Chicano life styles as chiefly the product of various external restraints imposed by virtue of their location in the class and caste systems of American society.

Cell 3: Chicano Students as "Copers"

Conceptual View

This view holds that Chicano student life styles are *functional* adaptations to primarily external constraints. Culture, from this perspective, is dynamic and adaptive. Chicano culture is the result of generally successful attempts by Chicanos to cope with certain structural and environmental conditions. Arciniega, in his examination of the urban Mexican American, views Mexican-American life styles as functional adaptations to the opportunity structure of the total societal system and as directly attributable to minority status.[11] The group's failures as well as its strengths can be seen as the result of attempts to cope with the institutions of the larger society. Mexican-American culture is viewed as inherently capable of developing even more positive adaptations to societal institutions as positive changes occur in these institutions.

This view of Chicanos as "copers" is implicit in Romano's notion of an "historical culture" which results from an "historical confrontation

11. Tomás A. Arciniega, "The Urban Mexican American: A Socio-Cultural Profile," ERIC-CRESS, New Mexico State University, 1971.

with life." [12] Romano rejects the pejorative stereotype of a monolithic "traditional culture" in favor of "a more realistic concept of multiple histories and philosophies" that develop out of different situations within which Chicanos carve their histories.[13] Such a pluralistic view of Chicano culture recognizes that "people of Mexican descent have adjusted to life in the United States in many different ways." [14] Examples of this perspective are not easy to find in the educational and social science literature. There is, however, a growing body of literature by Chicano academicians on cultural pluralism that can be said to be consistent with this view.[15]

Educational Approach

The educational system which is suggested in accordance with this view of Chicano student life styles has as its basic goal the promotion of cultural pluralism. The present public school system should be restructured to provide the Chicano student with the basic knowledge, skills, and political awareness to adequately work within the societal institutions while at the same time promoting constant institutional changes to improve the opportunity structure.

Bicultural schools and a bicultural curriculum are essential basic elements of this type of school system. English and Spanish are utilized as media of instruction in the classrooms with the idea of creating proficiency in both languages. Mexican-American culture is reinforced along with the Anglo cultural system. Both Chicano and Anglo students will complete their schooling knowing both languages and cultural systems. Under this type of educational system, the present public school would be changed to meet the needs of culturally different students. Thus, changing the methods and structure of the school system is seen as a more viable approach to education than changing the child to "fit" the school as it presently exists.

Schools under this educational system are to be representative of the communities they serve in the ratio of Chicano administrators, teachers, and counselors. There will be special emphasis placed on de-

12. Romano, "The Anthropology and Sociology of Mexican Americans: The Distortion of Mexican-American History," *El Grito*, 2 (Fall 1968), 25.

13. Romano, "The Historical and Intellectual Presence of Mexican Americans," *El Grito*, 2 (Winter 1969), 41.

14. Ibid., p. 42.

15. John A. Aragon, "An Impediment to Cultural Pluralism: Culturally Deficient Educators Attempting to Teach Culturally Different Children," unpublished paper. Cultural Awareness Center, University of New Mexico, 1971; Arciniega, "The Urban Mexican American"; and Philip D. Ortego, "Moctezuma's Children," *El Grito*, 3 (Spring 1970), 39–50.

veloping schools as microcosms of the "ideal pluralistic society." The assumption is that all students can profit from a bicultural curriculum which begins in the first grade and continues through high school.

Cell 4: Chicano Students as "The Oppressed"

Conceptual View

Whereas in cell 3 Chicano life styles are seen as chiefly adequate adaptations, in cell 4 they are seen as mainly *dysfunctional* responses to conditions imposed by the larger society. This view argues that Chicano life styles have been largely disrupted by various means of oppression. Present Chicano cultural patterns are considered to be degenerated reflections of a once-virile life style which has undergone complete subjugation.

A recent popular version of this view is found in the model of "internal colonialism." Blauner applied this model to the Afro American, suggesting that "despite the variation in political and social structure" between the classic colony and the black ghetto, "a common *process* of social oppression" characterizes both.[16] This "colonization complex" involves: (1) forced, involuntary entry; (2) the "colonizing power carries out a policy which constrains, transforms, or destroys indigenous values, orientations, and ways of life"; (3) "an experience of being managed and manipulated by outsiders in terms of ethnic status"; and (4) racism.[17] Moore contends that the case of the Mexican American more closely approximates classic colonialism than does that of the Afro American, because Chicanos were originally indigenous to the Southwest and in the majority.[18] The view of the Chicano as a colonized Mexican has appeared frequently in the more recent writings of Chicano social scientists[19] and by those involved in the Chicano movement.[20] There is even some evidence that the colonial analogy has played an important role in the development of a dominant Chicano ideology.[21]

16. Robert Blauner, "Internal Colonialism and Ghetto Revolt," *Social Problems,* 16 (Spring 1969), 396.

17. Ibid.

18. Joan W. Moore, "Colonialism: The Case of the Mexican Americans," *Social Problems,* 17 (Spring 1970), 464.

19. Mario Barrera, Carlos Munoz, and Charles Ornelas, "The Barrio as Internal Colony," *Urban Affairs Annual Review,* 6 (1972); Jose B. Cuellar, "De Eso Que Llaman Chicano Social Science: Toward an Operational Definition," paper presented at The Caucus of Chicano Social Scientists, annual meeting of the Southwestern Social Science Association, San Antonio, Texas, 1972.

20. Deluvina Hernandez, "La Raza Satellite System," *Aztlan,* 1 (Summer 1970), 13–36.

21. Cuellar, "De Eso Que Llaman Social Science," p. 8.

Educational Approach

The approach that follows from the view of Chicano students as "the oppressed" is to completely do away with the present educational system because it has been part of an oppressive national structure and to replace it with a system based on equality. School systems as they presently exist must be completely restructured and programs developed which reinstate the worth of the Chicano culture along with those of other oppressed groups.

Education must be organized to liberate Chicanos from their internal colonial condition. "Free schools" and alternative institutions are to be encouraged until such time as revolutionary changes can be brought about in the societal institutions. Basic changes in the economic and political systems must also be made in order to more equally distribute wealth and power in society.

With the above four views in mind, we can now turn to the public school system as it exists today and examine the perspective that seems to predominate among educators and educational administrators—the "pathological" view.

The "Pathological" View in the Literature

In the early part of this century, a biological model was frequently used to explain why minority group members were lower class and "low achievers." After the Binet test of IQ was introduced in 1905, group differences were discovered in test scores.[22] Attempts to control for cultural and environmental factors still yielded systematic differences in average group IQs between Blacks and Whites and between Chicanos and Anglos. Because environmental influences had seemingly been held constant, so the reasoning went, then the remaining differences could only be explained in terms of heredity. Thus, it followed that Blacks were genetically inferior to Whites and Mexican Americans were innately inferior to Anglos.

This biological explanation is no longer found in the social science journals; it smacks of racism, a position with which no social scientist would want to align himself. Since the mid-1930s another perspective has replaced the biological model, one no less dangerous in its implications.[23] Liberal social scientists were quick to replace the genetic inferiority model with the cultural deprivation model to account for "low achievement" by minority group members both educationally and

22. Vaca, "The Mexican American in the Social Sciences 1912–1970" Part II: 1936–1970, *El Grito,* 4 (Fall 1970).
23. Vaca, "The Mexican American in the Social Sciences, 1912–1970," Part II, p. 28.

occupationally.[24] Chicanos are now seen as carriers of a deficient culture which inhibits achievement among group members.

The literature in the field of education is replete with references to the Chicano student as "pathological." Johnson, in his work on *Teaching the Culturally Disadvantaged,* suggests that most Mexican-American children are impeded in school because of two basic philosophies in their culture. The first, exemplified in the expression "Dios dirá," takes the responsibility for influencing future events off of the individual and places it on God, thus thwarting individual initiative, planning for the future, and ambition. The second philosophy of life, represented in the saying "Hay mas tiempo que vida," works hand in hand with the first to encourage procrastination and improvidence— sometimes referred to as the "mañana syndrome." [25]

These value orientations toward fatalism, lack of initiative, and present gratification are seen as perpetuated by the Chicano family structure. The Mexican-American child, Johnson reminds us, owes his primary loyalty to his family, which is likely to have a rigid patriarchal structure. This familism tends to create certain problems in school.

> Many teachers have complained that Mexican-American children exhibit a lack of initiative—they depend on being told explicitly what to do and how to do it. Perhaps this lack of initiative is due to the subordinate role the individual must assume within the Mexican-American family structure.[26]

The literature goes on to suggest that because the family structure is patriarchal, boys are raised with the idea that they must develop into a man and behave *a lo macho.* The role of the *Macho* "accounts for the bravado in so many young Mexican males, the need to defend honor and the urge to establish a masculine image before women." [27] This cultural emphasis on "machismo" is seen all too often by educators as the source of many problems for the Chicano youth in school. Because the role of the male as *macho* is an *expressive* role and does not perform any real *instrumental* functions, the emphasis on masculinity is seen as a cultural handicap which impedes success in school.[28] Furthermore, according to Johnson:

24. Stephen S. and Joan C. Baratz, "Early Childhood Intervention: The Social Science Base of Institutional Racism," in Norman R. Yetman and C. Hoy Steele, eds., *Majority and Minority* (Boston: Allyn and Bacon, 1971), p. 473.

25. Kenneth R. Johnson, *Teaching the Culturally Disadvantaged: A Rational Approach* (Palo Alto, Cal.: Science Research Associates, 1970), p. 72.

26. Ibid., p. 71.

27. Ibid.

28. For the distinction between "instrumental" and "expressive" roles, see Talcott

The clear understanding of identity and male role may also explain why some women teachers have trouble disciplining Mexican-American boys. It may be one reason why so many Mexican-American boys drop out of school early: a boy is *macho* if he is working, earning money, and standing on his own two feet.[29]

Miguel Montiel, in his review of the literature on the Mexican-American family, notes that such "uncritical use of concepts like *machismo*—has relegated all explanations of Mexican family life to a pathological perspective." [30] This perspective views *machismo* as the underlying cause of many problems faced by Mexican Americans and as one of the many traditional cultural traits that this group must overcome if it is to become upwardly mobile.

Most typically, the value orientations associated with the traditional Mexican-American culture are contrasted with middle-class Anglo values, and the two cultural systems are thus set up as dipolar dichotomies. Miles Zintz summarizes the differences between the values of Spanish-speaking children and those of their Anglo teachers in Figure 4.[31]

But the literature does not stop at simply drawing distinctions between value orientations; there is always the added suggestion, either implicit or explicit, that traditional Mexican values are dysfunctional and thus need to be changed. The change, of course, must always occur in the direction of the middle-class Anglo values that characterize the school setting and that are necessary prerequisites for achievement later in life in the occupational sphere. Horacio Ulibarri takes this view in his monograph on "The Effect of Cultural Difference in the Education of Spanish-American Children" when he suggests that

Spanish-American children, in general, are in need of a new orientation to:

1. Acquisition of the Anglo value of achievement and success.
2. Time orientation that will be precise according to the hour and minute, but also placing great emphasis on planning for a definite future in this "temporal life."
3. Scientific interpretation of natural phenomena.
4. Acceptance of change and a zeal in looking forward to change.
5. Social relationships, whereby their "docility" and "timidity" will evolve into a desirable degree of aggression.

Parsons and Robert F. Bales, *Family Socialization and Interaction Process* (New York: The Free Press, 1955).

29. Johnson, *Teaching the Culturally Disadvantaged*, p. 71.

30. Montiel, "The Social Science Myth of the Mexican-American Family," *El Grito*, 3 (Summer 1970), 56.

31. Zintz, *Education Across Cultures*, pp. 241–43.

FIGURE 4. TYPICAL CLASSIFICATION OF MAJOR DIFFERENCES BETWEEN
MEXICAN-AMERICAN AND ANGLO VALUE SYSTEMS

Mexican-American Values	Anglo-American Values
Children from traditional Spanish-speaking families may be said to have accepted these general patterns:	American school teachers are sure to place great value on these practices:
Subjugation to Nature	Mastery over Nature
Present time orientation	Future time orientation
Status based on ascription	Status based on achievement
Particularistic perspective	Universalistic perspective
Emotional	Affectively neutral
Low level of aspiration	High level of aspiration
Work for present needs	Work for future success
Sharing	Saving
Nonadherence to time schedules	Adherence to time schedules
Reaction to change	Acceptance of change
Nonscientific explanation for natural phenomena	Scientific explanation for all behavior
Humility	Competition
Obedience to the will of God	Individuality and self-realization

Source: adapted from Zintz, *Education Across Cultures*, pp. 241–43. Zintz' summary is based on Parsons, *The Social System* (Glencoe, Ill.: The Free Press, 1951), pp. 198–99, and Saunders, *Cultural Difference and Medical Care*, pp. 111–40.

6. Economic efficiency, whereby they will learn the value of money and acquire the ability to spend it wisely.
7. A more universalistic outlook on life so that they will see the total picture instead of ascribing importance to the separate details.
8. Acceptance of scientific medical practice.[32]

Public school educators, perhaps influenced by both the educational literature and popular stereotypes, are operating under the same sort of subcultural model, which depicts Mexican-American life styles as deficient and sees the school as the inculcator of values of the dominant society. In his study of the public school system of the Southwest, Carter found that

The vast majority of educators interviewed for this study and most of the relevant literature argue that Mexican-American children are culturally deprived or disadvantaged, that their home environment does not provide the skills, personality characteristics, or experiences necessary for a child's

32. Ulibarri, "The Effect of Cultural Difference in the Education of Spanish-American Children," as cited by Zintz, *Education Across Cultures*, p. 244.

success in school. This view provides most schoolmen with plausible explanation for the failure of Mexican Americans in school.[33]

The implication of this "cultural deprivation" view, Carter suggests, is that the school system as it presently exists is satisfactory and it is the Chicano child's home environment that is the source of all of his problems in school.

A more popular version of the "pathological" view is found in the literature on the "culture of poverty." [34] This concept has had widespread appeal perhaps because it avoids the "racist" label by not identifying cultural pathology as unique to any particular racial or ethnic group but as found among the poor in Western capitalist societies everywhere. Oscar Lewis, credited with the popularization of the "culture of poverty" notion, describes this condition as "a subculture of Western society with its own structure and rationale, a way of life passed down from generation to generation along family lines." [35] The causal factor in this model is the subculture of the poor. Their life styles serve to perpetuate an endless cycle of poverty and deprivation. If the problems of the poor are to be solved, then it stands to reason that the poor must change their ways.

The "Pathological" Model as a Status Quo Ideology

To fully understand how this paradigm of a "pathological" subculture achieved preeminence in the educational and social science literature would require a more thorough examination into the sociology of knowledge than this paper warrants. An attempt will be made only to suggest some of the major factors involved in the emergence of the "pathological" perspective.

Most of the original research done on Mexican Americans consists of impressionistic studies of Chicanos in small town or rural village settings.[36] These studies were conducted according to the traditional

33. Thomas P. Carter, *Mexican Americans in School: A History of Educational Neglect* (Englewood Cliffs, N.J.: College Entrance Examination Board, 1970), p. 35.

34. Oscar Lewis, *La Vida: A Puerto Rican Family in the Culture of Poverty—San Juan* (New York: Random House, 1966); John Burma, ed., *Mexican Americans in the U.S.: A Reader* (New York: Pitman, 1970); and Edward C. Banfield, *The Unheavenly City: The Nature and Future of Our Urban Crisis* (Boston: Little, Brown, 1970).

35. Lewis, *La Vida*, p. xliii.

36. For example, Saunders, *Cultural Difference and Medical Care;* Edmonson, *Los Manitos;* Florence R. Kluckhon and Fred L. Strodbeck, *Variations in Value Orientations* (New York: Row, Peterson and Co., 1961); Madsen, *The Mexican Americans of South Texas;* and Arthur J. Rubel, *Across the Tracks: Mexican Americans in a Texas City* (Austin: The University of Texas Press, 1966).

anthropological concern with value configurations and adopted cultural determinism as their guiding paradigm. To these anthropologists and sociologists, Chicanos were very similar to the peasant people reported in the studies of rural villages in Central and South America. Armed with the Robert Redfield's ideal-type construct of the "folk society," [37] these social investigators found exactly what they were in search of—traditional, rustic peasant communities living a feudal existence. Their descriptions of the cultural traits they encountered (see Figure 4) are no different from anthropological descriptions of the culture of subsistent agrarian society in medieval feudalism.

What the anthropologists and other cultural determinists fail to point out is that culture is a dynamic thing which develops in adaptation to the group's environment. Thus, an agrarian subsistence economy may very well give rise to cultural patterns characterized by a present time orientation, lack of deferred gratification, low aspirations (because work must satisfy present needs), and an emphasis on ascriptive status (because accessibility to new roles is very limited). Some Chicanos are living in isolated rural areas, but they are not typical of Chicanos in the Southwest because almost 80 percent of Chicanos are situated in urban areas.[38] To generalize the findings of some anthropological study of a small rural community and apply them to Chicanos in the entire Southwest is a gross methodological error that has resulted in repeated misconceptions and stereotypes.

Why then does the stereotype of Chicanos as docile peasants persist? Gaviglio suggests that this stereotype is simply a sociological updating of "the popularized folk mythology of traditional American racism." [39] Although this assertion may be a very true one, the analysis does not go deep enough to explain the persistence of this folk mythology itself. Vaca comes closer to an in-depth explanation by attributing ideological reasons to the prominence of the cultural determinism model.

> It seems certain that the major reason for the triumph of cultural determinism in the 1950's was ideological. For only by viewing the causality of the social ills of the Mexican American as stemming from within him —his cultural baggage—all complicity was removed from American society. . . . With such a theoretical view, social welfare agencies, the police, hospitals, schools, universities and the numerous other institutions with which Mexican Americans were forced into contact were completely absolved of any oppressive policies, leaving the Mexican American to stand

37. *The Folk Culture of Yucatan* (Chicago: The University of Chicago Press, 1941).
38. Leo Grebler, Joan W. Moore, and Ralph C. Guzman, *The Mexican American People: The Nation's Second Largest Minority* (New York: The Free Press, 1970), p. 113.
39. Glen Gaviglio, "The Myths of the Mexican American," in Glen Gaviglio and David Raye, eds., *Society As It Is: A Reader* (New York: Macmillan, 1971), 422, 424.

in relief as the sole perpetrator of his economic, social, and his political plight.[40]

This is not to suggest that there exists some grand conspiracy deliberately conjured up by Anglos to oppress Chicanos. The oppression is more subtle, sometimes unrecognized by the oppressor himself, and not limited to Anglos as its sole perpetrators. The perpetuation of the "pathological" stereotype of Mexican Americans has more to do with economic and power relationships in society than with vulgar racism.

Romano calls attention to a "cultural mystique" adopted as a rationale by those in positions of power and privilege to account for the inequality that exists between themselves and those who are subordinate to them. This explanation is shared by members of minority groups who have by one means or another attained positions of influence and participate in the exploitation.

> Members of minority groups who have joined in the exploitation of their own group, or in the exploitation of other groups, traditionally have made use of certain words to describe the condition and behavior of those who are "beneath" them in the social order. That is to say, once they occupy some position or role in society that is above abject poverty they all too often speak of those who remain in such straits as people who are fatalistic, resigned, apathetic, tradition-oriented, tradition-bound, emotional, impetuous, volatile, affected, non–goal-oriented uncivilized, unacculturated, non-rational, primitive, irrational, unorganized, uncompetitive, retarded, slow learners, underachieving, underdeveloped, or just plain lazy.[41]

By using such adjectives to describe the members of subordinate groups, Romano contends, "they thereby place the reasons or causes of 'inferior' status somewhere within the minds, within the personalities, or within the culture of those who are economically, politically, or educationally out of power." At the same time, the explanation that those in power give for their own "success" is in terms of "goal-oriented behavior, a competitive urge, responsibility, a long cultural tradition, etc. etc."; that is, causes that are found within themselves.[42]

Implication for Public Policy

The impact of this "pathological" view on the educational system has been most devastating for minority groups who do not share equally in the middle-class culture of the dominant group. The cultural

40. Vaca, "The Mexican American in the Social Sciences," Part II, p. 46.

41. Romano, "Minorities, History, and the Cultural Mystique," *El Grito,* 1 (Fall 1967), 7.

42. Ibid., pp. 7, 8.

mystique, when carried into the classroom, has had the effect of defining the minority pupil as inferior and placing the responsibility for his failure on his home environment and group culture. The application of this perspective to public policy has been to create programs designed to intervene in the child's socialization process and even alter the child's home environment. Early childhood education and other compensatory education programs have been developed and currently take the lion's share of federal monies for educating the disadvantaged.

But, from most available indications, these intervention programs have failed.[43] One such interventionist program is Head Start. In their evaluation of the Head Start approach, Stephen and Joan Baratz point out that this program "has effectively disregarded or attempted unknowingly to destroy that which is a viable cultural system. . . . Head Start has failed because its goal is to correct a deficit that simply does not exist." [44] Faced with the realization of the failure of these compensatory programs, Baratz and Baratz suggest possible types of response that might be anticipated:

1. an increased preoccupation with very early intervention, at birth or shortly thereafter, to offset the allegedly "vicious" effects of the inadequate environment . . . ;

2. the complete rejection of the possibility of intervention effects unless the child is totally removed from his environment to be cared for and educated by specialists;

3. the total rejection of the environmentalist-egalitarian position in favor of a program of selective eugenics for those who seem unable to meet the demands of a technological environment—scientific racism.[45]

These alternatives, which follow as extreme consequences of the subcultural view of minority group behavior, are frightening in their implications. They signal the urgent need for a radically different approach to the problems of minorities, an approach that will basically alter the position of minority groups vis-à-vis the institutions of American society.

43. Baratz and Baratz, "Early Childhood Intervention," pp. 482–88; B. Caldwell, "The Fourth Dimension in Early Childhood Education," in R. Hess and R. Bear, eds., *Early Education: Current Theory, Research and Action* (Chicago: Aldine Press, 1968), p. 81.
44. Baratz and Baratz, "Early Childhood Intervention," p. 484.
45. Ibid., pp. 484–85.

Toward a More Humanistic Paradigm

The conceptual scheme presented in this paper examined the perspectives on Chicano student life styles found among educators today. It is clear from a review of the educational literature and the existing educational programs that public school efforts reflect basically a "pathological" approach to the education of Chicano students. This approach is based on the assumption that the problems encountered by Chicano students in school have their origins within the students' ethnic group culture. Solutions to the problems of Chicano students, therefore, are to be found in efforts to resocialize the student into the dominant culture. Whether one calls what needs to be changed their "mexicanness," their "value orientations" or, what is more in vogue today, their "cultural disadvantage," the intent is clear: in order to accept the Chicano student, society dictates he must first be "demexicanized."

This "pathological" view has not remained unchallenged. Romano will probably be proven correct in his assertion in the opening editorial setting the theme for *El Grito* (a journal of Mexican-American thought) that "only Mexican Americans themselves can accomplish the collapse of this ["pathological" view] and other such rhetorical structures. . . ." [46] The critiques of the "pathological" view by Chicano academicians have become increasingly more frequent.[47] But critiques will not suffice to bring an end to such a pervasive perspective. A new paradigm is needed to replace it, one that focuses its sights on the institutional structures of the larger society as the source of problems encountered by minorities.

It is imperative that public education shift its emphasis away from a prevailing point of view that insists that the chief impediments to success for the Chicano stem from the negative influences of home, family, and culture, and move toward a more humanistic view. It is our hope that the specifics of this new paradigm will emerge as the topic of a future paper. Some of the basic assumptions on which this paradigm should be built would include the following:

46. Romano, editorial, *El Grito,* 1 (Fall 1967), 4.

47. See Romano, ibid., and his "Minorities, History, and the Cultural Mystique," also his "The Anthropology and Sociology of Mexican Americans"; Montiel, "The Social Science Myth," Carlos Munoz, "Toward a Chicano Perspective of Political Analysis," *Aztlan,* 1 (Fall 1970), 15–26; Raymond A. Rocco, "The Chicano in the Social Sciences: Traditional Concepts, Myths, and Images," *Aztlan,* 1 (Fall 1970), 75–98; Vaca, "The Mexican American in the Social Sciences," Parts I and II; and Cuellar, "De Eso Que Chicano Social Science."

1. The roots of the educational problems of the Chicano are not culturally based.

2. The chief impediments to success by Chicanos in school cannot be attributed to deficient home or peer environments but to the various external restraint systems imposed on the group by virtue of its subordinate position in society.

3. The focus of research instruments should be shifted from the students' ethnic subculture to the structure of the educational and other societal institutions.

4. Educational systems must be restructured to reflect what "should be" and less "what is" in American society.

5. To be effective, changes in the educational system must be accompanied by changes in the political and economic sphere so that wealth and power are more equally distributed in society.

Full development of such a humanistic paradigm will require more than conceptual papers such as this. We now need very extensive research on the institutional structures of American society.

David E. Wright / Esteban Salinas / William P. Kuvlesky

Opportunities for Social Mobility
for Mexican-American Youth

Mexican-American youth in the Southwestern United States are stated currently to be orienting themselves toward their future quite differently from their Anglo counterparts.[1] One major cause of these differences is said to be the fact that these youths are being socialized in two different types of cultures. The Anglo youth is portrayed as being relatively more future- and success-oriented; the Mexican-American youth is more present- and humanistic-oriented. Stating these differences somewhat more extremely, the Anglo youth is said to be achievement-oriented, and the Mexican-American youth is said to value other things more highly—material goods, family ties, having a good time, honor, masculinity (as envisioned by the concept of "machismo"), and living for the present. To the Mexican-American adolescent, inac-

David E. Wright, Esteban Salinas, and William P. Kuvlesky, Department of Rural Sociology, Texas A & M University. Revised version of a paper presented at the Workshop on Southwest Ethnic Groups: Sociopolitical Environment and Education, sponsored by The Cross-Cultural Southwest Ethnic Study Center at The University of Texas at El Paso, July 27–29, 1972. The research included in this paper was supported by the Texas Agricultural Experiment Station as a contribution to TAES project H-2611 and USDA (CSRS) project S-61, "Human Resource Development and Mobility in the Rural South." Support for the paper was also provided as a contribution to TAES project H-2586 and regional project NE-58, "An Economic and Sociological Study of Agricultural Labor in the Northeast States."

1. See Celia S. Heller, *Mexican-American Youth: Forgotten Youth at the Crossroads* (New York: Random House, 1966); Talcott Parsons, *The Social System* (New York: The Free Press, 1951); William Madsen, *The Mexican Americans of South Texas* (New York: Holt, Rinehart & Winston, 1965); and James G. Anderson and William H. Johnson, "Sociocultural Determinants of Achievements among Mexican-American Students: An Interim Report of the Mathematics Education Program," National Conference of Educational Opportunities for Mexican Americans, Austin, Texas, 1968.

43

tivity and leisure are dignified and worthwhile goals. Thus, if he appears somewhat passive or adaptive rather than active in his behavior as compared to his Anglo cohort, such behavior only indicates a fundamental difference in the world views of the Anglo and Mexican-American cultures. Our recent studies directly challenge this stereotypical image.

There has been considerable hypothesizing and speculation about the aspirations and status projections of youth, particularly as they are said to vary among ethnic groups and social classes. Simplified, the suggestion is that youth from ethnic minorities and lower socioeconomic class origins have *lower* levels of aspirations and expectations than do youth from mainstream, middle- and upper-class Anglo origins.[2] Such speculation has gone even further in regard to Mexican Americans, imputing that many supposed features of Mexican culture have influenced their aspirations by fostering low-level goals and apathy toward opportunities for social mobility.[3]

Concepts and Methods

Our studies on the orientations of youth have been facilitated by using a conceptual framework that distinguished between what a person *desires* (aspiration) with regard to a specific object and what that person *anticipates* (expectation) will actually occur with respect to that same object. Aspiration is synonymous with "goal." If that person *desires* one thing but *anticipates* another, he is said to be experiencing *anticipatory deflection*—i.e., the difference between aspiration and expectation. Aspirations (desires) can vary in strength—that is, some persons may be more strongly committed in their aspirations to their

2. See Herbert H. Hyman, "The Value Systems of Different Classes: A Social Psychological Contribution to the Analysis of Stratification," in Reinhart Bendix and Seymour N. Lipset, eds., *Class, Status, and Power: Social Stratification in Comparative Perspective,* 2nd ed. (New York: The Free Press, 1966), pp. 488–99; Hyman Rodman, "The Lower-Class Value Stretch," *Social Forces,* 42 (December 1963), 205–15; Bernard C. Rosen, "Race, Ethnicity, and the Achievement Syndrome," *American Sociological Review,* 26 (February 1959), 47–60; Parsons, *The Social System;* Ozzie G. Simmons, "The Mutual Images and Expectations of Anglo Americans and Mexican Americans," *Daedalus* (Spring 1961), 286–99; Richard M. Stephenson," Mobility Orientations and Stratification of 1,000 Ninth Graders, "American Sociological Review," 22 (April 1957), 204–12; and Milton J. Yinger, "Contraculture and Subculture," American Sociological Review, 25 (October 1960), 625–35.

3. John H. Burma, "Introduction" and "General Characteristics," in John H. Burma, ed., *Mexican Americans in the United States: A Reader* (Cambridge, Mass.: Schenkman, 1970), pp. XIII–XVIII, 3–6; Heller, *Mexican American Youth;* Parsons, *The Social System;* Simmons, "The Mutual Images and Expectations"; and Horacio Ulibarri, "Social and Attitudinal Characteristics of Spanish-Speaking Migrant and Ex-Migrant Workers in the Southwest," *Sociology and Social Research,* 50 (April 1966), 361–70.

goals than others; this variable quality of aspirations is labeled *intensity of aspiration*. There is also a variable quality associated with expectation; specifically, persons vary in how certain they are of obtaining their expectations—*certainty of expectation*. This simple conceptual scheme—aspiration, expectation, deflection, intensity, and certainty—can be applied to any status area; for example, education, occupation, income, residence, military plans, and family and marital plans.[4] The majority of the status projection research at Texas A & M has been performed in relation to education and occupation, and to a lesser extent in relation to family and marital plans.

Detailed descriptions of our status projection research have been published elsewhere.[5] In sum, the findings are that the ethnic groups showed a great deal of similarity; indeed, the similarities outweighed the differences. The specific findings were that the youth in general held high level expectations, tended not to anticipate deflection from their goals, were strongly committed to their educational and occupational goals, and were rather certain of attaining their expectations. Although these similarities were judged to be of primary importance, the following *differences* should be noted. First, fewer Mexican Americans and Anglos held high-level expectations than did Negro youth. Second, more Mexican-American youth expressed strong commitments to both educational and occupational goals than did other youth. And third, more Mexican-American youth were uncertain about attaining their expectations than were Negro or Anglo youth.

Implications

When invited to participate in the Workshop on Southwest Ethnic Groups, we accepted our host's invitation to go beyond the findings and to speculate as we wished about the implications of the research. Thus, we frankly "go out on a limb" to speculate about what will occur, although we attempt to correlate our speculation with available research findings. Mexican-American youth are given prime attention from this point forward because, although many of the comments made are generally applicable to all youth and although the sponsor for the workshop is concerned with more than a single ethnic minority, in the Southwest the Mexican American is the most noticeable minority.

In preface to our speculations, it should be noted that we are gen-

4. William P. Kuvlesky and Robert C. Bealer, "A Clarification of the Concept 'Occupational Choice,'" *Rural Sociology*, 31 (September 1966), 265–76; Kuvlesky and George W. Ohlendorf, "A Rural-Urban Comparison of the Occupational Status Orientations of Negro Boys," *Rural Sociology*, 33 (June 1968), 141–52.

5. Kuvlesky "Status Projections and Ethnicity: A Comparison of Mexican American, Negro, and Anglo Youth," *Journal of Vocational Behavior*, 1 (April, 1971), 137–51.

eralizing about Mexican-American youth at large rather than merely about those in Texas. Until similar study can be extended to youth in other areas, the findings of this study serve as tentative generalizations relevant to the majority of Mexican-American youth. It bears noting that the nation's Mexican-American population is largely concentrated in the five southwestern states of Arizona, California, Colorado, New Mexico, and Texas, and that approximately two-fifths of these people reside in Texas; hence, the findings *are* representative of a large portion of these youth. And, we believe that at least in relation to status projections and conditions of economic deprivation, the youth we sampled are representative of Mexican-American youth in other areas.

Stereotypes

Many of the implications of these findings are obvious, but a few in particular deserve comment. Findings that Mexican Americans have high social achievement goals do not simply contradict some widely shared assertions about lower class youth; they are a direct, critical attack on the aged stereotypes of Mexican Americans as being a non-motivated, backward, lackadaisical people who give their commitment to presumed subcultural goals outside the predominant themes of this society (dozing in the sun, attending carnivals, praying in churches a great deal, and so forth). What about all the expert literature that has supported such conclusions? [6] How are the incongruities between our findings and these other often dated observations explained? The following are set forth as possible explanations.

First, it is conceivable that studies portraying Mexican Americans as having significant subcultural variation with respect to these goals, that is, lower level goals, are simply mistaken. [7] Second, our studies are fairly

6. See Parsons, *The Social System;* Heller, *Mexican-American Youth;* Madsen, *The Mexican Americans of South Texas*; and James G. Anderson and William H. Johnson, "Sociocultural Determinants of Achievements among Mexican-American Students."

7. The findings reported here are pertinent to comments by Burma ("Introduction," "General Characteristics," and "A Comparison of the Mexican American in Subculture with The Oscar Lewis Culture of Poverty Model," in *Mexican Americans in the United States*) and Julian Nava ("Cultural Backgrounds and Barriers That Affect Learning by Spanish-Speaking Children," ibid.) in which they attempt to explicate the subcultural variation present *within* the Mexican-American minority itself. Both believe that in speaking of value orientations of Mexican Americans, an effort should be made to differentiate the minority in terms of how closely the segments of the minority approximate or diverge from the characteristics and qualities of Mexico and its culture; those segments most like Mexico will have value orientations different from those segments more like the Anglo-oriented society of the United States. Both men go on to state that those segments of the Mexican-American minority which will have value orientations most like the traditional Mexican culture

recent, while much of the standard literature on Mexican Americans is comparatively dated; perhaps both sets of data are accurate and there have been recent, dramatic changes in the outlooks of Mexican Americans—as some have put it, a giant awakening has taken place. Third, it could be that we social scientists are so normally inclined to discern and describe differences that we have neglected to search for similarities among groups of people. Thus, it is possible that while certain subcultural differences between Mexican Americans and other groups do exist, certain similarities also coexist among them. A combination of these latter two explanations is probably the closest to a full account.

Opportunities

Our findings indicate that Mexican-American young people have high educational goals; and, although we do not have the necessary evidence to thoroughly substantiate how their parents feel about this, there is reason to believe that they positively endorse the high goals of their children. Our own experiences in conversations with parents during the personal interviews with Mexican-American high school dropouts supports this. "I want my children to get an education—for many reasons, one, that they will not have to work as hard as I have" is a statement heard from many Mexican-American parents. However, the extent to which these youth, in general, can receive support from their parents is highly questionable on at least two grounds. First, in respect to financial supports, it is well documented that a great many Mexican-American families are in extreme poverty condition;[8] for youth from such families, a college education—indeed, a *high school* education, is a great "ambition" luxury. Second, because so few Mexican-American adults have had high school and/or college education experience, they are not familiar with the new life their children will face if they move ahead of them and are therefore at a disadvantage in helping to prepare their children and may even fear estrangement as a result. The

are those living in rural areas along the Mexican border where Mexican Americans are heavily concentrated and in which there is a heavy influence of agriculturally related employment. The counties from which our Mexican-American respondents were selected fit all four criteria—rural, proximity to Mexico, predominantly Mexican American, and agriculturally dependent. Yet we find the youth from these counties to be highly success-oriented—not at all what Burma and Nava suggested!

8. See Harley L. Browning and S. Dale McLemore, A Statistical Profile of the Spanish-Surname Population of Texas (Austin: University of Texas, Bureau of Business Research, 1964); Frank G. Mittleback and Grace Marshall, *The Burden of Poverty* (Los Angeles: University of California, Mexican American Study Project Advance Report 5, 1966); and W. Kennedy Upham and David E. Wright, *Poverty among Spanish Americans in Texas: Low-Income Families in a Minority Group* (College Station: Texas Agricultural Experiment Station, Departmental Information Report 66-2, 1966).

parents are in all probability strongly convinced that their children should continue their education, but the positive incentives they can offer are few and their anxieties and fears probably great.

An area quite worthy of attention, perhaps especially in light of this research effort, is the vocational educational system. Mexican American youth have high educational and occupational goals and yet a disproportionate number of them, relative to Blacks and Anglos, are in vocational educational programs.[9] Additionally, while there is evidence to indicate that lower-class youth in general tend to be channeled toward vocational education and not encouraged to go on to college, this "channeling" appears to hit Mexican Americans particularly hard[10]—Why? Are not the goals of our educational system supposedly directed toward "enabling the student to attain his individual goals"? How is vocational education perceived to aid this minority? The tendency to push it as a general palliative for the disadvantaged—irrespective of individual differences in abilities and motivation—would not seem to serve the individual needs or societal needs well.

Even when Mexican-American youth decide to pursue a college degree, they tend to select a school near home; thus, they continue to be isolated from the larger society. Consider for example that most of the major state-supported universities in Texas have an average of 2 percent or less of Mexican-American youth in their student body composition; exceptions to this are Texas A & M University, Pan American University, and the University of Texas at El Paso—all of which are located in areas of Texas where the sparse population is predominantly Mexican American.

A similar isolation of Mexican Americans occurs in reference to occupations. With the vast majority of their parents employed in lower level occupations for example, agricultural laborers, common laborers, waiters, janitors, and so forth—and with the availability of meaningful summer jobs for Mexican-American students rather limited, these youth have little opportunity to learn about the availability of alternative jobs, let alone what is required to attain their goals. Such a situation is scarcely conducive to facilitating mobility.

In short, Mexican Americans have been largely isolated by class, residence, and language from the educational and occupational realms they wish and expect to enter. This isolation results in a lack of in-

9. Center for Vocational and Technical Education, What School Administrators Should Know About Vocational Education for Disadvantaged Youth in Urban Areas (Columbus: Ohio State University Press, 1971); George W. Mayeske, *Educational Achievement Among Mexican Americans: A Special Report from the Educational Opportunities Summary Division of Operations Analysis, National Center for Educational Statistics* (Washington, D.C.: Government Printing Office, 1967).
10. Mayeske, ibid.

formation that would aid them to make plans to secure their goals. Coupled with this is a wariness about and lack of understanding of the "red tape" involved in working within the system to obtain facilitation from it (it should be noted that this is characteristic not only of Mexican Americans, but of the lower classes in general).

Goals, Means, and Adaptive Behavior

Summarizing to this point, most disadvantaged youth have not only high goals but high expectations. Further, these youth and especially Mexican-American youth are strongly committed to their goals. However, considering the *existing resources* upon which these youth can draw and the *current* social structuring of access to opportunity, it can be concluded safely that many of them are not going to achieve their goals; in the current state of affairs, many have no chance at all. For reasons outlined above, these statements are especially true of Mexican-American youth. The directions for needed changes are clear; substantial change in structures influencing opportunity are needed now.

But what if these changes do not occur, or do not come fast enough —what then? We shift to a consideration of how individuals and groups adapt to situations of goal blockage, utilizing a sociological scheme that revolves about societal *goals* and the *means* to those goals, and that presents a typology of adaptive behavior.[11]

Two aspects of culture are important here. The first concerns the prescribed goals the society defines as legitimate for its members; the second concerns the system of prescriptions pertaining to the acceptable means of reaching for these goals.

Societies differ in three important ways concerning these goals and means. First, they differ according to just what their goals and means actually are; for example, the goals for the United States differ from those of India. Second, societies vary in which of their goals and means are held as legitimate to which members of the society; for example, India has a differentiated set of goals—people of one caste seek goals that differ from those sought by members of other castes. And third, societies vary in the amount of emphasis given to goals relative to that given to means. From all the variations possible along these dimensions, just one type of society is singled out for consideration: the extreme type that holds out the *same* goals and means to *all* its members regardless of their location in the social structure of that society. Depending upon whether or not the members of this type of society accept the prescribed goals and means, the following types of behavior are possible.

11. Robert K. Merton, *Social Theory and Social Structure* (revised and enlarged edition) (New York: The Free Press, 1957).

FIGURE 5.

	Type of Behavior*	Goals	Means	Implication, Example
	I. Conformity	+	+	Stable, uniform society.
	II. Innovation	+	−	Unacceptable means to attain goals—crime, demonstrations, etc.
Deviate from the prescribed modes of behavior	III. Ritualism	−	+	Abide by the rules, give proper appearance—bureaucrats.
	IV. Retreatism	−	−	Withdrawal from society—hippies, hobos.
	V. Rebellion	− +	− +	Reject or change both goals and means, can be peaceful or violent.

* Key: +, accepts; −, rejects. Merton, *Social Theory and Social Structure* (New York: The Free Press, 1957).

To further set the stage for a discussion specifically about Mexican Americans, the following short description of the United States in terms of this scheme is necessary. The ideology of a society often expresses these cultural aspects of goals and means. The ideology of the United States is permeated with themes of individual struggle and the consequent economic success that is held forth as a legitimate goal for all members. The themes go further than this, however; not only is economic success held as a legitimate goal for everyone, but individual worth tends to be defined in terms of this economic success, or at least in terms of continued striving for it. The seeking of economic success becomes not merely a legitimate goal, but in fact a moral obligation of the members of this society. The theme of individual success is so heavily stressed in the United States that by comparison the morally acceptable means for achieving success are slighted. This distortion produces a milieu in which there is no room for failure for many—a milieu in which many persons begin to abandon the prescribed means for achieving their success goals for whatever means possible.[12]

Future Patterns of Behavior

Our research has confirmed that Mexican-American youth (and others) from the most disadvantaged conditions possible in this nation are success-oriented; they accept the goals of this society and are

12. Ibid.

strongly committed to them. Failure to be upwardly mobile in the future cannot be blamed upon any absolute lack of personal desire or personal commitment. And there is indication that these youth additionally accept the societally prescribed means to their goals, as evidenced by their educational projections, education being a standard, effective, and widely condoned channel of mobility—that is, they indicate an acceptance of prescribed means *so far!* [13]

In terms of the above scheme of behavior, it would be tempting to say that historically and presently the behavior of Mexican Americans in general and in terms of the above goals-means scheme has been that of conformity. This statement, one could argue, can be supported in that the history of the Mexican-American people in *their* behavior in response toward the rest of this society has been peaceful, nonaggressive. If they desire these goals as we indicate but still have not attained them as demographic data indicate, it is simply because they have not tried hard enough through the accepted means. It would be tempting to make such statements, but they would be grossly inaccurate. An accurate statement is that Mexican Americans, similarly to other minorities, have been denied *access* to the societally prescribed means, or, having employed them, have still failed to achieve success due to prejudicial and discriminatory hiring, paying, and promoting practices. [14]

The question is posed again: What is going to happen if changes in the structures of opportunities do not occur, or do not come soon enough? What is likely to happen in the future when most of these youth begin to fail to achieve their highly desired goals (which are held to be legitimate and even expected of them) because the legitimate avenues for mobility are blocked or ineffective?

To us, the major lines of activity have already been sketched. Most future activity of Mexican Americans in pursuing their goals can be expected to be conformist in orientation. That is, the majority of Mexican Americans can be expected to continue striving for those goals

13. T. A. Arciniega, *Public Education's Response to the Mexican-American Student* (El Paso, Texas: Innovative Resources Incorporated, 1971) has utilized this scheme by Merton in a sensitive effort to locate, describe, and explain the behavior patterns of various segments of the Mexican-American population. Arciniega's interest is different from our own in that he attempts to utilize the entire scheme and to describe historical and current conditions; we are more concerned with only a portion of the scheme and attempt to project future trends. Arciniega concludes his article with a description of the various modes of orientation toward school taken by Mexican-American youth. In short, this brief article is "must" reading from both a theoretical and a pragmatic perspective.

14. Leo Grebler, Joan W. Moore, and Ralph C. Guzman, *The Mexican-American People: The Nation's Second Largest Minority* (New York: The Free Press, 1970); Peter M. Blau and Otis D. Duncan, *The American Occupational Structure* (New York: John Wiley, 1967).

through the accepted means—or, perhaps more accurately, they will continue to attempt to gain access to those means and to make the means more effective. However, it appears warranted to predict a considerable and dramatic increase in forms of "innovative" behavior. Increasing effort is being given to discover and utilize new and different collective means for development rather than the traditional individual, quiet struggle. Maclovio Barraza, a Mexican-American leader, speaking to the Cabinet Committee Hearings on Mexican American affairs, expressed this position boldly and succinctly when he said, "Along with the other disadvantaged people, the Mexican American is growing more and more restless. He is patient, but it's running out. He may soon be forced to seek dramatic alternatives to his patience —alternatives that seem to bring more generous responses . . . than obedient restraint in face of adversity and injustice." [15] These dramatic, innovative changes which Barraza calls for still remain to be brought into full play: sit-ins, demonstrations, and other forms of militant behavior; increased political activities ranging from more emphasis on voter registration and more informed and block voting to the formation of political organizations; perhaps some increase in certain forms of violent or illegal activities that would enable individuals to enjoy goals on an individual basis; certainly increased efforts to coalesce with other minorities, especially with Blacks.

Perhaps no less important than increases in innovative behavior will be the expected increases in forms of "rebellious" behavior, although the *amount* of these activities can be expected to be relatively small. It must be remembered that rebellion is defined here in terms of rejecting the goals and means of the society and *substituting new ideals* for these, and that this behavior may be peaceful or not. Surely such substitution is implied when Chicano activists state that many of their subcultural values must be preserved and incorporated in the value complexes of the larger society.

In short, heightened activism at all levels of participation concerned with issues of occupation, education, welfare, and discrimination would appear to be in store for the future. The deep commitment of the youth whom we have studied, if applicable to similar Mexican-American youth as we believe it to be, indicates a sustaining force for more militancy and more activism, not less; perhaps this society has seen to date only the "advance guard of the movement" and "La Causa." The problems to be faced go beyond those encountered by the Mexican-American individual or single family. There are problems that pertain to the Mexican-American ethnic minority as a whole and that must be resolved for the minority as a group, presuming it

15. Armado Rendon, "La Raza—Today Not Mañana," in John H. Burma, ed., *Mexican Americans in the United States,* pp. 307–24.

can be organized and take on structure and identity. These difficulties relate to internal factionalization of the minority and consequent lack of unity and internal communication; this lack of unity is accompanied by lack of group awareness, lack of definitions of clear *common* purpose and consensus on methods, and—not the least of all—lack of power, both economic and political.[16] The needs with respect to these difficulties are self-evident. In sum, we are predicting continued conformity behavior among Mexican Americans as the major pattern of behavior, but accompanied by a dramatic increase in innovative behavior and activism despite the problems of disunity outlined above. The specific nature and consequences of this activity and their relationship to the difficulties of disunity deserve careful consideration. The traditional rallying cry of an unorganized minority that feels it has suffered inequities states that "to accomplish meaningful results will require pressure, aggressiveness on the part of the minority itself and this will require greater unity. We cannot rely on someone else to champion our cause; we must do it ourselves. Thus, we must unite, organize, and remain active; this will take time, and delays and setbacks must be expected. But we shall overcome!" The implication of the call to unity and action is that *calling* for it will make it inevitable, and the inequities will then begin to be resolved.

Although there is little disputing that it would be to the overall advantage of Mexican Americans to achieve unity in pursuing their collective goals, this does not mean that they will or are likely to do so. The difficulties of achieving unity and organizing are substantial enough to support scepticism about the success of the movement—it may well fail. However, the *attempt* to unite will in all probability produce long-run opportunity gains for the minority.

On that note of dissention concerning the feasibility of a solid front, we turn to a further specification of alternative outcomes and predictions of their likelihoods. Of course, it is possible that Mexican Americans could largely return to the earlier states of somnolence that existed before the recent developments of group identity and the movement simply die out, but such a course of events is highly unlikely. Another conceivable but very improbable alternative outcome is that Mexican Americans will achieve unity and consensus across all factions on goals and means, become quite aggressive as a group, and provoke a backlash or even instances of open warfare between themselves and the dominant society with no resultant improvement in their circumstances. This, too, however, appears unlikely because most people—Mexican American or otherwise—tend to be pragmatically oriented toward their individual comfort and hence are rather reluctant to make the

16. Ibid.

sacrifices necessary for such militant action, because of the already mentioned deep splits among Mexican-American groups themselves, and because the society *is* making adaptive changes itself toward the Mexican-American minority.

A total picture of the most probable future of the Mexican-American movement is a composite including all of the individual components mentioned. Factionalism of Mexican Americans will continue because of distinctive ethnic differences within the minority itself, differing interests, and the inability to overcome such differences. At the same time that factionalism can be expected to continue—maybe even to increase—there will be a heightening of efforts by the factions to bring about facilitation for achieving their own special interests. And, as stated before, the major portion of the Mexican-American people will remain more or less seemingly apathetic to the movement, unwilling to make the individual sacrifices of time, resources, and comfort necessary to engage in a struggle, *but*, however, ready and willing to take advantage of the new opportunities to mobility as they are made available to them by the partial successes of those groups actively engaged in the movement. The overall situation will be rather cyclical in nature, alternating between periods of sporadic events that provoke bursts of intense attention and activity on the one hand and, on the other, periods of inactivity and listlessness. There will be successive periods marked by considerable unity over specific issues, unity which will then dissolve into periods marked by continued factionalism and drifting apart until the next issue. Gains in opportunities available to Mexican Americans will follow in a comparable manner; at times they will come in a flood, at others in a trickle.

This total picture of the future course of events with respect to the activities of Mexican Americans is one reflecting the general patterns of minority group operations, and a most recent example of the pattern is the Black movement to date. One speculative point of difference between the overall patterns of the Black and the Mexican-American movements is worthy of comment here. Though it is plausible that the issues at the source of the Black movement will some day be resolved with some degree of finality, such is not the case with the Mexican-American movement; there will continue to be an influx of immigrants from Mexico who will continually replenish the lower ranks of the Mexican-American minority and thereby rekindle the issues of the Mexican-American movement.[17] Such a substantial influx of Blacks is not likely to occur.

17. Burma, "A Comparison of the Mexican-American Subculture with the Oscar Lewis Culture of Poverty Model"; Jack D. Forbes, "Mexican Americans," *Mexican Americans in the United States*, pp. 7–16.

It is apparent that we have been orienting our discussion toward the probable long-range consequences. *The overall, very long-run implication of the Mexican-American movement appears to be a striving for and an eventual achievement of assimilation into the broader United States society and not a situation of general and widespread ethnic and cultural separatism existing for the Mexican-American majority.*[18] Several Mexican-American organizations are founded on explicitly formulated goals of assimilation; the latent implications of the stated goals of most Mexican-American organizations suggest underlying goals of assimilation.[19] Our own data affirm that the majority of Mexican-American youth are oriented toward the "good things" of the broader society; that is, toward assimilation goals rather than goals of separatism.

This is not to say that there are no Mexican Americans who have separatism as a goal; indeed, there are—however, the point being stressed is that they are a minority. Further, of this minority holding the goal of separatism, the portion intensely committed to this goal and also willing to make sacrifices to attain it are even smaller. It is from this small minority, seriously committed to the goal of separatism, that the most radical and extreme forms of behavior can be expected; and it bears repeating that this group is a very small minority. However, before efforts at separatism are disregarded, one should consider the broader consequences of such efforts. Some attempts at separatism are a standard mode of adaptive behavior among the usual responses of a minority and serve the useful—in fact, necessary—purposes of helping to gain attention for the minority and of acting as a point around which ethnic identification can take place. Beyond these broad services, the efforts of separatists do at times result in demonstrable redress of grievances and the preservation of some subcultural values and ideals.[20]

18. The word "assimilation" is used here in the sense of more equal access to the avenues of mobility and less discriminatory practices against the ethnic minority —greater "social justice'—and *not* in the sense of stripping minorities of their ethnic identity.

19. Paul Sheldon, "Mexican-American Formal Organizations," in *Mexican Americans in the United States*, pp. 667–72.

20. Arciniega has made a critique of this presentation (at the workshop where it was presented) most perceptively on the following grounds: in making our projections of future trends, we have held the *goals* segment of the goals-means scheme constant and looked only at how Mexican Americans might adapt themselves in striving for these goals. Arciniega states that the goals portion itself is also changing because of direct attempts to redefine the goals and also indirectly as a consequence of minorities utilizing "deviant" modes of behavior to attain their goals. His analysis is correct; our only response to Arciniega is that we attempted to discern what the major, overall pattern of events would be. There should be little doubt that the goals of this society are being redefined, or at least being given greater specification. We did not feel ourselves competent to investigate these aspects at

The Short Run

The long-range result is eventual assimilation, but return to the more immediate situation of those persons who hold high-level aspirations yet are unlikely to attain them. Beyond the modes of adaptive behavior that have already been covered, there are other, less visible adaptations that are likely to occur. As the youth we studied begin to be frustrated in their efforts to achieve their goals, they may simply lower the level of their goals, or lessen the intensity of their commitment to these goals, or both. A more probable outcome, and there is preliminary empirical research to indicate this, is that the youth will continue to maintain both their high-level goals and their deep commitment to them, but lower their expectations of what they will actually achieve.[21] Concomitant with this pattern, there will probably occur the well-documented pattern of shifting the goals these youth will have failed to attain onto their future children, socializing them in turn to have high goals and expectations.[22]

We feel it necessary to direct some comments toward what all this may mean in terms of concrete events for the individual. For many of the individuals concerned, it appears that much personal frustration lies ahead. Their aspirations and expectations are simply higher than they will be able to attain—too high to be attained in general even where dramatic positive changes in opportunity occur in the structure of society. The tension generated by this frustration will have to be addressed very directly by both the Mexican-American ethnic minority and by the larger society, to attempt channeling it into productive uses in order to avoid a variety of social costs. But how?

One vital area for immediate ameliorative attention is the educational system. Youth have high educational goals *and* expectations, but are unlikely to attain even their expectations in the current system.

---

this time. Further, it may be that the goals of the society are more stable—less subject to change over time—than the means to attaining the goals. Nevertheless, Arciniega is correct and his suggestions are particularly worthy of research.

21. Katheryn A. Thomas and Nelson L. Jacob, "A Longitudinal Analysis of Change in Occupational and Educational Orientations of East Texas Boys: a Racial Comparison," paper presented at the annual meeting of the Rural Sociological Society, Washington, D.C., 1970.

22. Elizabeth Douvan and Joseph Adelson, *The Adolescent Experience* (New York: John Wiley, 1966); Arthur B. Shostak and William Gomberg, eds., *Blue-Collar World: Studies of the American Worker* (Englewood Cliffs, N.J.: Prentice-Hall, 1964); Robert Coles, *Children of Crisis: A Study of Courage and Fear* (Boston: Little, Brown, 1964); and Melvin L. Kohn, "Social Class and Parent-Child Relationships: "An interpretation," *American Journal of Sociology,* 58 (January 1963), 471–80.

The schools do not address the problems encountered by Mexican-American youth—problems of language usage, lack of attention to Mexican-American heritage, isolation of these youth and communities from the Anglo society, lack of encouragement and social support, and exclusion of the Mexican-American community from the schools—even within areas of high Mexican-American concentration.[23] There are good reasons for focusing upon the school systems as a locus for change: the shortcomings and deficiencies of the school systems are well documented; Mexican Americans have the highest rate of dropouts and of failure to complete school of any group, and consequently the lowest levels of school attainment; Mexican-American youth have high educational goals; and, as stated earlier, a higher education has been and remains one of the surest channels (though not without problems) for upward mobility in this country. One thing that is not needed in relation to education is a program aimed at generally "instilling high aspirations" or "raising the level of the aspirations" of these youth; their aspirations are already high. Programs of social change that will facilitate achieving their aspirations in some degree will provide what is needed. And such programs as these latter mean, at the very least, aid to families and communities in addition to substantial school reforms.

Some youth with low-level or seriously incongruent aspirations for mobility but with high levels of talent and capability may be helped by simply being encouraged to aim higher, but only if guidance and support is provided to help them locate and realize opportunities that exist. What about the youth with high achievement aspirations but low capabilities—undoubtedly the more common type: how are they to be dealt with best in their own and the larger society's best interests?

Conclusions

Beyond individual, familial, and governmental efforts and resources that should be used to help the Mexican-American minority achieve parity in our society, another source of help is the formal voluntary organization, which can perform many diverse services such as dissemination of information, interpretation of events, the pursuing of benefits or advantages through public pressure, the safeguarding of the

23. United States Commission on Civil Rights, *Ethnic Isolation of Mexican Americans in the Public Schools of the Southwest,* Mexican American Education Study, Report 1 (Washington, D.C.: Government Printing Office, 1971); *The Unfinished Education: Outcomes for Minorities in the Five Southwestern States,* Mexican-American Educational Series, Report 2 (Washington, D.C.: Government Printing Office, 1971); *The Excluded Student: Educational Practices Affecting Mexican Americans in the Southwest,* Mexican-American Educational Study Report 3 (Washington, D.C.: Government Printing Office, 1972).

interests of the group, and diffuse social support for members.[24] A well-known example of such organizations serving the particular interests of an ethnic group is the National Association for the Advancement of Colored People (NAACP). Use of the NAACP as an example here serves a dual purpose: not only does it attempt to protect the interests of Blacks, but it is also well-known nationally and is looked to by Blacks and others as well as a central, unifying force on a wide range of issues concerning Blacks. By comparison, no such broad-based, multifunctional organization exists to represent the Mexican American people as a whole.[25] In summary, by comparison with Anglos, Mexican Americans tend to be isolated from the broad mainstream of this society and the avenues to mobility in that society; by comparison with Blacks, Mexican Americans lack recognized, effective organizations to coordinate, to inform, and to aid them in seeking their goals.

The Mexican Americans are a diverse people, with many differences in values, interests, styles of life, and so on. Factionalism occurs in reference to finer ethnic distinctions (Spanish Americans, combinations with American Indians, native citizens of the United States, Puerto Ricans, and others), location in the class structure, age, occupational interests, and in some cases, length of residence in this country. To date, to the best of our knowledge, there has not yet emerged a central, unifying Mexican-American organization. Although La Raza Unida party and the United Farm Workers Union (UFWU) have at times come close to serving this function, they tend to perform narrow singular purposes and rather narrow economic and political interests.

The partial effectiveness of UFWU in achieving recognition and higher wages in California and Florida, and incidences of effectiveness by La Raza Unida (in Crystal City, Texas, for example) have gained considerable publicity for Mexican Americans and have encouraged the formation of many other groups that are explicitly organized for the purpose of advancing the interests of Mexican Americans along many different fronts. Such effectiveness has also resulted in statements, formally or informally, from already established organizations to the effect that they wish to help. The ability to accomplish significant results by either the new organizations or the established sympathizers remains to be measured. We know little as sociologists about how Mexican-American youth view these organizations in relation to their social goals, or whether or not (or which organizations) they are likely to support or join.

24. Peter M. Blau and W. Richard Scott, *Formal Organizations: A Comparative Approach* (San Francisco: Chandler, 1962); and Seymour M. Lipset, *Political Man: The Social Bases of Politics* (New York: Doubleday, 1960).

25. Sheldon, "Mexican-American Formal Organizations."

A similar position can be developed on leadership among Mexican Americans.[26] Compared to charismatic leaders such as the late Martin Luther King, Congressman Julian Bond, Mayor Charles Evers, and others among the Blacks, Mexican Americans have fewer clearly visible and accepted leaders who maintain allegiance across the many Mexican-American factions. Some such examples are perhaps Cesar Chavez and Reyes Tijerina—although it is debatable as to whether or not the *methods* employed by these two men—perhaps even their goals—are accepted by all or even most factions. To what extent are these actual leaders becoming symbols of a larger and broader movement and symbols (hero figures) for Mexican-American youth?

Finally, in considering impediments faced by Mexican-American youth as they pursue their achievement goals, the problem of a language handicap should be given priority.[27]

And, despite linguists' claims that a language handicap is a problem shared by Blacks, other ethnic groups, and lower-class youth in general, as well as by Mexican-American youth, there is little disagreement that this problem is the most severe for Mexican Americans.[28] There is little likelihood that Mexican-American youth in substantial numbers can advance through a college education until the language problems can be overcome. And there is equally little chance that these language difficulties will be overcome if the educational systems continue to resist bilingual programs as they have done and may still be doing now—even given the fact that there are a number of promising programs involving bilingual education for American Indians and Mexican Americans that exist through stimulation by federal encouragement and funding. In general, it is doubtful —at least propositional—whether the school functionaries at the local level have dramatically altered their longstanding negative orientations about the use of a "foreign" language in their schools. What may appear to be a significant trend toward bilingual programs in terms of funding being utilized may be a deceiving surface effect—little may have changed in most local schools in this regard.

It would be interesting to see to what extent Spanish is actually used in general in formal school relations within predominantly Mexican-American areas. Of course, the issue is broader than a willingness to

26. George Rivera, Jr., "Recognition of Local-Cosmopolitan Influentials in an Urban Mexican-American Barrio," in *Mexican Americans in the United States,* pp. 273–77.

27. William P. Kuvlesky and Victoria M. Patella, "Degree of Ethnicity and Aspirations for Upward Social Mobility among Mexican American Youth," *Journal of Vocational Behavior,* 1 (July 1971), 231–44.

28. Fernando Peñalosa, "The Changing Mexican American in Southern California," *Sociology and Social Research,* 51 (July 1967), 405–17.

tolerate use of Spanish in school; it is really the extent to which the school staff can relate meaningfully to the students—their needs, interests, and backgrounds. Outside of Crystal City, it is probable that Mexican-American youth are still taught predominantly by Anglo teachers and that the proportional increase in use of Mexican-American teachers in these situations has been relatively small over the last five years. Is it any wonder that the Mexican-American dropout rate is so high and that, according to our research, Mexican-American youth feel they were not encouraged to stay in school?[29] The surprising thing is how hope persists as it does in these circumstances—the Mexican-American dropouts we studied generally wanted to finish high school and many wanted to go further. Most of them still hoped for social mobility through occupational attainment. It is likely that their hopes will die in the future.

Concluding Remarks

The implications could be carried further; this is left to the reader and to those interested in extending research in this area of concern. By way of a summary conclusion, it should be noted that data were presented that portray Mexican-American youth as generally being success-oriented and deeply committed to their goals; such a portrayal is a direct counter to the many negative stereotypes of these youth. Furthermore, awareness of this intensity of commitment provides a basis for predicting a sustaining force for the movement and for seeking innovative forms of behavior in pursuing individual and collective minority group goals. Finally, it was indicated that the educational system was a logical and much-needed area for immediate ameliorative reform. Our data argue strongly against general programs, which are insensitive to differences in individual desires, capabilities, and needs, against present and continued unrestricted use of vocational education programs, and also against programs aimed at raising aspirations.

29. Sherry Wages, Katheryn Thomas, and William P. Kuvlesky, "Mexican-American Teen-age School Dropouts: Reasons for Leaving School and Orientations toward Subsequent Educational Attainment," paper presented at the annual meeting of the Southwestern Sociological Association, Houston, 1969.

John H. Haddox

American Indian Values

So often we tend to speak of Indians as a homogeneous group, as when we speak of Indian religion or Indian art, and we do this at great risk of error, inaccuracy, or oversimplification.

Among over 600,000 Americans Indians there are more than 315 tribal groups (which at one time had over three hundred languages, at least fifty of which are still in use) living in all fifty states in urban and rural settings (with approximately two-thirds living on reservations). Vine Deloria, Jr. notes that tribes range in size from the huge Navajo tribe with over 130,000 people controlling 16,000,000 acres of land to the Mission Creek of California with fifteen people and a tiny bit of land. There are among Indians an amazing variety of mores, customs, traditions, degrees of acculturation, economic status, needs, wants, and values. In many ways the Indians were more culturally diverse than their European and American conquerors. In *The Indian Heritage of America*, Alvin M. Josephy, Jr., points out that "From Alaska to Cape Horn, in fact, the Indians of the Americas are as different from each other as Spaniards, Scots, and Poles—and, in many cases . . . they are even more different." [1] Furthermore, the non-Indian invaders of Indian lands fostered divisions among Indians and encouraged intertribal hostilities.

Even in the same general areas tribal differences were (and sometimes still are) striking. For example, there were the contrasting life styles of the largely nomadic Sioux and the largely agricultural Pawnees who once lived near each other on the great plains, or the aggressive Apaches, the peaceful Hopis, and the Navajos, who fell

John H. Haddox, Department of Philosophy, The University of Texas at El Paso.

1. *The Indian Heritage of America* (New York: Alfred A. Knopf, 1968), p. 9.

somewhere in between the first two as far as militancy goes, all living in the southwest—in New Mexico and Arizona.

Further, Indians (with few exceptions) have ever struggled for the individual freedom to remain Indians as well as for tribal survival. In 1753 Benjamin Franklin, in a letter to a Peter Collinson, complained that nature provides for Indians so bounteously with such little labor that even though they are intelligent enough they "have never shown any inclinations to change their manner of life for ours." He then notes that when an Indian child has lived and learned in white society "if he goes to see his relations and make one Indian Ramble with them, there is no persuading him ever to return." [2]

Yet despite the unquestionable fact that Indians have displayed almost no propensity for acculturation or assimilation, these have been the policies of the whites who have had varying degrees of power over them. The fact is that the "solution" to what these whites have considered to be "the Indian problem" has been to try to turn the Indian into a White, in culture if not in color. Edgar Cahn notes that "It was the Indian's great misfortune to be conquered by a people intolerant of cultural diversity. The Indian looked different, spoke a different language, had his own religion and customs; Americans saw him as an anathema and were chagrined when he refused to conform to 'civilization.'" [3]

Later guilt over the theft of a continent stimulated the formation of white policies of assimilation that would in time, hopefully, eliminate evidence of this theft. However Indians have vigorously rejected the melting pot, fearing that their very Indianness, with all it implies, would be melted away. They do not want to be melted and come out culturally White. As Earl Shorris puts it, "Conquered and loved, butchered and smothered, the Indian staggers into the battle for a pluralistic society; he has seen death in the melting pot." [4]

Now, as never before, many Indians are caught up in a dedicated battle for their survival as Indians. Of course there is always the danger that an ardent drive for self-determination and "Red Power" might descend to narrow, fanatical Indian parochialism. However, among even some of their strongest and most determined spokesmen,

2. Wilcomb E. Washburn, ed., *The Indian and the White Man* (New York: New York University Press, 1964), p. 49.

3. Edgar S. Cahn, *Our Brother's Keeper: The Indian in White America* (New York: New Community Press, 1969), p. 32. There were, of course, exceptions. Francis Leupp, commissioner of Indian Affairs in 1905, wrote: "I like the Indian for what is Indian in him. . . . Let us not make the mistake, in the process of absorbing them, of washing out what is distinctly Indian." (Quoted in Hazel W. Hertzberg, *The Search for An American Indian Identity* [Syracuse, New York: Syracuse University Press, 1971], p. 17.)

4. *The Death of the Great Spirit* (New York: New American Library, 1972), p. 61.

like Vine Deloria and Mel Thom, there is a beautiful humanistic breadth of concern. In struggling for the cultural, social, political, and economic freedoms for the American Indian they are fighting for us all. Deloria explains that it matters little that compared to other groups Indians are few in number: "What is important is that we have a superior way of life. We Indians have a more human philosophy of life. We Indians will show this country how to act human. . . . What is the ultimate value of a man's life? That is the question." [5]

Now, what are some central elements in an American Indian philosophy of life? Before attempting to answer this question we must emphasize once more the fact of tribal cultural diversity. This means that some of the elements of an "Indian" philosophy of life presented here will be characteristic of certain tribes and not of others, but there are a substantial number of shared values.

First of all, it is clear that for Indians freedom has been and is a fundamental value—and here freedom not so much in the negative sense of lack of restrictions (though given the fact of a century or so of repressive governmental control, this is imperative) but more in the positive sense of the ability to be, to live, to create in one's own way. On this point Deloria has commented wryly, "Of course if our way of life turns out to be better, more human, than yours, that would be your problem. Not ours. We would never force anyone to live as we do. We never have." [6]

This "way of life" features a strong sense of community, generosity, and interpersonal harmony, all of which are an outgrowth of the prevalence of the extended family or clan among Indians. The tribe is often like one family with a majority related either by blood or by "adoption in the Indian way" (usually a relatively informal system wherein parents state their love for and acceptance of a person as their "son" or "daughter").[7] In this manner, strong personal relationships among Indians multiply.

S. Gabe Paxton, Jr., commenting on the effects of an extended or kinship family on Hopi students says, "The Hopi child is never allowed to feel isolated or abandoned, for he always has several groups of relatives to whom to turn for comfort and reassurance. The tendency to treat children as a group apart from adults, strongly developed

5. From the book *Touch the Earth: A Self-Portrait of Indian Existence* by T. C. McLuhan. Copyright © 1971 by T. C. McLuhan. Published by E. P. Dutton & Co., Inc. (Outerbridge & Lazard, Inc.) and used with their permission.

6. Quoted in Stan Steiner, *The New Indians* (New York: Dell, 1968), p. 269.

7. The author of this article was highly honored to have been adopted by his Pawnee Mother, Alice Morris, and given the name "Kiwakutiwati" (Walking Fox), so acquiring an impressive number of wonderful brothers, sisters, aunts, uncles, and cousins.

in White American culture, does not exist among the Hopis. A child is regarded as an important member of the community." [8] (For a lovely example of this attitude in another tribe: the Navajo give a party to celebrate a baby's first laugh.)

In books on his life as an Indian boy, Charles Eastman (whose Sioux name was Ohiyesa) explains that his early education was based on observing, exploring, and feeling. Further, these experiences fit into his life as a whole. He notes that his parents taught him very little directly, but a great deal indirectly by example and by means of stories. (In these stories there was no explicit moral drawn, but the storyteller would often make a moral point as part of the tale itself.)

Among Indians of all ages, kinship ties lead to a strong community sense. A tribal people sees a community as a loosely and freely unified whole, without denying the importance of the individual who discovers himself or herself through warm, personal relationships. As Steiner puts it in speaking of the tribal person: "He lives within himself, but not for himself. The distinction is vital. Everything in tribal life is based on the community's protection of the individual. The tribe shelters a man's family within the umbrella of the kinship family. The tribe nourishes a man's well-being in time of failure with its built-in brotherhood and neighborliness." [9]

In most tribes "chiefs" are distinguished and honored, but they rarely have much power or even authority. Richard Brandt has noted, for example, that among the Hopi, chiefs are traditionally "the servants of the people" and some members of the tribe have declined the honor.[10]

A quality most prized among Indians is generosity, good examples of which are in the traditional "give-away dances" at pow-wows or handgames where persons dancing carry gifts to friends—maybe a sack of sugar, or one of flour, or a bolt of cloth, or perhaps some beadwork or a hand-sewn or woven article of clothing. Also at such occasions, often when persons shake hands one passes a dollar, or a few, to the other. A Pawnee Indian friend once commented that the best thing about having something is to be able to give it away. However, the "giving" is better termed "sharing" because it is such a ubiquitous practice. Indians simply take care of each other in a per-

8. Quoted in Steiner, *The New Indians*, p. 147.

9. Ibid., p. 140. In Adolf F. Bandelier's *The Delight Makers* (New York: Dodd, Mead, 1918), he explains that the Indian "keeps secrets in the same manner that he lives—namely, in groups or clusters." (p. 13)

10. Richard B. Brandt, *Hopi Ethics, a Theoretical Analysis* (Chicago: University of Chicago Press, 1954), pp. 24–25.

sonal way (which is pretty far removed from our white society's practice of impersonal contributions to a Community Chest or a United Fund).

In an article on Indian values by Popavi Da, former Governor of San Ildefonso Pueblo in New Mexico, he notes that "no one goes hungry within an Indian group if there is food available because each family shares with the less fortunate group." [11] Although a result of the strong family and community sense among Indians is generosity and a lack of economic competition (with the communal ownership of property an enduring tradition), they enjoy personal, often playful competition as in costume or fancy dancing contests or in handgames.

The Hopi seems to epitomize a common Indian tendency to prize cheerfulness, cordiality, hospitality, cooperation, and contentment and to eschew selfishness, economic competition, resentment, and aggression.

Further, Indians tend to be very much present-oriented, concerned primarily with the here and now. The languages of some Indian tribes have verbs with only a present tense, with any references to a past remembered or to a future projected implied by the context of a statement. Indians tend to see the past and future as elements of an extended present. Deloria thus writes, "I say, enjoy life right now. Live a full life, right now. Share with your neighbors, right now. What a man does with his life right now is what he will do in the future. That's the Indian way. So you might say the Indian is 'future-oriented' in the present. The urban man says he lives for the future. He doesn't really. He lives by the time clock and the calendar and the bank check. As a result he hardly lives at all. Now or ever." [12] (Similarly, Charles Eastman has noted that for the Sioux work was not valued in itself; more highly prized was the immediate enjoyment of the beauty of life as it was lived.)

Just as Indians' concepts of time are unusual, so are their understandings of justice. Many legal decisions are made by tribal councils (which usually play economic, social, and religious roles within the tribe as well as juridical). The councils stand in an unusually close personal relationship to individual tribal members, with, in some cases, the council seen merely as an extension of the individual. In *The American Indian Today*, editors Stuart Levine and Nancy O. Lurie note that Indian political and juridical processes are so dem-

11. "Indian Values," in *The Living Wilderness*, 34, No. 109 (Spring 1970), 26.

12. Quoted in Steiner, *The New Indians*, p. 122. On this point Steiner notes: "Where the unity of time is shattered he too is at the mercy of the time clock. Where his tribal memory is forgotten he too has lost his history and has to depend on the pages of books written by strange hands." (p. 122)

ocratic that they "make even a New England town-meeting seem dictatorial in contrast." [13]

Sometimes the authority of tribal leaders is religious, as in the New Mexico Pueblo *caciques*, who are concerned with both the spiritual and material well-being of their tribal members. (This is similar to the *caciques* in some Mexican villages who are deemed to have *brujo*—supernatural or magic or sometimes bewitching—powers.)

Punishment for Indians is not for the sake of revenge but for restitution, whenever possible, of whatever has been stolen or injured. Popavi Da explains: "In the field of justice, instead of applying punitive action to a criminal, Indians focus on rehabilitating him. The man who stole a cow is asked by the Pueblo authorities to replace the animal with two cows, one given to the man whose cow he stole, the other given to the governing body of the village, which has also been injured by the anti-social act. If a man's arm is broken in a fight, the sentence, for the one who caused the accident is to do the work of the injured man until his arm heals." [14]

In November 1969, a number of Indians took over Alcatraz Island, the old prison site. Before they were forcibly evicted in June 1971, they issued a statement explaining their claim to the island. With delicious irony they offered $24.00 in glass beads and red cloth for its purchase (following a precedent set by the white man about 300 years ago for purchasing islands). The remainder is too well-put to paraphrase:

> We will give to the inhabitants of this island a portion of that land for their own, to be held in trust by the American Indian Affairs and by the bureau of Caucasian Affairs to hold in perpetuity—for as long as the sun shall rise and the rivers go down to the sea. We will further guide the inhabitants in the proper way of living. We will offer them our religion, our education, our life-ways, in order to help them achieve our level of civilization and thus raise them and all their white brothers up from their savage and unhappy state. We offer this treaty in good faith and wish to be fair and honorable in our dealings with all white men. . . .
>
> We feel that this so-called Alcatraz Island is more than suitable for an Indian Reservation, as determined by the white man's own standards. By this we mean that this place resembles most Indian reservations in that:

13. *The American Indian Today* (Deland, Florida: Everett/Edwards, 1968), p. 6.

14. "Indian Values," p. 26. In the last century Thomas Wildcat Alford, Shawnee, presented a code of justice for his tribe which includes: "Do not kill or injure your neighbor, for it is not him that you injure. You injure yourself. Do not wrong or hate your neighbor, for it is not him that you wrong. You wrong yourself. Moneto, the Grandmother, the Supreme Being, loves him also as she loves you." (Quoted in Steiner, *The New Indians*, pp. 150–51.)

1. It is isolated from modern facilities, and without adequate means of transportation.
2. It has no fresh running water.
3. It has inadequate sanitation facilities.
4. There are no oil or mineral rights.
5. There is no industry and so unemployment is very great.
6. There are no health care facilities.
7. The soil is rocky and non-productive; and the land does not support game.
8. There are no educational facilities.
9. The population has always exceeded the land base.
10. The population has always been held as prisoners and kept dependent upon others.

Further, it would be fitting and symbolic that ships from all over the world, entering the Golden Gate, would first see Indian land, and thus be reminded of the true history of this nation. This tiny island would be a symbol of the great lands once ruled by free and noble Indians.[15]

The American Indian reverence for life is more than just a concern for human life. For Indians every living thing is sacred, so all of life, both plant—trees, corn, flowers—and animal—bison, deer, birds—are to be cherished. In fact all of nature—the sky and stars, and especially the land—are to be treated with reverence. The Indian accepts the man–nature relationship of harmony-with-nature wherein all natural forms, living and nonliving, interrelate without domination, as opposed to the mastery-over-nature thesis that prevails in our western societies wherein man is seen as the superior force in nature, the other elements of which he can utilize (or destroy) as he sees fit.[16]

In 1796, an unidentified Indian chief told the governor of Pennsylvania, "We love quiet; we suffer the mouse to play; when the woods are rustled by the wind, we fear not." [17] More recently Chief Luther Standing Bear, an Oglala Sioux, presented a similar idea beautifully: "We did not think of the great open plains, the beautiful rolling hills, and winding streams with tangled growth, as 'wild.' Only to the white man was nature a 'wilderness' and only to him was the land 'infested'

15. "Proclamation: to the Great White Father and all His People," in McLuhan, *Touch the Earth,* pp. 164–65.

16. Popavi Da, in "Indian Values," p. 25, has pointed out that when in the fall of the year the Indians are hunting for pinons to eat during the winter months, they always search for pack rats' nests where there are always large stores of nuts that they can take; but, he notes, they always replace the nuts with corn or wheat to support the rats as a trade for the nuts.

17. Quoted in McLuhan, *Touch the Earth,* p. 5.

with 'wild' animals and 'savage' people. To us it was tame. Earth was bountiful and we were surrounded with the blessings of the Great Mystery. Not until the hairy man from the east came and with brutal frenzy heaped injustices upon us and the families we loved was it 'wild' for us. When the very animals of the forest began fleeing from his approach, then it was that for us the 'wild west' began." [18]

With their attitude toward nature, as was noted earlier, Indians could not understand the white man's avarice or his penchant for destroying fields and forests and virtually whole species of animal life. As Steiner summarizes, "The Oriental contemplated nature; the white man conquered nature; but the Indian lived in nature." [19]

Thus, interestingly, Indians' concern for the present did not exclude nature conservation. In our majority society the ecologist continually speaks of preserving our environment for the future; the Indian, with present-oriented reverence for nature, simply did not have to worry about future conditions in this area.

Some persons have argued that the Indian preserved nature only because he did not have the industrial means at his disposal to lay waste and ravage the earth as members of the majority society have done with their machines. However such positions are simply further indicators of the widespread ignorance of Indian attitudes and values in this society. These attitudes are what are really important as motivators to preserve and develop certain facets of our society without destroying others. This is, then, not a matter of ignoring or denying the role of technology in our modern society; rather it is a matter of seeing technology as possibly a means of enhancing rather than of degrading our environment. With the earth seen as mother of all life,

18. Ibid., p. 45. Chief Standing Bear also comments more abstractly: "The man who sat on the ground in his tipi meditating on life and its meaning, accepting the kinship of all creatures and acknowledging unity with the universe of things was infusing into his being the true essence of civilization. And when native man left off this form of development, his humanization was retarded in growth." (p. 99)

19. Steiner, *The New Indians*, p. 166. An old holy Wintu woman colorfully laments the destruction of nature by the white man: "The white people never cared for land or deer or bear. When we Indians kill meat, we eat it all up. When we dig roots we make little holes. When we build houses, we make little holes. When we burn grass for grasshoppers, we don't ruin things. We shake down acorns and pine-nuts. We don't chop down the trees, kill everything. The tree says, 'Don't. I am sore. Don't hurt me.' But they chop it down and cut it up. The spirit of the land hates them. They blast out trees and stir it up to its depths. They saw up the trees. That hurts them. The Indians never hurt anything, but the White people destroy all. They blast rocks and scatter them on the ground. The rocks say, 'Don't. You are hurting me.' But the White people pay no attention. When the Indians use rocks, they take little round ones for their cooking. . . . How can the spirit of the earth like the White man? . . . Everywhere the White man has touched it, it is sore." (In McLuhan, *Touch the Earth*, p. 15.)

land was and is itself considered sacred. Indians have traditionally held that one can no more buy and sell land than one can buy or sell the air of the sky or the water of lakes or rivers. All these are given to all by the Great Spirit. Thus a chief of the northern Blackfeet responded to offers for the purchase of his land by the white man: "As a present to you, we will give you anything we have that you can take with you; but the land, never." [20]

The Indian, then, found his life consisting of a web of relations, person-with-person and person-with-nature, a source of great joy. When the young Henry David Thoreau announced in his graduation address: "This curious world we inhabit is more wonderful than it is convenient; more beautiful than it is useful . . . more to be admired and enjoyed than used" he expressed an attitude largely lost in modern society, except in the Indian.[21] The joy of the Indian is not mere "enjoyment"; as Deloria comments, it is more like "celebration." (Clyde Warrior, among others, expressed his dismay over a loss of joy among Indians resulting from their loss of freedom in a white society, along with a slight hope that, with a recovery of a measure of autonomy, the native joyousness would return.)

The gusto, the *joie de vivre* of Indians, which in some tribes is subdued by harsh circumstances of today's world but never wholly lost, is both a cause and an effect of their creative, artistic achievements. In addition to the traditional gorgeous bead- and decorated leatherwork (and in southwestern tribes, especially, the silver jewelry), most Indian art is related to ritual, religious or secular. There are songs and dances for every occasion, for every part of life, sometimes expressing the most profound feelings and beliefs, sometimes just for fun.

Orpingalik, an Eskimo Indian shaman and poet, explained that "it is as necessary for me to sing as it is to breathe. . . . Songs are thoughts, sung out with the breath when people are moved by great forces and ordinary speech no longer suffices. . . . When the words we want to use shoot up of themselves—we get a new song." [22]

On a more mundane level is the revealing statement of William

20. Quoted in McLuhan, *Touch the Earth*, p. 53.
21. On this point Joseph Wood Krutch, in *Baja California and the Geography of Hope* (San Francisco: Sierra Club, 1967), comments: "Beauty and joy are their source in a natural part of him. . . . Joy is the only thing of which indisputably the healthy animal, and even the healthy plant, gives us an example. And we need them to remind us that beauty and joy can come of their own accord when we let them . . . [and] . . . it seems to me that Joy and Love, increasingly fading from human experience, are the two most important things in the world." (pp. 86, 88)
22. Quoted in Knud Rasmussen, "The Netsilik Eskimos, Social Life and Spiritual Culture," *Report of the Fifth Thule Expedition 1921–1924*, 8 ,No. 1–2, Copenhagen, 321.

Brandon, editor of a book of American Indian songs and poems: "If the Pawnees had operated a General Motors, each worker would have had his time-clock-punching song, his assembly-line song, and so on, and the management would have been at least as attentive to the songs as to the rate of production, probably more so." [23]

Indian poetry, often presented as chant, reveals the tremendous richness of Indian languages. Concrete images and a wealth of symbols are utilized in place of terms expressing abstract concepts. A well-known example was the use by the Aztecs of Mexico of the image of a face being at one with a heart to symbolize forthrightness or honesty. (Certain North American tribes had similar symbols to express this concept.) A lovely illustration of Indian imagery is contained in the last words of Crowfoot, a Blackfoot Indian who died in April 1890: "What is life? It is the flash of a firefly in the night. It is the breath of a buffalo in the winter time. It is the little shadow which runs across the grass and loses itself in the Sunset." [24]

From the foregoing it seems clear that the American Indian tends to value a person more for who he or she is than for what he or she has, and gives preeminence among the virtues to a loving openness of person-with-person and person-with-nature. Now, concerning the matter of religion, there is an even wider variety of positions taken among tribes than on other issues. There were hundreds of different religions among the many tribes at one time; even now there are a significant number of widely shared teachings and practices among them and, even where there are differences, there is almost no sense of exclusiveness.

Few Indians make a sharp distinction between religion and what one might term the secular aspects of life. For most, all of life has a sacred character to one degree or another and the Indian has integrated religion into most of his activities. Thus a shaman (sometimes identified as a "medicine man") was and is today in some tribes usually more a priest than a doctor, but his roles have included those of healer, seer or prophet, priest, counselor, and educator.

Further, Indian religions have had little concern for prohibitions, negative moral codes, guilt, sins, and confessionals. Religion for Indians has often consisted of celebrations of nature with, as noted be-

23. *The Magic World, American Indian Songs and Poems* (New York: Wm. Morrow & Company, 1971), p. xii. Phil George, a Nez Perce, articulates a common Indian attitude when he exclaims that dancing leaves him "mentally and physically refreshed . . . more human, more loving, more peaceful." (In Steiner, *The New Indians*, p. 158.)

24. Quoted in McLuhan, *Touch the Earth*, p. 12. *In the Sky Clears—Poetry of the American Indians* (Lincoln: University of Nebraska Press, 1951), A. Grove Day discusses at some length the qualities of Indian poetry and the motives of Indian poets for writing it on pp. 2–6.

fore, the universe and its myriad inhabitants viewed with awe-filled reverence. Evil and pain and death often result from a disturbance of the harmony of one with nature. Supernatural forces are seen as the most natural things on earth. All natural—especially living—beings possess supernatural powers. Along with a pantheon of supernatural beings in nature, some tribes also believe in a supreme being, so terms like "theist" or "Pantheist" do not apply in any simple fashion to their religion. Again, depending on the tribe, rites and rituals, fasting, sacrifices, and visions were and are elements in many Indians' religion.[25]

As far as the effects of Christianity on Indians' religious life go, it is important to note that even though the depth and breadth of Christian influences among diverse Indians have varied considerably, they have played a major role in the post-conquest history of many tribes. This is obvious in the sense that missionaries—largely Roman Catholic in Mexico and in the once Spanish and later Mexican territories of what is now the southwestern United States, in northern regions once settled by the French, and from various Protestant denominations in many different areas—did at times struggle for the freedom and rights of Indians. (Perhaps most notable among these were Bishops Bartolomé de las Casas, Juan de Zumárraga, and Vasco de Quiroga in Mexico, who generally respected and often praised the Indians under their care.)

There were, of course, many attempts, often successful, though at times superficially, to convert them to Christianity. Some tribes, like the Hopi, were extremely hostile to such activities, viewing Christianity as an alien, destructive force.

After making such critical remarks as: "Christianity came along and tried to substitute 'giving' for [Indian-style] sharing. There was only one catch: giving meant giving to the church, not to other people. Giving, in the modern Christian sense, is simply a method of shearing the sheep, not of tending them" and after urging the expansion of the Native American Church (of which more later) or the development of a national Indian Christian Church, Vine Deloria (whose father is an Episcopal minister and who spent four years in a seminary himself) finally comments: "I believe that an Indian version of Christianity could do much for our society. But there is little chance for such a melding of cards."[26]

Others have struggled for such a melding, like the Catholic Indians of the Pueblo of Isleta in New Mexico who (overcoming some objec-

25. See Erna Ferguson, in *Dancing Gods, Indian Ceremonials of New Mexico and Arizona* (New York: Alfred A. Knopf, 1942), which presents a fascinating description of dance as prayer for many tribes.

26. *Custer Died for Your Sins* (New York: Macmillan, 1969), pp. 121, 124.

tions from certain Catholic authorities) have included in their religion many of their tribal beliefs and attitudes and practices—like dancing before and inside of the church. Andy Abeita, then governor of the Pueblo proclaims, "We are good Catholics. But we are Indian Catholics. Let me tell you what that means. Let me tell you one thing. When the Anglo prays, he prays for what he wants, for himself. When the Indian prays, he prays for other people. The last words of the Indian prayer are these: 'If there is anything left let it be for me.' . . . It is our way. We shall keep it that way." [27]

There are many similar examples, like Pawnee Baptists and Methodists, who point out that they worship the same Supreme Being, Tirawa, that they and their ancestors had always worshipped, but from Christians they learned of Jesus Christ.

In fact some Indians believe that their Christianity is more real, more authentic, more truly Christian than the white man's, because they can live by its teachings better in their loving communities than can the isolated white man in his urban, covetous society. Deloria comments that for most white men religion is a matter of ideas in their head, where they remain, while for Indians religion is a matter of feelings in their heart, from which issue generous actions.

At times Christianity has been a strong force for Pan-Indianism, with members of diverse tribes with formerly different beliefs joining together as Christians in an ecumenical sense. However most advocates of a spiritual Pan-Indianism insist that in the Christian form most truly Indian elements disappear. As Hazel Hertzberg explains, "To Christianize and to civilize the Indian were identical processes [for most Christian, especially but not solely, Protestant, missionaries]. In adopting Christianity, Indians were expected . . . to conduct their family life according to Christian ideals of a patriarchal, nuclear family, live in a house like other Americans, forego their dances, work hard, keep clean, learn the value of money, be thrifty, stay away from liquor, believe devoutly in private property, and live and think like other church-going Americans." [28]

One may be appalled to see many of these traits described as "Christian ideals," but many Indians were taught this and a majority (naturally enough, one might add), even among those who favored some degree of Pan-Indianism, rejected this avenue to unity.

Another avenue has been through the spread of the Native American Church, a loosely organized intertribal religion which contains and combines certain Christian beliefs and rituals with traditional Indian beliefs and the use of peyote (a hallucinogenic cactus) buttons

27. Quoted in Steiner, *The New Indians*, p. 105.
28. Hertzberg, *The Search for an American Identity*, p. 21.

as a sacrament of sorts.[29] In 1918, James Mooney wrote: "The Indian, under the influence of this peyote religion, has given up the ideas that he and his tribe are for themselves alone, and is recognizing the fact of the brotherhood of the Indian race particularly, and beyond that the brotherhood of mankind." [30]

At this time, although it has suffered from both local and national factionalism (with some members narrowly Native American Church fundamentalist in their approach and others moving closer to traditional Christian beliefs), it is the largest Indian religious body and Deloria, for one, predicts that "eventually it will replace Christianity among the Indian people." [31] However, many Indians today are continuing their attempts to develop Indian Christian churches and others are returning to or preserving (as with many Hopis) their pre-Christian beliefs.

In any event, the essential role that religion (in the various forms discussed above, and others) has played and continues to play in Indian life was beautifully expressed in 1911 by Charles Eastman, (Ohiyesa) a Santee Dakota Sioux: "In the life of the Indian there was only one inevitable duty—the duty of prayer—the daily recognition of the Unseen and Eternal. His daily devotions were more necessary to him than daily food. . . . Whenever . . . [the Indian] comes upon a scene that is strikingly beautiful or sublime—a black thundercloud with the rainbow's glowing arch above the mountain, a white waterfall in the heart of a green gorge; a vast prairie tinged with the blood-red of sunset—he pauses for an instant in the attitude of worship. He sees no need for setting apart one day in seven as a holy day, since to him all days are God's." [32]

At this time an ever-increasing number of Indians are aware of the

29. In 1921 a group of Winnebago peyotists stated the following beliefs: "We recognize all people who worship God and follow Christ as members of the one true church. We believe that all earthly sects are all human organizations. We abominate creeds as relics of the 'Dark Ages' in dividing the followers of a Risen Savior into contending factions and wee [sic] seek for union in worship and in spirit. We do not condemn the practices of any but in so far as the same tend to spirituality believe in the same. We believe in the sacrament and the sacramental bread and wine, but in so much as the use of the same is forbidden to Indians, we of the people who cannot obtain or use the same have adopted the use of bread as peyote and water as wine. We find consolation and encouragement in Romans the fourteenth chapter and second verse and the rest of the said chapter as to this practice. The following are tenets of our religion: One Lord, one faith, one baptism, one God, the Father: To those who are faithful in both kingdom of nature—heaven and earth. Our hope is glory, honor and immortality. Ephesians fourth chapter, fifth and sixth verses." (Quoted in Hertzberg, pp. 276–77.)

30. Quoted in Hertzberg, p. 252.

31. *Custer Died for Your Sins*, p. 113.

32. Quoted in McLuhan, *Touch the Earth*, p. 36.

fact that unity is essential for the achievement of the power needed for their values and beliefs and culture—for they themselves—not just to survive, but to flourish. This means Indians getting together, organizing, speaking out, making demands and, some argue, turning to actions like the recent occupation of the Bureau of Indian Affairs building in Washington, D.C.

There is also a sort of Pan-Indian spirit that seems to have developed in recent years simply because contacts (at pow-wows and ceremonials and at Indian clubs formed in cities and schools) and communications (through tribal and other newspapers and through the ever-increasing number of books by Indians) have fostered a sense of Indian identity along with tribal identity.

A few Pan-Indian movements have been motivated by religious factors, as was the case of the Ghost Dance rituals of the 1890s, and though most have been secular, there is, generally speaking, a strong spiritual drive involved. As Deloria proclaims: "We will survive because we are a people unified by our humanity; not a pressure group unified for conquest." [33]

In any event, the concept of Pan-Indianism is very important for Indians whose numbers (Indians are not "vanishing," by any means) and powers are growing. These powers are especially those deriving from determined activities on the part of tribal leaders and the strong support of more and more non-Indians who, embarrassed over the knowledge of iniquitous white actions against the Indian and attracted by their ideals (real or imagined), are becoming ever more vocal and active.

With ever-increasing vigor Indians are now demanding the freedom and opportunities to manage their own economic and political affairs with the possibilities for leadership in these spheres that they have always lacked. This involves the development of economic institutions that are controlled by Indians themselves. (There are some impressive examples of such achievements, like the electronic components factory on the Yankton Sioux Reservation, the Mescalero Apache "Cattle Corporation," and a variety of economic operations on the White Mountain Apache Reservation including motels, tourist facilities, cattle ranching, and modern farming. In all of these cases the enterprises are tribally owned and communally operated.)

In the political arena, until recently Indians have been relatively inactive, with voter registrations low and candidates few and very far between. However, here again, major changes are taking place as Indians realize that political power can only come from numbers, so the tradition of intertribal cooperation is being expanded to include

33. Deloria, *Custer Died for Your Sins,* p. 224.

intertribal policy unity. (Edgar Cahn mentions that if the BIA is to be the force that it might be for the Indian and not the force that it is, it "must be reorganized, even taken out of [the Department of the] Interior, and given more independence.")[34]

Further, in the cultural sphere Indians are advocating a "leave us alone" policy.[35] Even Indians desiring to enter the United States mainstream rarely are willing to do this at the expense of their cultural identity. At least the freedom to choose the desired degree of cultural assimilation in the wider society must be present.

A young Indian poet, David Martin Nez, expresses this attitude in a poem *New Way, Old Way*: "We shall learn all these devices the White Man has. We shall handle his tools for ourselves. We shall master his machinery, his inventions, his skills, his medicine, his planning; but we'll retain our beauty. And still be Indian." [36]

It is significant to note here that the development of Pan-Indianism (as a source of unity) has not often been at the expense of tribalism (a source of diversity). Most Indians today realize that an emphasis on race is consistent with Pan-Indianism as is an emphasis on culture with tribal diversity—and that both of these are important.

Indians are insisting that models for societies and cultures founded on their various tribal antecedents are preferable to those that they have observed among white men, and that they should be inspired by these models. Writing of Indian youth, Deloria notes that they "suddenly realize that outside of hula hoops and Cadillac fins, the white society had nothing, absolutely nothing, to offer them spiritually." [37] He also carefully differentiates between nationalism that is a positive concern for the preservation and development of one's tribe and a violent militancy, the effects of which are destructive for both Indian and non-Indian. An excellent example of a nonviolent but so far successful Indian nationalistic achievement is the Rough Rock Demonstration School, where the staff is 87 percent Navajo and English is taught as a second language, Navajo legends, literature, history, arts, and crafts are taught both to adults and to children, and the Indian community is in complete control. As Earl Shorris points out: "It is, at first glance, merely a progressive school—immaculate floors and

34. Cahn, *Our Brother's Keeper*, p. 189.

35. In the 1870s, Crazy Horse, the Oglala Sioux mystic and warrior who fought General Custer with Sitting Bull, announced: "We do not want your civilization! We would live as our fathers did, and their fathers before them." (Quoted in McLuhan, p. 67.) Many Indians today are echoing that cry.

36. In Steiner, *The New Indians*, p. 131. Used by permission of the author, former student The Institute of American Indian Arts, Santa Fe, New Mexico, a Bureau of Indian Affairs School.

37. Deloria, *Custer Died for Your Sins*, p. 95.

smudges on the hands of the children. But underlying the laughter is the most aggressive plan for community control of education undertaken by Indians in this century. Its ally is the OEO, which provides a large part of the school's annual budget of nearly a million dollars. The enemy is the Bureau of Indian Affairs, which watches the erosion of its major area of power quietly, waiting for an error." [38]

Finally, it is important to note that along with this Indian and tribal nationalism, a strong patriotism regarding the United States has been common among Indians. Even many who have been appalled by and angry over U.S. government policies still have hopes that this land may finally make real the ideals expressed in its political documents. Meanwhile, quite a few are willing to serve (and have served with distinction) in the Armed Forces—the pride of Indians in their servicemen is well-known.

Now, with great dedication and hopes growing, Indians are claiming their American birthright. A recent Cherokee tribal declaration includes the pledge: "We will go on until our lands and our homes are safe. Until we live within the full and just protection of the law. Until we live as the American authors of the Constitution and the Declaration of Independence intended each of the nationalities in this country to live. As dignified men. As free men. As men equal to all other men." [39]

Finally, just as Indian unity is valued, along with tribal variety, by more and more Indians, so too is an enthusiasm for the possibilities of new ways seen to be consistent with a respect for the values and achievements of the old. Modern scholars, especially anthropologists, have been amazed at the extent of Indian tribal memory—a vast store of preserved lore: history, traditions, myths, and beliefs. Josephy has pointed out that "numerous Indians still cling to traits that are centuries, if not millennia, old and cannot be quickly shed, . . . many find it difficult, if not impossible so far, to substitute individual competitiveness for group feeling; . . . many yet feel a sacred attachment to the land and reverence for nature that is incomprehensible to most whites." [40]

Indians today do insist that they really are not so different from their ancestors, and a fairly large number of college- and university-educated Indians are giving new life to and making vital modern applications of their traditions, some of which are ancient. Indian youth tend to respect the ideas and opinions of their elders in a striking way. Wahleah Lujan, a Taos Pueblo college girl, thus an-

38. *The Death of the Great Spirit,* p. 177.
39. Quoted in Steiner, *The New Indians,* p. 10.
40. *The Indian Heritage of America,* p. 19.

nounces: "If I were living in a dream world what would I want? I would want my people to be able to hold on to our beautiful way of life. I would want my people to hold on to their ways, somehow, and yet be able to be on the same shelf, or level, as the white man. I would want my people to be able to compete with this white man, and yet be able to come back to the pueblo, to live our way. If I were living in a dream world that is what I would want. But why is that almost impossible? . . . I hope most of all, by venturing out, to show my people one can be modern, and yet be very much a part of the old way." [41] The fact that these approaches are now in fact being combined in diverse ways seems to indicate forcefully that a new day is beginning to dawn at last for the American Indian after a long, dark, bitter night.

41. Quoted in Steiner, *The New Indians*, p. 289.

Darrell W. Krueger

The Effect of Urban-Industrial Values
on the Indian Life Style

A major problem confronting traditional people in the modern world is the value crisis they face as they are increasingly exposed to beliefs, attitudes, and values different from their own. This value crisis is called many things, including identity crisis, culture shock, and future shock. Whatever one calls it, the results and ramifications of the conflict between the old and new values for the people involved is significant, for their traditions and very identity are at stake.

The American Indians are facing and have faced this problem for some time. More and more, their values are being challenged by constant contact with a value system quite different from their own. The purpose of this paper is to analyze the results of the penetration of the urban-industrial way of life on the Pima Indian Reservation in Southern Arizona. First, there will be a short analysis of what is left of the traditional Indian political way of life; second, the penetration of the urban-industrial political style on the reservation will be analyzed; and third, the results of this penetration will be considered.

Darrell W. Krueger, Department of Political Science, Northeast Missouri State University. This paper represents the results of more than a year's research on an Indian Reservation in Southern Arizona. It was first presented at the Western Political Science Association Convention, Albuquerque, New Mexico, in April 1971. It also, in somewhat different form, is found in the author's doctoral dissertation. During the year of research a survey of some 200 respondents was conducted, visits were made to numerous meetings, taped-recorded interviews with tribal leaders were conducted, and many documents such as tribal council meeting minutes were read.

Significant Differences in Indian and Urban-Industrial Political Styles

One of the first surprising things that strikes a middle-class Anglo visiting an Indian reservation is the similarity between the Indian life and his own. Modern homes are being constructed, water systems installed, roads repaired, yards cleaned, and gardens planted. Even when visiting political meetings, similarities are apparent. For example, parliamentary procedures are used in conducting meetings. A chairman, of one type or another, presides over the meetings; testimony is asked for and given; votes are taken. People appear to be everywhere engaged in activities with which an outsider can readily identify.

Differences, however, are also apparent. The pace of life is much slower and conversation is lighter. The operation of the political system appears to be inefficient and political actors noninvolved.

On closer observation, one becomes aware of major differences between the Indian's political behavior and his own. Observation of the political life styles of the Indian and those of the urban-industrial man suggests the following categories of differences: Pima political life is consensus-oriented, while the urban-industrial life is majority-rule-oriented; the Pimas are oriented toward persons but the "urbans" are concerned with things; Pimas have functional diffuse political roles, while urban men prefer specific political roles; politically, the Pima Indians have a fluid concept of leadership and authority and urban man has assigned leadership; finally, the Pima way is politically nonhierarchical and the urban-industrial way is hierarchical. Each of these categories of differences is considered at length in the following section.[1]

Consensus Orientation versus Majority Rule

The *informal* decision-making process and political values on the reservation are very democratic, but in the consensus style. In small groups the decision-making process is unstructured. The goal, in such meetings, is to arrive at the best possible decision or means of accomplishing a goal rather than to push for a particular decision that may benefit one group or another. Discussions may last until every-

1. In no case are there strictly dichotomous political norms between the Pima political life style and the urban-industrial political life style. Each, however, tends toward different poles. Nonetheless, given concrete examples, the tendency may appear to be reversed. In these cases exceptions are found but they are not the rule. Exceptions, however, are becoming increasingly evident because of the acculturation of the Indians into the political life style of urban-industrial man.

one has had his say; in fact, some meetings last far into the night. Participants nod their heads in agreement as the speakers argue for or speak out against a particular point. Discussion ends when a consensus has been achieved. When the decision has been made, no vote is necessary to determine what feeling predominates.

This form of consensus democracy contrasts sharply with the ideal of majority rule democracy found outside the Indian community; the bargaining process of the majority rule democracy would be foreign in this atmosphere. In fact, even in a *formal* group setting, theoretically governed by "outside" rules, instances are observed where the informal process determines the outcome of a decision. For example, at a district meeting a vote was observed during which seven people voted for a proposal and two against. Nonetheless, the motion failed because of thirteen abstentions. A premature motion had been made and a consensus had not been reached. The delegates in the room knew, after the vote, that the motion had failed. Nothing needed to be said to deny explicitly the technicality that the motion had carried under the "outside" rules supposedly governing the meeting.

The political values of the Indians are also highly democratic. When a randomly selected sample of 196 residents on the reservation were asked if they agreed or disagreed with the following statements (see Figure 6), an overwhelming number of respondents' answers demonstrated strong democratic values.

FIGURE 6. INDIAN EXPRESSION OF DEMOCRATIC ATTITUDES

Question	Agreed	Disagreed	Don't Know
Tribal improvement should be the concern of only a few leaders in the tribe.	20%	73%	7%
Every citizen should have an equal chance to influence government policy.	83	5	12
Democracy is the best form of government.	76	5	19
The Minority should be free to criticize government decisions.	70	14	16
It is not very important to vote in local elections.	17	67	16
It is very important to vote even when many other people vote in an election.	82	6	12

Personal Orientation versus Thing Orientation

The Pima Indian is highly person-oriented. He still maintains in his everyday life an admiration for personal contact and intimate friendship. Strangers who approach the Indian do well to remember that the impersonal and formal approach will be less successful than a personal informal approach.

On the reservation, the "Indian way" is to develop personal relationships that are unstrained by forces of modern life. When the relationships are materialistically or thing-oriented, the fundamental elements of personal relationships become strained. Two examples demonstrate the Indian preference for personal relationships: the nature of the court system of the reservation and a comparison of the community health representative with the community aides.

The judges on the reservation are well-known and often have intimate knowledge of the cases they are trying. If a problem of a broken family or of assault and battery as a result of intoxication are involved, they probably will have been aware of the situation for some time. In trying the case, it is not uncommon for the judges to plead with the accused, reminding him of his past and of the responsibilities he has to his family and community. Seldom is a court case strictly formal and impersonal; although formal procedures are followed, they do not get in the way of personal involvement of all concerned. Often outsiders criticize the process as being too informal and protest that "the judge spends most of his time giving sermons rather than trying the case." This, however, is an indication of the inability of non-Indians to empathize with the personal orientation of the tribal people toward each other.

Community health representatives have for the most part been well-received in the communities and have gained considerable influence among the people, but community aides have been the center of much criticism and controversy. The turnover in community health representatives is low (not one was replaced in six months of observation), while the turnover in community aides is high (all seven quit their jobs during six months of observation, and replacement was difficult because there were few applications for the jobs). One explanation for this might be the difference in goods and services provided by each group rather than the personalities involved or the fact that one service might be more useful than the other.

The work of the community health representatives is personal and intimate. They "translate the Public Health Service's health programs and resources into terms understandable by the Indian community through home visits and participation in other PHS programs." [2] They contact people who are sick and in need of not just food but also personal attention. They see that proper attention is given to health in the home and visit people at a time when death occurs.

On the other hand, the community aides serve as the primary field staff for the entire program. "Their function is to disseminate infor-

2. Richard I. Hirshberg and Janet F. Abrams, *Local Utilization of Federal Assistance Programs for American Indians* (Menlo Park, Cal.: Stanford Research Institute, 1970), p. 81.

mation about what resources and services are available in the total community and to act as liaison with the recipient of these services." [3] As a Stanford Research Institute report indicates, this role has become one of "transmitting information and policy downward" rather than representing "the people in bringing their ideas to the reservation level." [4] Thus, those who operate at the level of bringing ideas from the people to the supervisors have been successful, while those who perform the impersonal function of representing their superiors to the people have not been well-received.

One further point indicating the Indians' preference for personal relations rather than materialistic achievement is that Pimas are subjectively less affected by their economic situation than are those on the "outside." Despite the fact that over 60 percent of the families interviewed had annual incomes less than $3,000, only 40 percent of the respondents felt that their economic situation was unsatisfactory. This suggests that the community has not developed the materialistic attitude characteristic of Anglo society.

Functionally Diffuse Roles versus Functionally Specific Roles

The differences between the community health representatives and the community aides have an additional dimension that merits consideration. Community aides have functionally specific demands placed on them. They need, for example, to fix the water system or to tell all the people about the next community meeting or to provide the lumber to fix a house. All of these tasks demand particular performances which can be judged as fulfilled or unfulfilled. The tasks of the community health representatives, however, are such that a variety of means are available to individual representatives in fulfilling the demands placed on them. Their roles are functionally diffuse; they therefore feel competent and successful no matter how they decide to go about comforting either a sick person or someone who has lost a loved one. The performances of these tasks cannot be measured as easily as jobs demanding specific performance criteria.

This also suggests that the Pimas tend to behave in diffuse ways even when the roles would seem to call for specificity. Even where specific performance criteria are established for a job, the individual filling that job is allowed to perform the role in many different ways. Only when performance standards are unquestionably far below the acceptable means is a person dismissed. Even then, people are not fired without numerous chances and without great agony on the part of the Indian employer.

3. Ibid., p. 79.
4. Ibid., p. 79.

Political roles in the tribe are also handled in this manner. Given certain goals, the committeemen, tribal councilmen, governor, and lieutenant-governor are allowed to fulfill their responsibilities in a variety of ways. It is the outsider and those Indians who have been completely acculturated into the urban-industrial way who are most critical of the way these roles are being performed.

Fluid Conception of Leadership and Authority versus Assigned Leadership

The early political history of many Southwest Indian Tribes repeatedly stressed cooperative labor principles. Most projects, i.e., hunting expeditions, ditch-digging, and other agriculture pursuits, were performed by means of cooperative work forces. No general leader presided over these undertakings; leadership was determined by the situation. It was assumed that the person who was most qualified to run each specialized function was the person looked to for leadership. It was not until the threat of the Apache grew that a chief was placed over the tribe. The first chief, however, was nothing more than a war chief selected to lead the Pimas against the Apache.[5]

> All this work was done under a supervisor—sometimes they needed two for a big job. When they got through at night the boss would lecture them on how good work they had done. He would tell them that now they should go home and plant more than last year and try to make good. He encouraged them. Every time they work together on a job he makes a speech when it is over.[6]

The fluid concept of leadership is still evident on the reservation. Many young people have been selected by tribal elections to tribal leadership positions because they have acquired the capabilities of dealing with the white man on his level. However, when it comes to decisions that are strictly related to the people on the reservations, such as open and closed range, a noticeable shift in leadership is evident. Here the old leaders are called upon to discuss the problem and, in reality, to make the decision, even though, in theory, the tribal council which is filled with many younger people constitutionally should be deciding the problem.

Furthermore, leadership shifts constantly with the issues within the tribe. The most influential persons in particular areas will be those who are most informed about the problem and who have been recognized by the tribe as possessing special knowledge or skills. When

5. Robert A. Hackenberg, *Economic and Political Change Among the Gila River Pima Indians,* a report to the John Hay Whitney Foundation, March 1955, p. 48.

6. Ibid., p. 28.

dealing with tribal health problems, the health board chairman, the head community health representative, and the Public Health Service director all play predominant roles. If a problem exists regarding a particular industrial park director, the economic developer and the attorney play predominant roles.

Nonhierarchical versus Hierarchical Structure

The fluid concept of leadership, as well as the personal orientation of the Indian way, reinforces the basic nonhierarchical orientation of the tribe. The hierarchical leadership is a product of the "outside" which has been placed on the Indians. Initially, the Indians needed to have a chief, a headman, to negotiate with the outside. Later, although the organization changed, hierarchical leadership was still foreign to the Indian and was meant to meet foreign demands.[7]

American Indians never understood completely the differentiated structure of the "outside." Early in their history, they found it difficult to understand why the negotiator of the whites always had to look for direction from a higher source. They also had difficulty perceiving why those who broke the treaties were not necessarily the same ones who made them.

Policy-making among the Indians is not as differentiated in an hierarchical form. Once a policy was legitimated by consensus, all were responsible for the decision and shared in authority. When this nonhierarchical attitude is united with the fluid concept of authority, it is easy to see why authority and power relationships appear to shift so dramatically with each policy situation on the reservation.

The Penetration of the Urban-Industrial Way into the Reservation

Even though an observable "Indian way" still exists on the reservation, it is constantly under attack by the urban-industrial influences outside the reservation. The greatest penetration comes primarily from two separate sources: that of a foreign political structure with corresponding values, and the modern communication system. These forces have produced a gap between the behavior of the Indian and the values of the outside structure. As a result, a growing lack of identity and a serious occurrence of pathological social behavior are apparent.

7. Edward H. Spicer, *A Short History of the Indians of the United States* (New York: Van Nostrand Reinhold, 1969), pp. 15–16, 70.

Political Structure and Urban-Industrial Values

The first imposition of outside political values came in 1852, when the first federal bureaucracy was established to deal with the Pimas and the first agent was assigned to the reservation. Penetration of outside values continued with the conversion of two-thirds of the tribe to Presbyterianism from 1870 to 1914. Hackenberg observed:

> Organization was generated through the establishments of the role of village elder, who eclipsed the traditional chief as a figure of authority and a leader in community affairs. Elders were elected to serve as leaders and guardians of the public morality in each of the churches Cook founded throughout the reservation during the 1890's.[8]

One of the most important penetrations of structure was the forced allotment of ten acres per individual along the river running through the reservation between 1914 and 1921. The allotment was meant to give personal property to the Indian so he would feel responsible for his own welfare and as the "Protestant ethic" and "capitalism" suggest, rise above his deprived conditions. The allotment did not make the Pima self-sufficient, but it did help destroy the Indian way of life.

> The social effect of giving every Indian ten acres (as much as eighty acres to some families), where most families had previously possessed less than ten acres, was to separate the members of the community from each other spatially. Previously, families in a community located their houses near each other in a common village. After allotment they moved their houses onto the land they owned, like white midwestern farmers. Allotment ended the old Indian village.[9]

The last major penetration came with the adoption of the constitution and by-laws of the community on May 14, 1926; these established a pattern of government that in many ways was in direct opposition to the pattern prescribed by the "Indian way." First, leadership was to be assigned rather than "fluid." A council, a governor, a lieutenant-governor, and so forth were the ostensible governing body of the community. The tribal council was, of course, to be the supreme authority. Second, the method of selecting leadership and making decisions was declared to be by majority vote instead of by consensus. This process of selection is foreign to the Indian. Councilmen, under this system, are nominated for the position at a district meeting. Once nominated, the candidates are given time to campaign (however, few do). An election with poll-watchers and judges is then held

8. Hackenberg, *Economic and Political Change,* p. 62.
9. Ibid.

by secret ballot. The successful candidate is the one polling the majority of votes. The procedure for selecting the governor and lieutenant-governor differs in that those who desire to run must file for candidacy. After filing, the candidates campaign from community to community; later, a nominating convention is held that selects the two final candidates for each position. These candidates may continue to campaign until the election is held, and the candidate getting the majority of votes is elected.

The process of making decisions under the 1926 constitution and by-laws was also foreign to the Pimas. In tribal council meetings all issues must now be formally settled by majority vote. The subject is first discussed and the tribal council has an opportunity to question key witnesses. After the discussion, a motion is made on the matter and then settled by a majority vote. The entire proceeding is controlled by parliamentary procedure.

The new constitution also established a hierarchy of authority. It placed the tribal council at the top of reservation government with the power to prescribe the executive powers of the governor and to legislate the duties and jurisdiction of the judiciary. The council also now appoints all standing committees and approves special committees appointed by the governor. The secretary and treasurer are appointed by the council, which also declares vacancies when a governor, lieutenant-governor, chief judge, associate judge, or council-man resigns, moves, or is removed for cause. The council establishes all election laws and ordinances and is the final election judge. It can expel, by a vote of twelve members, elected officials who are found to be guilty of improper conduct or gross neglect of duty or have failed to perform the duties of their office for a period of sixty days. The council enacts ordinances which define what constitutes improper conduct; a crime or gross neglect of duty. Furthermore, any official committee or board member appointed by the council may be removed or discharged by a majority vote.

The constitution also establishes the governor as the chief executive administrator; the lieutenant-governor, in Ordinance 21, is placed inferior to the governor. The districts are also placed in inferior positions to the tribal council.

Finally, with the hierarchical lines of authority came specific role assignments that were directly opposite to the formerly diffuse concept of roles. Many roles assigned to councilmen have already been described. Beyond these, prescriptions have been set for the roles of all major offices. It is interesting to note that in all cases the specific role assignment concept has not been achieved, to the chagrin of many outsiders who feel that specific role assignments are necessary for a smooth-running machine.

With the prescription of foreign structure came the pressure to change the behavior of the Indian to conform with the rules of the structure; outside observers cannot forget their own value system when they observe the Indians' performances. Although the Indian may try to adjust the structure itself in a way quite consistent with the Indian way, outsiders will not allow him to operate by such unconventional means. The superintendents of the Bureau of Indian Affairs, attorneys' study teams, and many others, when asked for advice generally, encourage rather the changing of the "Indian way" to the established structure. The outsider then attempts to teach the Indian how to run the urban-industrial structure in an urban-industrial way. With these pressures and the lack of adequate comprehension on the part of the Indian, his ability to resist change is limited. Perhaps if he understood the problem of these pressures, he would be better able to resist them and decide for himself which course he should follow.

Communication as a Stimulus to Change

The second challenge to the Indian way is provided by the modern communication system. Instruction on how to live the urban-industrial life reaches individuals on the reservation by means of radio and television, travel, education, and work off the reservation. Often the message is unclear; some of it is propaganda; but the media continually tell the Indian to change his way and to adopt the urban-industrial way. Although some communication from outside does not necessarily act to propagate the urban-industrial life style, but provides important information that enables the Pima Indian to choose between his apparent alternatives, there is little communicated that provides a positive view of the Indian life style.

The educational system in which the Pima has been schooled over the past century has propagated the urban-industrial way. This school system transmits the values and orientations of Anglo Society. When the 196 respondents of the Gila River Reservation were asked "Speaking generally, what are the things about this country that you are most proud of?" only 1 percent could *not* name anything. Yet when asked "What are the things that make you most proud to be a Pima (Maricopa)?" 25 percent could *not* name any particular characteristic. The strong systems affect of the Gila River Indian Community people at the national level is probably a result of the educational system. When asked "Do you remember how much time was spent in school studying current events and the government of the country?" 74 percent of the people responded that at least a little time had been spent on these subjects.[10] On the other hand, very little time probably was spent on Indian materials, although no question was asked about this subject.

Newspapers, radio, television, travel, and employment off the reservation provide a more rounded view of the urban-industrial way. However, the contact that the reservation actually has with these things is limited: 20 percent of the respondents read the newspaper at least once a week, 37 percent listened to the radio or watched television at least once a week, 40 percent went to a nearby "Anglo" town weekly, 67 percent had traveled outside the state of Arizona, and only 51 percent of the people had worked off the reservation for a year or more.[11] It could be expected that because the reservation is so close to urban centers the contact with the outside would be greater; at any rate, in spite of these somewhat limited contacts with the outside, the percentages are sufficiently high for a good deal of information to be transmitted frequently to the reservation. No doubt this information places challenges on the Indian way.

Some Results of the Penetration of the Urban Industrial Way on the Reservation

The constant challenge of the Indian way by the outside world has had some devastating effects on the Indian. Many Indians now face an "identity crisis." Many feel that they cannot control their own destiny. And probably as a result of these stresses there is a startling amount of pathological social behavior on the reservation.

Lucian W. Pye examined the problem of identity crises that transitional peoples face. He hypothesizes that

> the struggles of large numbers of people in any society to realize their own basic sense of identity will inevitably be reflected in the spirit of the society's political life, and thus, more specifically, that those conscious and subconscious elements most crucial in determining the individual's identity crises must have their counterparts in the shared sentiments of the policy.

Furthermore, he adds, "We must assume that in transitional societies in which the socialization process fails to give people a clear sense of identity there will be related uncertainty in the political culture of the people." [12]

One of the basic measures of the identity crisis is trust in human

10. Darrell W. Krueger, *The Political Integration of the United States Indians: A Case Study of the Gila River Reservation* (doctoral dissertation, University of Arizona, 1971), pp. 60–62.

11. Ibid., pp. 45–107.

12. *Politics, Personality and Nation Building* (New Haven and London: Yale University Press, 1962), pp. 52–53.

relationships. The individual facing an identity crisis "cannot be sure about the actions of others because he cannot be sure about himself." [13] Among the Pima-Maricopa Indians, distrust is prevalent. The respondents were asked "Some people say that most people can be trusted. Others say you can't be too careful in your dealings with people. How do you feel about it?" A startling 48 percent answered "It depends." Only 25 percent answered "Most people can be trusted."

Another evidence of distrust is reflected in the feelings an individual has about influencing others. If he distrusts others, he must distrust his own capacity in influencing others, and hence his feelings of impotence.[14] The Gila River Indian Community respondents showed a relatively low sense of efficacy in tribal affairs. When asked whether they felt they could do something about an unjust tribal regulation, 38 percent answered they could not. When asked whether or not they felt they could do something about an unjust national regulation, 58 percent answered they could not.

In summary, an observable difference exists between the political life styles of the Indian Community and the urban-industrial political style. The differences between the two, however, are becoming blurred with time. The political values and attributes of the urban-industrial way are propagated through regular contact with the outside, they are taught by the educational system, by the outside observers, and by those Indians who have been completely acculturated into the other value system. Nonetheless, remnants of the Indian way are still preserved, primarily in the private culture of the home. What is left of the Indian way of life is passed from generation to generation by the socialization of the children into family life. This life style, however, is gradually fading away, as demonstrated by change of dress, the loss of ability by many to speak an Indian language, and the gap between what people say they will do and what they do. As a result, the political integration of the Indians into the political system of the United States is becoming increasingly easier because the difference in political values, although still evident, are disappearing.

The Indians have had to pay a great price for their rapid change in values. All struggle for a new identity. Many are successful, but some find it impossible; this is evidenced in the increase in drinking and the suicide rate.

As in so many cases in which people undergo rapid change, the Pimas have not yet turned to nationalism. Perhaps if the Indian way is to survive at a significant level on reservations, more nationalism will have to emerge.

13. Ibid., p. 55.
14. Ibid.

Joseph H. Stauss/Bruce A. Chadwick/Howard N. Bahr

Red Power:
A Sample of Indian Adults
and Youth

Introduction

The 1960s was the decade of protest, especially among the youth, and the significant increase in social and political action has been heavily documented. A variety of causes have been supported, but civil rights for Black Americans and the Vietnam war are two that have attracted large numbers of supporters.[1] In contrast to the extensive literature available about protest activities by Black Americans and White supporters for their civil rights, very little is known about other minorities' use of protest as a tactic to influence the administrators of bureaucracies and the public in general. The social science literature is almost devoid of empirical studies of their attitudes and their participation in protest activity. Therefore, the first intent of this paper is

Joseph H. Stauss, Department of Sociology, University of Arizona, Bruce A. Chadwick, Brigham Young University, and Howard M. Bahr, Washington State University. The study from which the data for this report were obtained was supported by the National Science Foundation (GS-3248) and was conducted at the Washington State University Urban Research Station in Seattle, Washington.

Financial support from the Graduate College Faculty Research Support Committee at the University of Arizona that allowed continuation of this research is gratefully acknowledged.

1. P. G. Altbach and R. S. Laufer, *The New Pilgrims: Youth Protest in Transition* (New York: David McKay, 1972); R. Flacks, "Who Protests: Social Bases of the Student Movement," in Julian Foster and Durward Long, eds., *Protest: Student Activism in America* (New York: William Morrow, 1970); S. Surace and M. Seeman, "Some Correlates of Civil Rights Activism," *Social Forces,* 46 (December 1967), 197–207; and R. H. Somers, "The Mainsprings of the Rebellion: A Survey of Berkeley Students in November, 1964," in S. M. Lipset and S. Walin, eds., *The Berkeley Students Revolt* (Garden City, N.Y.: Doubleday, 1965).

to report a study documenting the level of support and the use of protest as an influence tactic by Indian people living in an urban area.

Steiner reports that the term "Red Power" was first used by Clarence Tallbull in 1966 at an annual convention of the National Congress of American Indians.[2] Robert Day, utilizing newspaper accounts in an analysis of Indian activism, reports that the unique aspect of Indian activism is its nonviolent nature.

> In applying their obstructive tactics, the Indians have carefully attempted to avoid all forms of violence, except an occasional fight, while tenaciously demonstrating against the law, rule, or practice in question.[3]

There are notable exceptions to this nonviolence theme, such as the recent destruction of the Bureau of Indian Affairs offices in Washington, D.C. But even in this case the preference for nonviolence is evidenced by the numerous Indian leaders who denounced the tactics of violence and destruction while supporting the objectives. Therefore, a second purpose of this study is to examine the attitude of Indian people toward the use of violence in fighting for their civil rights.

Day makes the point that Indian activism has developed because of the efforts of young people. According to him, college students have provided the leadership and impetus for increasing Indian activism. The formation of the National Indian Youth Council (NIYC) is cited as a major step in the emergence of Red Power and activism. Perhaps Day and other authors have been influenced by the literature concerning Black civil rights and Vietnam war protests because in both cases the struggle was conducted primarily by young people. Personal observation and participation in Indian protest activities have caused the authors, however, to question the assumed major role of the young in Indian protest, at least in urban areas, and thus the third objective of this study is to determine the difference between young (high school students) and old (adults) in their support of Indian activism. (Indian high school students rather than college students were sampled because of the limited number of the latter.)

The study was conducted in Seattle, Washington during the summer and fall of 1971. Of a proposed sample of 753, 269 interviews were completed including 122 by Indian adults and 147 by Indian youths; 33 respondents refused to participate, 364 could not be located, and the remainder were excluded for various reasons.

The interviews, conducted by trained Native-American interviewers, probed to identify support for as well as participation in protest

2. Stan Steiner, *The New Indians* (New York: Delta, 1968).

3. Robert C. Day, "The Emergence of Indian Activism," in Howard M. Bahr *et al.*, eds., *Native Americans Today: Sociological Perspectives* (New York: Harper and Row, 1972), pp. 507–32.

activity in two local controversies. Fort Lawton, an approximately 300-acre tract of land in the Seattle metropolitan area having frontage on Puget Sound, was declared surplus by the U.S. Army. The Indian community in Seattle claimed the land under an old law that permits certain tribes to reclaim land taken from them when the government no longer needs it. The city of Seattle also claimed the land for a park, creating competition between the two groups. Several protest activities including two occupations of the Fort grounds occurred before a portion of the land was leased to the Indian community for development as a culture center. A second rallying cause concerned the fishing rights of several tribes in the Seattle area. Fishing by the Indians is opposed by various state agencies and conservation and sportsmen's groups. Each year during the salmon runs, various protests and counterprotests by White sportsmen's groups occur, frequently resulting in fights, beatings, and arrests.

Because of personal observations of a limited number of youths participating in past protest activities, items pertinent to past participation were omitted from the youth questionnaire. Also, several factors such as lack of transportation may have prevented willing and even eager young people from protest activities, making a comparison of such behavior between young and adults unreasonable. The youth questionnaire contained several items concerning aspirations, academic achievement, and experiences in and perceptions of the public school system.

As Figure 7 indicates, a fairly large number of urban Indians (32 percent of the adult respondents and 27 percent of the youth) had actually participated in protest activities in support of the Indian com-

FIGURE 7.   PROTEST ACTIVITIES OF SAMPLE OF ADULT URBAN INDIANS

Item	Yes	No
Have you ever attended any meetings concerning the Fort Lawton issue?	32%	68%
IF NO, if you were asked to attend meetings concerning Fort Lawton, would you go?	81	19
Have you participated in any demonstrations or marches supporting the Indian claim to Fort Lawton?	27	73
IF NO, if you were asked to participate in a rally, demonstration, or march supporting the Indian claim to Fort Lawton, would you?	68	32
Have you ever participated in marches, rallies, or demonstrations supporting the Indian claim to Puyallup River fishing rights?	11	89
IF NO, if you were asked to participate in a rally, demonstration, or march supporting the Indian claim to Puyallup River fishing rights, would you do it?	63	37

munity acquiring Fort Lawton. A very high percentage (81 percent and 68 percent) of those who had not engaged in such activities indicated a willingness to do so. Both the level of past participation (11 percent) and the willingness to participate (63 percent) are considerably smaller in behalf of the Puyallup fishing rights. The greater support for local activities that affect the respondent, such as Fort Lawton as compared to support for activities outside the direct experience of the respondent (Puyallup fishing rights). is consistent with previous protest research. Nevertheless, these findings do indicate that a sizable number of adult Indians living in Seattle have become involved in actual protest activities for Indian causes. The fact that a large body of individuals expressed a willingness to become involved suggests that, to the extent Indian leaders can identify problems and acquaint the Indian population with these problems, they can marshal a substantial number of individuals willing to protest, seeking change or redress.

Figure 8 presents the responses to items indicating some support for protest activities including violence. Both the adults and the youth exhibited considerable support for protest activity by agreeing with items such as "I feel that civil rights marches, as long as they are peaceful, do a lot of good," and disagreeing with items such as "Indians spend too much time in 'civil rights' activities, protesting, and demonstrating, and neglect their work." Adult respondents, however, rejected the use of violence. They denied the need to employ it and quite strongly agreed that fair treatment could be obtained without resorting to violence. While analyzing the adults' responses, the conclusion emerged that "Red Power," as voiced by urban Indians, avoids violence as an influence tactic or as a frustration reduction mechanism. This is quite different from the Black Power movement. Those adult Indians who have engaged in protest behavior and/or are willing to engage in such behavior reject the use of violence. On the other hand, the youth sample indicated significantly more support for the use of violence.

This suggests that the young are more eager to engage in protest activity including violence. However, when the adults and youth are compared on the six nonviolent items, the adults are more supportive of protest on every item. The differences in two of the six items are statistically significant. Together these two findings indicate, much to our surprise, and inconsistent with the body of Black civil rights and war protest literature, that adults are more militant than youth in support of protest behavior. There is also a strong rejection by adults of violence as an acceptable tactic. On the other hand, the young who are not as actively supportive of protest do not share their elders' disdain for violence. The young are *not* as supportive of protest, but if

FIGURE 8. MEAN RESPONSES TO ITEMS SUPPORTIVE OF PROTEST BEHAVIOR
FOR INDIAN ADULTS AND YOUTH

Item	Mean Response Youth	Adult	T Values
Indians spend too much time in "civil rights" activities, protesting and demonstrating, and neglect their work.	−1.3*	−2.2	3.3ᵃ
Those Indians who take over places like Fort Lawton or Alcatraz do their cause more harm than good.	−0.6	−1.6	3.0ᵇ
I feel sure that civil rights marches, as long as they are peaceful, do a lot of good.	1.6	1.9	0.8
Demonstrations and protest are the best ways to get more rights for Indians.	−0.2	0.0	0.7
If the Indians want equal treatment and "red power" we are going to have to work for it just as the Blacks have.	2.0	2.1	0.8
I support the Indians' fight for fishing rights on the Puyallup River.	2.5	2.9	1.6
Whites used violence to subdue the Indians; it is only right that Indians use violence, if necessary to regain their rights.	1.6	−0.1	5.1ᵃ
Indians today can gain fair treatment without resorting to violence.	0.9	1.6	2.2ᶜ
I would resort to physical violence if necessary, to help regain fishing rights on the Puyallup River.	0.5	−0.8	3.5ᵃ

a = significant at the .001 level.
b = significant at the .01 level.
c = significant at the .05 level.
* Responses varied from +5 (total agreement) to −5 (total disagreement). Therefore, a negative sign indicates disagreement with an item while the remainder represent agreement.

they were to participate, they would be considerably more willing to utilize violent tactics.

Discussion and Conclusions

The findings of this study indicate that despite lack of representation in the social science literature, minority groups other than Blacks have utilized protest activities in attempting to improve the quality of their lives. Specifically, a very high percentage (nearly 40 percent) of adult Indians living in the Seattle metropolitan area have engaged in Red Power activities. Even more significant is the large reservoir of potential activists who expressed a willingness to participate if given the opportunity. These findings indicate quite strongly that Red Power is a real and vital factor in this urban community. As issues appear and leaders take up the challenge, it is anticipated that more and more Indians will utilize protest to exert an influence on the policies that affect their lives.

It was discovered, contrary to the literature on Black protest, that the Red Power advocates rejected the use of violence as a protest tactic. Many respondents told the interviewer that violence is not the "Indian way." This is not to say that every Indian activist rejects violence—there are cases in which Indians have utilized violence and destruction. But it does indicate that any attempt to marshal large numbers of Indian people for violent protest would be a difficult task, at least in the Seattle area. The organizers of potentially violent activities could do much better to look for recruits among high-school-aged Indians. One important avenue of further research would be to follow up on these young people to determine whether their attitudinal behaviors change as they leave school and enter the occupational world. Will they be more supportive of protest as adults? And, even more importantly, will they maintain their propensity for violence or will the experience of the "real" world after school moderate their idealism and passions? Hopefully this type of longitudinal research will be forthcoming.

It was quite a surprise to discover *less* support for protest among the young as compared to the adults. This is a rather startling finding in the light of the large amount of literature reporting the opposite trend. This reversal of previous findings should be accepted with caution, however, and additional research conducted to verify the extent to which the Indian experience is unique compared to other minority groups. The nature of the adult Indian's daily experience in the city, the aspect of being on the "firing line" against the lack of BIA, Indian Health Service facilities, or discriminating employers, and so on may result in the emergence of strong support for protest activity aimed at alleviating current conditions.

In addition, the "realities" of being a numerically small minority coupled with a history of military genocide may contribute to the adult Indians' rejection of violence, because the retribution following such actions frequently outweigh the positive effects. At the same time, the youth are somewhat insulated by the public school system, with its promise of a bright future, and to a large extent they have not faced the same frustrations the adults have. Thus, they do not feel the strong need to support protest activities. Again, additional research is suggested to pursue the factors associated with the emergence of Indian adult and youth support for Red Power programs.

In summary, it was discovered that a significant number of Indian adults living in the Seattle metropolitan area have engaged in protest on behalf of Indian causes. Two significant differences between youths and adults emerged; the young were *less* supportive of protest but *more willing* to use violence than the adults.

The Political Behavior
of Chicanos and Native Americans

The pattern of political behavior of Chicanos and Native Americans within the U.S. political system has characteristics peculiar to these two minorities that set them apart from other American ethnic groups. They are the only minority societies that came into the U.S. nation-state as a result of expansion and territorial conquest. Furthermore, this conquest has occurred in relatively recent times, considering the events at Wounded Knee, South Dakota in 1890, which marked the end of the long period of armed struggle against White encroachment. Similarly, the Treaty of Guadalupe Hidalgo of 1848 and the Gadsden Purchase of 1853 amputated half of the territory of Mexico while promising to the Mexican Americans cultural autonomy, land rights, and privileges acquired prior to the acquisition by the U.S. of the Southwest and the West.

These treaties were later severely curtailed, obviated, or in some instances totally nullified (for example, consider the forcible reloca-tion of Indians and preempting of Mexican land grants by claims of the new American settlers). An analogy can thus be made and a par-allel drawn between these two conquered polities. Chicanos and Native Americans, unlike any American immigrant minority or even the Blacks (who were carried or induced away from their land, property, and sociopolitical institutions), have characteristics of a territorial minority. That concept is generally alien to the American political experience, but very familiar in the European, Asian, and African political scene of shifting borders, expanding polities, and consequent change in sovereignty over conquered territories and people.

In the case of both Chicanos and Native Americans, the concept of territoriality and race survives to this day in whatever diminished form. Ethnic consciousness of the common tradition, history, and culture based on linguistic unity (in the case of the Mexican Americans) and tribal and linguistic unity (in the case of each Indian society) reinforced the active or inactive, direct or indirect resistance to the processes of political integration resulting from the change of sovereignty. Furthermore, the accident of racial differences between both groups and the immigrating Anglos (as they have been known in the American Borderlands) was juxtaposed on ethnic consciousness. It prevented, slowed, or postponed for generations the political integration of these two groups within the Anglo-American nation-state. In fact, their integration has not been accomplished even with the expansion of Civil Rights legislation and the belated acceptance of the concept of cultural pluralism.

Thus it is largely through this ethnic-racial nexus that these two American territorial minorities avoided cultural assimilation and sociopolitical integration within the U.S. It is hence posited here that the past failure to assimilate these minorities irrevocably destroyed the possibility of melting them into Anglo America. As cultural and political reawakening began occurring among Chicanos and Native Americans in the 1960s, these societies became determined to retain their societal structure and cultural identities. Their integration would now occur on a group level rather than on the individual level of immigrant Americans of the turn of the century.

Thus, ironically enough, they emerged victorious from the melting-pot phase and have the potential to play a bigger role as groups in the pluralistic America of tomorrow than do other ethnic groups. These stipulations are nevertheless predicated on one hand on the allocation of sociopolitical rights by the larger American community to these groups and on the other hand on political participation in decision-making and formulation of public outputs by the members of the two minorities.

Integration could not and did not happen as a result of the past and recent sociopolitical relations of these groups with Anglo-American society, or at best happened only marginally. Let us therefore examine the general characteristics of political behavior of each group in the light of these peculiar circumstances recognizing, however, that they were treated somewhat differently by the expanding political system into which they were absorbed.

The initial and still operative Anglo-American policy toward the Indian tribes was delineated through the establishment of the reservations, run until recently in a rigid paternalistic fashion from Washington, D.C. As long as the Indians lived on reservations, they were separate and apart from the society, although expected to acquire basic characteristics of the white society, its mores and life style. Those Indians immigrating out of reservations in dire pursuit of jobs and social mobility were expected to join the melting pot, a model only recently questioned or challenged by social scientists. On the political level, the perfunctory integration of Indians within the American political system was considered neither desirable nor mandatory under the constitution even after the extension to them of voting rights by the Congress.

Even this political step did not usher the concept of pluralism, common control, and autonomy that the Native Americans are only now trying to implement. In case of the "detribalized" Indians, they were presupposed to melt individually into the American society and react to it politically. It is against this background that the Native-American political behavior has to be appraised. By and large, neither individually nor as a group did Native Americans become integrated into the American political system, the "support" of various presidential candidates notwithstanding. On the reservations, they participated only in internal tribal politics and not in BIA policy-making. Individual detribalized Indians seldom became politically integrated because of discriminatory barriers, apathy, and alienation resulting from the non-implementation of systemic constitutional guarantees. It is only recently and more dramatically in Washington, D.C., Wounded Knee, South Dakota, and elsewhere that the newly emerged Indian elite has focused on the problems of cultural pluralism and political autonomy. The American Indian Movement charts new directions for Native-American political participation, both within and without the reservations and in the larger American political scene. In their chapter, Joyotpaul and Jean Chaudhuri address themselves to these problems and trace their directions against the background of the dismal failure of previous federal policies directed toward Native Americans. They illustrate the bewildering array of outputs causing either neglect or injustice, half-measures conceived of ethnocentrism that do not alleviate the hopeless socioeconomic position of the Indians but only deepen the critical situation of this minority.

Although Mexican Americans of the Borderlands have not been resettled into reservations, they were reduced to the role of conquered people and progressively deprived, especially in the nineteenth century, of their ancestral rights and privileges solemnly guaranteed under the Treaty of Guadalupe Hidalgo. Except for a small acculturated elite, the Chicanos essentially have remained, until today, outside the mainstream of political decision-making, and when integrated into the U.S. political system, they were cast into a role of supporters of a party that seldom translated its power into Chicano-oriented outputs. The juxtaposition of socioeconomic and ethnic cleavages that Karl Deutsch calls the "double trouble" syndrome of the social mobility and decision-making model is nowhere more glaring than in the American

Southwest. The ethnic and racial barriers to advancement, mobility, justice, and full-fledged participation not only in the larger society but also in their respective communities have resulted over the last century in a deeply rooted pattern of Chicano political behavior *vis-à-vis* Anglo-American society. Political apathy born of economic privation and restrictive sociopolitical outputs created by the Anglos prevented the Mexican-American community from reasserting its inherited and constitutional rights. The economic reality of poverty disarmed and postponed any effective attempts at political participation. Absolute control of all societal structures by the Anglos made the Chicano response a reaction to the existing situation and precluded, until recently, any solutions and structural reforms. Thus individual and communal political behavior was characterized by an overwhelming feeling of helplessness and alienation.

The emergence of *Chicanismo* in the 1960s, vigorously fostered by the growing ranks of college-educated Chicanos, has generated a transformation of traditional Mexican-American attitudes toward the American political system. It has also brought a new pattern of political socialization, a new awareness of community self-identity, and new boldly stated and far-reaching political aims. The traditional, however passive, support of the Democratic Party, largely due to socioeconomic considerations, is being reassessed in view of failure to generate outputs in response to Chicano demands. Thus, a third party quest has gathered momentum and culminated in the emergence of a Chicano party—La Raza Unida. Its history, tribulations, and purposes are reviewed by Armando Gutierrez against the background of rapidly changing patterns of Chicano political behavior.

His analysis of La Raza Unida establishes linkages between this party and other past and present parallel Mexican-American social institutions. Thus, La Raza Unida plays a role similar to other Chicano sociopolitical organizations designed to foster community aims against the encroachment of the Anglo-American society. Hence, this political party is not a dramatic departure from past societal forms—only the style of response is different as circumstances and times change.

Patrick McNamara examines the problem of assimilation of the Mexican Americans and Catholicism against the background of emerging *Chicanismo*. The Catholic Church—the paramount social organization of the Mexican-American community, which in the past offered comfort, solace, and refuge to communal cultural values—is now viewed as an institution largely unable and/or unwilling to adjust to Chicano sociopolitical demands. Thus the Church's insensitivity to the Chicano movement results in its being replaced as a dominant institution in the Chicano community.

Problems stemming from the systemic failure of the Anglo-American society to provide political equality and justice to racial minorities are common to the Chicanos, Native Americans, and Blacks. Stephen Herzog discusses in his paper the important issue of political coalitions among the ethnic groups in the Southwest, analyzing not only their weighty potential in American politics but also their difficulties stemming from systemic "divide and rule" tactics. The latter precludes any simple answers to the issue of political coalitions of the disadvantaged and discriminated minorities. They are altogether too often pitted against each other in competition for socioeconomic advantages, as was vividly portrayed in recent tragic events in Gallup, New Mexico, where the meager "concession" in decision-making granted by Anglos to the Chicanos led to an Indian-Chicano confrontation (kidnapping of the Chicano mayor appointed to the Board of Regents of the University of New Mexico and the subsequent suicide of an Indian activist).

The ease with which the Anglo structures can allocate values through political favoritism generates Indian intertribal responses and deepens the misery of the Native Americans. Thus, it is not very surprising that Anglo political tactics and outputs create feelings of separatism among the growing segment of both territorial minorities. Frustrated and not convinced of the future implementation of just economic and political solutions, they chart new directions.

The Chicanos, through the "Brown Power" movement, aim at an autonomous territorial polity based on their cultural heritage—"the Northern mythical land wherefrom the Aztecs came, *la tierra de Aztlán*"—a powerful romantic symbol which has been already translated into a *"plan espiritual de Aztlán,"* a political call for unity, organization, and liberation. This program concludes that "social, economic, cultural and political independence is the only road to total liberation from oppression, exploitation and racism." (Denver, Colorado 3/30/69)

The Native-American political reawakening and reassertion of Indian cultural heritage is aptly summarized by the late Clyde Warrior, the most legendary of all the new leaders of the Red Power movement:

It appears that what is needed is genuine contemporary creative thinking, democratic leadership to set guidelines, cues, and goals for the average Indian. The guidelines and cues have to be *based on true Indian philosophy geared to modern times.* This will not come about without nationalistic pride in one's self and one's own kind. This writer says this because he is fed up with religious workers and educationalists incapable of understanding, and pseudosocial scientists who are consciously creating social and cultural genocide among American Indian youth. . . .

The National Indian Youth Council must introduce to this sick room of stench and anonymity some fresh air of new Indianness. A fresh air of new honesty and integrity, a fresh air of new Indian realism, a fresh air of a new Greater Indian America.*

* Clyde Warrior, "Which One Are You? Five Types of Young Indians," Clyde Warrior Institute in American Indian Studies, undated pamphlet.

Joyotpaul Chaudhuri / Jean Chaudhuri

Emerging American Indian Politics:
The Problem of Powerlessness

Rhetoric to the contrary, the social sciences have paid scant attention to the contemporary problems of American Indians compared to that given other minorities, including Blacks and Mexican Americans. Even anthropologists who alone among social scientists have long been interested in Indians have, on occasion, treated contemporary Indian problems with academic disdain. Some are disappointed when the contemporary Indian does not measure up to the anthropologist's reconstruction of historic and idealized Indian roles. Exaggerated as it may seem, there is a new distrust of the anthropologist and social scientist among many Indians today.[1] The irrelevance of much social science to the resolution of real Indian problems, however, provides minor frustrations when compared to the realities of Indian powerlessness despite the civil rights movement and the cries for Indian power.

A corollary of Lord Acton's proposition can be properly drawn for the Indian experiences in American politics: powerlessness frustrates and absolute powerlessness frustrates absolutely. Even a superficial examination of Indian alcoholism gives one index of the degree of

Joyotpaul Chaudhuri, Department of Government University of Arizona, and Jean Chaudhuri, Tucson Indian Center. This paper was presented at the Workshop on Southwest Ethnic Groups: Sociopolitical Environment and Education, sponsored by The Cross-Cultural Southwest Ethnic Study Center at The University of Texas at El Paso, July 27–29, 1972.

1. Vine Deloria, Jr., *Custer Died for Your Sins* (New York: Avon, 1970), pp. 83–104.

frustration,[2] as does the high incidence of suicide among young Indians.[3]

Anthropologists have at least attempted to study Indians. Other social scientists have largely ignored them or buried them in aggregated data about ethnic minorities. Harrington's conscience-awakening *The Other America* barely touches on Indians, the poorest of the poor. Although Indians share many economic and political problems with others minorities, problems of the Indians are unique because of their numbers, their geographical dispersal, their occasionally common bonds (Pan-Indianism), their differences, and their individualized cultural histories and legal environments. This essay attempts, first, to outline some major areas where Indian sociopolitical problems are unique, and second, to discuss the obstacles to political power of the major categories of Indian groups.

Problem Area I: Property

The gulf between the Indian conceptions of land and the dominant common-law conceptions of property is the greatest among all American ethnic and or cultural groups. In Anglo-American common law, the shift of property notions from possession to ownership is a well-established idea.[4] Ownership as a bundle of highly abstract rights is distinguished from the ancient European conception of possession. The highly formalized and abstract notion of common-law property is part of the reason many non-Anglo groups persistently get into difficulties in their economic relations and contracts. Over and above this, in the case of Indians, there is an additional difficulty.[5] Even the earlier European ideas of possession are alien to traditional Indian

2. An unpublished report by a sophomore team from the University of Arizona Medical College contains the following findings abstracted from Tucson, Arizona police records and Pima County Hospital (Arizona) records for 1969. 16.3% of persons arrested for any reason were Indians, though Indians composed around 1.7% of the population. More particularly 23.8% of the alcohol-related arrests involved Indians. Finally, 1154 of the 1264 Indians arrested were cases involving drinking.

3. Although published studies of comparative Indian health statistics are few and far between, conversations with social scientists (including University of Arizona's ethnologist, Bernard Fontana) close to Papago history and culture makes it fairly clear that at the San Xavier and Sells Arizona public health clinics the following generalizations can, apparently, be made: with the coming of public health services, classic physical problems like dysentery have almost disappeared, while manmade problems like car "accidents," brawling, and suicide have steadily risen.

4. Joyotpaul Chaudhuri, "Toward a Democratic Theory of Property and the Modern Corporation," *Ethics*, 81, No. 4 (July 1971), 271–86.

5. See pages 67–72 of Emory Sekaquaptewa's essay entitled "The Legal Basis of Tribal Governments" in the research report of the *Eighteenth Arizona Town Hall*, Arizona Academy, Phoenix, 1971.

values in that they contain elements of English individualism. In contrast, among Indians, private ownership of personal tools, adornments, and occasionally songs did not exist—they were reserved for common tribal usage and disposition. Although personal tools and possessions were from time to time transferred from father to son in Indian patriarchies and from mother to daughter in Indian matriarchies, land did not pass from individual to individual but remained common property. Though these traditional attitudes about property are diffused today, they continue to cause frustrations with respect to the disposition of both tribal property rights and the individual allotments arising out of the General Allotment Act of 1887.

Tribal property rights both in history and often at the present time have been disposed by Indian "representatives" or "councils" in accordance with Anglo conceptions of contract. Although often legitimate in common law, these councils are usually at variance with traditional attitudes and their contemporary vestiges. Chief William McIntosh of the Alabama Creeks was killed by his own people for going beyond the tribal conceptions of property.[6] Today, groups of articulate young Indians often sharply criticize the perfectly "legal" common-law leases of Indian land for purposes of obtaining water on Papago land, mining on Navaho land, and raising cattle on Sioux lands in the Dakotas. Though some members of other minorities may not fully understand the legal meaning of leases, lease arrangements are completely outside the traditional Indian understanding of property and nature.

The effects of the General Allotment Act of 1887 provide additional examples of the general theme of cultural differences and the unique Indian situation. The general intent of the act was to bridge this cultural difference by forced parcelling out of many tribal lands into individual allotments. This act alone accounted for considerable loss of Indian lands. Bernard Fontana notes:

> When this law was passed in 1887, American Indians were still in possession of about 139,000,000 acres of land. When alloting ceased under provisions of the Indian Reorganization Act in 1934, Indians were in possession of 48,000,000 acres. In other words, from 1887 to 1934, Indians were dispossessed of an additional 91,000,000 acres of land.[7]

Even though allotments stopped in 1934, the frustration resulting from its effects still continues intensely today. In Oklahoma, where Indian land is mostly allotment land, the frustrations show up in the details of a variety of contexts: multiple heirs, absence of wills, BIA withhold-

6. See Grant Foreman, *Indian Removal* (Norman, Okla.: University of Oklahoma Press, 1932).

7. *Eighteenth Arizona Town Hall* report, p. 22.

ing lease money, endless partitioning of the original allotment. It is not unusual to find one heir's sub-allotment being completely surrounded by ex-allotments which have been sold or appropriated by Anglos—leaving undefined and contested right-of-way problems; and if the Indian is poor this constitutes an endless nightmare of legal snares.

Problem Area II: Education

Compared to the educational problems of other minority groups, the case of Indian education, like that of Indian property, is also unique. Although the segregation of Black students has its counterpart in Indian experience, the Bureau of Indian Affairs (BIA) schools provided a different context. Historically, assimilation at almost any cost was the original hope of Indian schools. For the most part their record on this score (even if one were to assume the moral validity of the goal) has been one of failure. Despite the brutal separation of parents from children who used to be sent hundreds of miles away and despite the forced prohibition against using one's own language, the schools were able to bring about two unintended consequences. The first was the nourishing of the seeds of Pan-Indianism among some Indians and the second was the contribution to the alienation and cultural disintegration among many of the rest. Additionally, what little successful vocational training Indians received often took place without taking into account the actual job opportunities available. More so than other minorities, Indians were not actively encouraged to go on to college by counselors and advisors. Traditionally, Indian groups had no regular access to policy-making in BIA schools; the schools were responsible to the federal bureaucracy and had no counterpart of the public school's elected school boards.

In the last decade the picture has changed only slightly. There is more of an effort to cut down on the distance travelled by Indian reservation students and occasionally a large tribe such as the Navajos can influence school policy. But by and large, schools like Chilocco Indian School in northern Oklahoma continues to be accountable to the BIA alone.

In addition to BIA schools, a considerable number of Indian students (40 percent in Arizona) are in public schools. This phenomenon was partly stimulated by the Johnson-O'Malley Act of 1934, which permits contracts between the federal government and public and private agencies working with Indian children at the local level. Even though the Act provides relief for schools "burdened" with Indian students, no corresponding mechanism for institutionalized Indian input into school policy is provided for. In short, despite some improvements in programs, Indians continue to be powerless in affecting their own educational policy.

Problem Area III: Hospitals and Health

What is true for Indian powerlessness in education is also true for Indian health. The Indian hospital has been the one symbol of hope the reservation Indian has in the area of health. In 1955 the administration of Indian hospitals was transferred from the BIA to the Public Health Service. Whatever administrative "efficiency" was achieved by their transfer, the result was an even lesser Indian input in hospital policy-making; Indians now face two bureaucracies instead of one. Though there are good doctors available under the PHS system, there is frequent rotation and turnover. Sustained medical care for complicated problems (diabetes, for instance) is not as easily available as treatment for cuts, wounds, and accidents. Apart from the quality of medical care, the ignoring of Indian needs in these special Indian hospitals exists in a variety of areas, including lack of courtesy for the typically large numbers of "relatives" who want to come and wait outside a room for long periods of time. Transportation to these hospitals is difficult to obtain for the poor and elderly. In addition, of course, the needs of urban Indians and unrecognized groups like the Yaqui Indians of Southern Arizona are by and large ignored.

Problem Area IV: Tribal Governments

The entire maze of Indian tribal governments, like each of the previous topics, deserves a more elaborate treatment than is possible here. However, in the way of illustration of Indian powerlessness, some general comments can be made.

Many contemporary tribal governments received their authority from the Indian Reorganization act of 1934, with some notable exceptions like that of the Navajo. Almost all of them, moreover, describe their powers in the language of Anglo-American constitutionalism. Although they may not always act as common-law deliberative bodies, nevertheless their spirit is not rooted in their own Indian traditions. The idea of majority rule is not an Indian conception. What comes closer to a common theme are notions of wide consultation and consensus, which are seldom achieved. It is not surprising that Indian participation in tribal elections is quite low and general awareness of the details of the tribal council's deliberations is largely missing in most tribes. Among the Hopis there are still villages that have not even participated in tribal elections.

Added to nonparticipation is the fact that the idea of "free elections" have come only recently for some Indian groups. Only in the last five years have the Cherokees, Creeks, and Seminoles of Oklahoma been allowed direct elections for their tribal chairmen. Even then, the ground rules for these elections had to be approved by the Secretary of Interior. In fact, the outgoing chairmen appointed by the Secretary actually drew up the rules, even though they themselves were either candidates for election as in the case of the Oklahoma Cherokees, or as in the case of the Creeks, where they were openly supporting one of the candidates! The rules were drawn up in such a manner that in the cases of the Cherokees and the Creeks, part-Indians casting absentee ballots could easily outnumber (there is some evidence that they actually did) and dominate those who by either blood or culture were Cherokees and Creeks.

Irrespective of the manner of elections, the jurisdiction and power of tribal governments is limited by the guidelines provided by the BIA. Tribal contracts and administrative acts generally need the approval of the BIA. This paternalism often makes tribal governments shy in using their authority and initiative even in areas where they could carry some potential clout. A case in point is the well-publicized "Ajo case" involving the death of Phillip Celaya, a Papago youth, at the hands of Pima County, Arizona, sheriff's deputies at the edge of the Papago reservation.[8] The hasty justice of the peace courts ruling exonerating the deputies within hours of Celaya's death received wide publicity. After extended protests by urban Indian groups and civil rights groups, a publicized autopsy and inquiry was made by judicial authorities. Throughout the events the Papago tribal council did not exert even its moral authority by requesting proper hearings and an inquest.

After having discussed Indian powerlessness in four areas, we can examine briefly the problems of powerlessness from four Indian group perspectives. These groups can be characterized as (1) reservation Indians, (2) Nonreservation tribes, (3) unrecognized Indian groups, and (4) urban Indians.

Reservation Indians

With the great diversity in cultures, attitudes, and problems, generalizations about Indians are more difficult to make than for most other minorities. However, among the four Indian groups, reservation Indians are relatively the most powerful. They do have land and they do have tribal budgets. However, many factors, including location and size, enter into determining political influence. The Navajos, because

8. For a news report, see June–August issues of the *Arizona Daily Star*. Also see *Akwesasne Notes* (the largest "Indian" newspaper), Summer 1972, p. 4: "Papago Youth's Death Angers Many."

of their size and their location in Northern Arizona and neighboring states, are able to wield considerable power. They could influence local elections and they can press the BIA harder than most tribes.

In contrast to the Navajos are numerous small reservations whose residential membership continues to dwindle. The Omahas of Nebraska, for instance, have engaged in considerable controversy among themselves regarding who should be considered a voting member. Small as the group is, it can be easily overwhelmed by absentee voting by Omahas and part-Omahas. The external effectiveness of the Omahas cannot be expected to be as great as the Navajos.

Size itself, however, is no guarantee of the political effectiveness of a tribe. The Navahos have developed considerable political sophistication in addition to their size. Witness the very effective lobbying in Congress by the Navajos which resulted in the killing of the Steiger bill—one proposed solution of the Hopi-Navajo land dispute. On the other hand, the Rosebud Sioux, a fairly large tribal group, have been plagued with more than the usual amount of bickering and have not been an effective political group. After Cato Valandra's scandal-ridden administration was replaced by a rival's in 1969, a tribal equipment officer resigned when his inventory showed that there "was practically no equipment for him to take care of." [9]

Nonreservation Tribes

Oklahoma Indians provide the best examples of nonreservation Indian tribal groups. Even though nonreservation Indians are often held up as examples of assimilation, their political problems are often greater than those of reservation Indians. This is especially true of Oklahoma rural full-bloods. Their lands, if they have any, are "allotment" lands, which are "individualized" and fragmented. Their tribal governments provide no legal aid in property conflicts because they are not "tribal" lands.

Because the PHS hospitals in Oklahoma do not deal exclusively with individual tribes, Indians cannot expect their tribal government to exert pressure in the case of wrongdoing or oversight. The smaller bands of Florida Seminoles, because of their organization on a reservation basis, have more effective political power over education and health than the much more numerous nonreservation Oklahoma Seminoles.

The Oklahoma Indians also have far greater problems than reservation Indians, with aggressive part-Indians claiming tribal suffrage and tribal benefits without reciprocal concern for the tribe or sustained involvement in their affairs and needs.

9. Editorial: *Indian Voice,* September–October 1971, p. 2, Santa Clara, California.

Unrecognized Indian Groups

Scattered throughout the United States are pockets of American Indians who have no legal status as Indians for a variety of reasons. A few, like the Menominees of Wisconsin, have been officially "terminated." Some, like the Yaquis of Arizona, never had legal status. (The Yaquis were originally refugees from Sonora, Mexico.) But most of the groups, because of their lack of political and legal sophistication, have lost their ancestral lands and are regarded as squatters. At the present time their only hope is special legislation on their behalf giving them tribal status and making them eligible for health and education programs. Vine Deloria, Jr. the well-known Indian author and leader, has been working hard for several such isolated groups. To date, there is only one precedent, though a major one, of success. Recently (October 1972) the Tonto Apaches of Payson Arizona succeeded in getting a bill passed in Congress creating the first new Arizona reservation since the Indian Reorganization Act.

Urban Indians

A majority of Indians now live in cities and towns and are regarded as "urban Indians." They are the most powerless of all Indian groups. They not only have all the disadvantages of other urban minorities but they are also the poorest and culturally the most distinct. As long as they remain in urban areas, they are cut off from standard Indian services. They are ignored by the establishment and by other minorities. In Tucson Arizona, the United Fund Drive budgets zero dollars for the Tucson Indian Center. Other cities like Chicago, with a respectable Indian population, allocate negligible amounts of community funds for urban Indians (43,000 in 1970) compared to traditional middle-class Boy Scout activities, which received $401,200.

The urban Indians are not only ignored by city hall, they are patronized and neglected by other minorities as well. In the rhetoric of minority and civil rights appeals, concern for the Indian is included and then forgotten. In urban "coalitions," Indians are always taken for granted. In Los Angeles, Blacks and Mexican-American political groups are too busy fighting for their share of the pie to include the Indians in their actual concern. Tucson Arizona, with 6,000 Indians, provides another example of how the urban civil rights movement and its benefits have by and large passed Indians by. The two major programs for fighting urban poverty and blight are the model cities program and the CEO (Council on Economic Opportunity—an Office of Economic Opportunity contractor). Even though the Indian population is comparable in size to Black and Mexican-American groups, Indians have a minimal voice in CEO and none in Model Cities. The director of CEO is a well-known Mexican-American leader who has a Black assistant director. Similarly, the model cities director is a Black whose first assistant is a Mexican American. Except for two Indian Center staff positions that are funded by CEO, no special attention is paid to Indians as a group.

Despite their powerlessness, Indians have not given up. There is considerable evidence of rising interest in politics. At the tribal level, splinter groups like the Navajo Rights Association or the Creek Centralization Committee keep pressuring tribal governments into being more responsive. At the national level, the venerable National Congress of American Indians, the most effective and visible national organization, keeps seeking wider constituency and to include more Indian groups in its membership.[10] The NCAI continues its efforts though it is plagued with problems—previous domination by Sioux and Plains Indians, the coolness of "traditional" Indians, and the scepticism of Indian groups insensitive to the need for nationwide Indian planning.

There is also the rising Indian nationalism or pan-Indianism nurtured by the camaraderie of Indian Schools, by shared Indian prophecies, and the spreading habit of "traditional conventions" (not powwows) such as those at Henryetta Oklahoma, Rosebud South Dakota, and Tonawanda New York. Pan-Indianism is often strongest among groups with the least unbroken maintenance of tribal traditions or with the longest exposure to Anglo influence, like the Mohawks and Onondagas of the northeast.

Less numerous but more visible (with the help of the media) are the "radical" groups, like American Indian Movement (AIM) and the smaller National Indian Youth Council. Skillful in the use of media, these groups have not bothered to build an Indian constituency. Occasionally, AIM is "successful" when operating in the familiar home territory of one of its leaders—usually a Plains Indian. Thus, for instance, in Nebraska AIM was able to mobilize many Sioux Indians into a mass protest against the public indignity suffered by an Indian who was forced to dance naked in the dance hall of a veteran's group. Elsewhere, AIM has not been as effective. In much of the Southwest, AIM has been unable and perhaps unwilling (because of its preoccupation with media) to build a real constituency. In October 1972 at the first organizational meeting of AIM in Tucson, eight persons showed up and three of them were Anglos! Perhaps with experience and planning this will change in the future.

At the national level, Indians are not numerous enough to form effective coalition with other groups. The student movement never

10. See Deloria, *Custer Died for Your Sins*, pp. 196–238.

bothered with the details of Indian problems. Many traditional liberals like Senator Jackson of Washington actually worked against Indian demands and requests. Only a handful of legislative leaders, liberal (Ted Kennedy) and conservative (Barry Goldwater and Paul Fannin, U.S. Senator from Arizona), have had anything close to a sustained sympathetic interest in Indian affairs—these are strange allies indeed.

In the meantime, although Indian political sophistication has a long way to go—Indians are plagued with a new romanticism which ignores the real world fostered by the "new" moviemakers, revisionists of Indian history, and some of the alienated young who have become fascinated with things Indian. The old traders at least left the Indians with beads and trinkets—even these are the objects of the new invasion by new friends as they are absorbed as adornments in the new life styles. If one feels any guilt, there is the catharsis provided by books like *Bury My Heart at Wounded Knee* or movies like *Little Big Man*. The outrage with the past smoothes over the ease of ignoring the present.

This new wave of interest in the Indian in song, literature, history, movies, and dress points unfortunately toward a romanticism that comes close to Tom Paine's characterization of Burke's mourning for the trappings of French society before the revolution as an admiration for the plumage while ignoring the dying bird.

Armando G. Gutiérrez

Institutional Completeness
and La Raza Unida Party

That Chicanos have not been served by governmental institutions goes without saying. The social and economic conditions for the Chicano throughout the Southwest are appalling. With a median level of school completed ranging from 6.0 in Texas to 9.0 in Califorina,[1] the Chicano has consistently lagged behind even Blacks in many socio-economic characteristics. In terms of income, the Texas Chicano has been the worst-off. In 1960, the median income of employed males 14 years of age and over was $2,029, or less than half that of the Anglo.[2] Other characteristics point to the same undeniable fact—Chicanos have continued to be looked upon and treated as second-class citizens.

These conditions have been with the Chicano ever since the Southwest became part of the United States. This, coupled with the constant immigration of hundreds of thousands of Mexicans, has necessitated some kind of adjustment on the part of the Chicano. After all, the Chicano who already lived here in the Southwest, as well as the new immigrant, had a variety of primary (such as food, clothing) and secondary (such as companionship, recreation) needs.

Given the disdain with which the Chicano was looked upon by the dominant white society, he could not rely on the institutions of the

Armando G. Gutiérrez, Department of Government, The University of Texas at Austin.

1. Harley S. Browning and S. Dale McLemore, *A Statistical Profile of the Spanish-Surname Population of Texas* (Austin, Texas: Bureau of Business Research, University of Texas, 1964), p. 59. See this book for a full-scale description of the socio-economic conditions of the Chicano, especially in Texas. See also *Civil Rights in Texas*, A Report of the Texas Advisory Committee to the U.S. Commission on Civil Rights (February 1970).

2. Ibid., p. 61.

Anglo to fulfill these needs. It not only was the case that many businesses and organizations, for example, did not allow him access to their services, but also it was very difficult and uncomfortable for the Chicano to use those institutions that did not overtly discriminate. On the one hand, there was the language problem. For the Chicano to make use of employment agencies or physicians, for example, required an expertise not only in the English language but also in behavior patterns which would elicit favorable responses from the Anglo clerks, secretaries, and officials. Most Chicanos had little knowledge in either of these areas. On the other hand, there was the problem of dissonance. In confronting situations, all of us are much more comfortable when we know (or at least have some idea) how others will react to us. The dissonance created by not knowing how others will react is often enough to keep us from encountering that situation at all. Thus, in many (perhaps most) of the situations in which the Chicano would have to interact with Anglos, he could not and cannot have even a reasonable idea of how he would be received. It was as likely that he would be thrown out and called a "greaser" as that he would be served.

But the needs of the Chicano remained. These needs, along with the aforementioned conditions, necessitated the creation of institutions[3] geared to handle his needs. That such institutions have existed for some time becomes evident when one examines the literature. Several Chicano authors, most notably Miguel Tirado and Salvador Alvarez, have documented a long organizational history of the Chicano people which dates back to the 1800s.[4]

That ethnic institutions not only existed in the past but flourish up to the present is testimony enough to the continued lack of faith of Chicanos in Anglo institutions. Spanish-language radio and television stations have increased rapidly in the last decade. Newspapers and periodicals have also flourished, as have the number of dailies which carry sections written in Spanish. Even as far away as Chicago, we find at least five Spanish radio stations and several periodicals written specifically for the Chicano population of the city, which numbers well over 250,000. Chicano credit unions and self-help groups can be found

3. For present purposes, "institutions" are defined loosely as formal or informal structures within the ethnic community that provide some service to that community's members. As such, it includes religious, political, commercial, service, communications, and recreational organizations. For a further discussion of the concept of institutional completeness, see Raymond Breton, "Institutional Completeness of Ethnic Communities and the Personal Relations of Immigrants," *American Journal of Sociology*, 70 (July–May 1964–65), 193–205.

4. Miguel Tirado, "Mexican-American Community Political Organization," *Aztlan*, I, No. 1 (Spring 1970), 53–78, and Salvador Alvarez, "Mexican American Community Organization," in Octavio I. Romano-V., ed., *Voices: Readings from El Grito* (Berkeley: Quinto Sol Publications, 1971), pp. 91–100.

in a variety of communities in and out of the Southwest. Such organizations have had an important impact upon the role of Chicanos in the politics of the region. As we examine this role, the relationship between customs and politics regarding the Chicano should come into focus. For now, let us begin to examine the specific case of Chicanos and politics in one Southwestern state—Texas.

The Chicano and Texas Politics

The support the Chicano population has given the Texas Democratic Party is quite impressive. McCleskey and Merrill, for example, point out that as late as 1969, some 88 percent of Chicanos expressed an orientation toward the Democratic Party. It must be noted, however, that of this large show of affiliation with the Democrats, only 30 percent expressed a strong orientation to the party. Thus, even though most Chicanos almost exclusively vote Democratic, most of this support appears to be *unenthusiastic*. In contrast, while Blacks express nearly the same degree of orientation toward the party—90 percent—only 27 percent of this group weakly identified with it. In the Black case, then, a majority feel a strong tie to the Democrats.[5] This fact will become particularly important later in our discussion. To say that even with such a large show of support the Democratic Party has seen fit to do little in the way of policy implementation for the Chicano would be a gross understatement. The poor social and economic conditions of the Chicano people evidence the fact. The Republican Party, on the other hand, has until very recently ignored the Mexican American. Apparently convinced that there was no way of drawing the Chicano away from the Democrats, the Republicans made no overtures at all to this community. In 1969, only 5 percent of the Chicano people professed support for the Republican Party.[6]

Not only has the Chicano been largely ignored in terms of solicitation and legislation in Texas, but he has also had little choice in the selection of the candidates. The mere logistics of the nominating process have excluded him. A variety of forces have been at work. First, the poll tax, until its invalidation in 1966, served to limit the voting power of the Chicano. For a man trying to feed and clothe his family on less than $3,000 per year, the $1.75 poll tax was far more than he could afford for the "right" to vote. Second, although the voter has until recently had only four months in which to register to vote—between October 1 and January 31—the filings for office were not due

5. Clifton McCleskey and Bruce Merrill, "The Political Behavior of Mexican Americans in Texas: A Preliminary Report," paper delivered at the Annual Meeting of the *Southern Political Science Association* (March 26–28, 1970), p. 14.

6. Ibid., p. 14.

until after this date. Because one would have no idea who would eventually be running for office, the thought of an upcoming election did not serve to mobilize any interest among Chicanos in order to get them to register. Third, and more specifically related to the nominating process, is the fact that a large portion of the Chicano population engage in migrant labor. Estimates have ranged in the past from 15 to 40 percent.[7] Fourth, a factor that has long been present but that is difficult to document is the widespread intimidation Chicano voters and potential candidates have suffered. Recently, Chicanos have seen two of three Chicano candidates in La Salle county lose their jobs as a result of their political activity.[8] It hardly seems a coincidence that the King Ranch in South Texas had never witnessed a split in its workers' votes until 1968, when the first poll-watcher was allowed on the ranch.

All of these factors have served to disenfranchise the Chicano. This exclusion is evidenced by their low voting turnout. We find, for example, that both Blacks and Whites have higher voting rates in the state than do Chicanos.[9]

Unable and unwilling to rely on the Democratic and Republican parties to satisfy their needs, Chicanos have, in keeping with a long tradition of creating their own institutions, created their own party. Having to depend on the resources available through Anglo institutions to improve the conditions in the Southwest, Chicanos have developed a leverage for getting at these resources. Rather than making demands directly upon the dominant institutions, La Raza Unida Party has provided a middle force for the fulfillment of needs. Hence, Chicanos, without having to learn English and change their ways, can make demands upon the party and the party can then mediate to achieve the ends set by its membership. In order to more fully understand the workings of the party, let us now take a closer look at it—its history, development, and future.

A Brief History of La Raza Unida Party of Texas

Although the incidents leading to the formation of a third party dedicated to Chicanos go back for a century or more, the most immediate, precipitating cause was the student walkout in Crystal City, Texas. To be sure, organizational work had been going on for some

7. See *Hearings Before the Senate Subcommittee on Migratory Labor* (Washington, D.C.: U.S. Government Printing Office, June 19, 1963).

8. From a discussion with José Angel Gutiérrez (March 26, 1972).

9. McCleskey and Merrill, "Political Behavior of Mexican Americans in Texas," p. 12.

time. In the summer of 1969, José Angel Gutiérrez returned to his home town of Crystal City and quickly recruited the aid of a VISTA couple, Linda and Guillermo Richey, to aid in the organization of the community. Four immediate goals were set by the group: (1) the extension of the educational system to the Chicano, (2) the implementation of democracy (majority rule) into local government, (3) direct confrontation with the local, white power structure, and (4) the creation of a program of rural economic development. Crystal City was chosen as the site for these organizational activities because of its similarity to so many other South Texas communities where Chicanos make up a numerical majority but have little or no political and economic power.[10]

In the Fall of 1969, the students finally became mobilized around the issue of popularity elections and other school-related problems. After several months of negotiation and compromise, they walked out of the schools in early December. For an entire month the students were out of school, and while out they worked at registering voters for the upcoming Spring school board elections.[11] With this mobilization of both student and parent support, the idea of an independent third party came to the fore.

Perhaps most important in this revolt against the Crystal City Independent School District was the fact that the base of organizational support came from the Chicano family. By mobilizing the entire family, any chance for internal factional strife was curtailed.[12] Thus, a solid base of support was developed for the upcoming elections.

The idea of the third party was discussed at length during the walkout, and preparation was made for its legal implementation. Finally, after weeks of legal advisement, the party was organized on January 17, 1970, with the petitioning of 88 (3 percent of the last general election's total votes) registered voters from Zavala County.[13]

An indication of the mobilization that had occurred for the elections is evident when we look at voter turnout. A total of 3,100 people were legally registered to vote in the Crystal City school district. Of this total 2,544 voters actually went to the polls. Prior to the 1970 election, the largest voter turnout in a school board race had been 1,705 in 1963.[14] In the city council election, a total of 2,222 people cast ballots. This total compares with the previous year's high of only 1,619

10. José Angel Gutiérrez and Gloria Garza, "Aztlan: Chicano Revolt in the Winter Garden" (unpublished, undated article).

11. *Zavala County Sentinel* (December 25, 1969).

12. John Shockley, "Crystal City: La Raza Unida and the Second Revolt" (unpublished, undated manuscript).

13. "La Raza Unida Party" (unpublished mimeo, January 17, 1970).

14. *Zavala County Sentinel* (April 9, 1970).

votes.[15] It is evident, then, that the party's large-scale drive at mobilizing the local populace had been successful.

At least as important as the victory itself, however, was the fact that a new consciousness had developed within Crystal City's Chicanos. This consciousness that one could indeed affect his political environment had spread from a small core of activists to the populace in general.[16] The hope of the party's organizers was now to spread that consciousness to other South Texas communities.

That such "Chicano consciousness" could indeed be exported was already becoming evident. In nearby Cotulla and Carrizo Springs, the fever of Crystal City had already spread, and in those communities' elections Raza Unida candidates had also been elected.

Soon, because of the changes that were rapidly being implemented within city government and within the schools, there was a rapid movement of Anglos out of Crystal City. By the Spring of 1971, nearly two-thirds of all the Anglo families had moved out of the city. Thus, in the Spring's city council and school board elections, the Raza Unida Party completed its sweep of local government. Though the party had been dealt a blow by the previous negative rulings of the Texas courts, the battle was by no means over.

The changes that have occurred in Crystal City since this complete takeover have been far-reaching. In the schools, bilingual education programs have been instituted in the lower grades, as has a free breakfast program. Throughout the school a program of bicultural education (a critical move in enhancing Chicanos' self-images and thus in lowering the dropout rate) has been put into operation. In addition, the make-up of the faculty and administrative staffs has changed profoundly. The most important administrative positions—principal, assistant principal, school superintendent, and so forth—have all been manned by Chicanos sympathetic to and understanding of the needs of the student body. All teachers in the schools are bilingual, and Mexican-American teachers are actually in a majority. The school district is also much more aware of and willing to search out and accept federal aid. Money has been received from a variety of public and private agencies. Moreover, the district has banned army recruiters from the schools (army recruiters are generally allowed into high schools to attempt to gather recruits) and made school records private, to keep the Selective Service System from operating effectively. A draft consultant has been hired.[17]

15. Ibid.
16. See Armando G. Gutiérrez and Herbert Hirsch, "The Militant Challenge to the Dominant Ethos: 'Chicanos' and 'Mexican Americans,'" *Social Science Quarterly* 53, No. 4 (March 1973), 830–45.
17. Shockley, "Crystal City: La Raza Unida," p. 13.

Outside the school system, important changes have also occurred. Training programs for city staff and for the police have greatly increased the efficiency and quality of these forces. Programs to extend sewage and water facilities to areas of the city long neglected have been put into operation. A concerted effort is being made to attract industry to the city. This, perhaps, is the most critical variable in the future of Crystal City. With the continued mechanization of so many farms, more and more migrants are being lured to the large urban centers in search of work. Crystal City hopes to attract industry to keep the migrants in the city. As yet, this particular dimension is unresolved. The competition for industry is, of course, quite strong and widespread.[18]

Beyond these questions of what and how to implement programs once one has gained power lies the fundamental question of securing control. The aim of Crystal City's organizers was not merely one town. Evidence since the LRUP's initial successes points to the undeniable fact that the party's popularity is spreading quite rapidly throughout the Southwest and beyond. At present La Raza Unida Party has branches in Texas, Colorado, California, Arizona, Washington, and Wisconsin.[19]

Thus, Crystal City's geographical boundaries are hardly the terminating point of a developing Chicano consciousness among the masses of Mexican Americans.

Today's Raza Unida Party

At present, the party has undertaken a campaign to go statewide in Texas. For the some million-and-a-half potential Chicano voters, the party may offer an alternative so long absent; specifically, the party ran candidates for statewide offices, including governor, in an attempt to gain a large enough backing to appear on the November 1972 ballot. As such, it organized precinct conventions in well over three hundred precincts throughout the state. These conventions were overt attempts to keep Chicanos from voting in the Democratic and Republican party primaries so that they would then be eligible to sign LRUP petitions.

In addition, the future appearance of the party on the state's election ballot was indeed assured. In the November 1972 general election, La Raza Unida's candidate for governor, Ramsey Muñiz, polled approximately 6.5 percent of the vote, well over the 2 percent required by law for the assurance of a place on the 1974 ballot.

18. Ibid., p. 15.
19. "What Is La Raza Unida Party?" (unpublished, undated mimeo).

But at the same time, the Raza Unida Party has already encountered numerous legal and practical obstacles. It in no way is deluding itself. Realistically, the outlook for the party, while not overly dark, is not particularly bright. Let us look at some of the major handicaps and problems the party faces.

1. Financial and manpower resources have been hard to come by. Money has come mainly from small individual contributions. A population with a median level income of less than $3,000 per year can hardly afford to spend money on anything but primary needs. The manpower the party has utilized has been almost exclusively voluntary.[20] As such, the mere logistics of supporting the party and its principal organizers become quite tenuous. This obstacle becomes even more pronounced when one recognizes that most of the support for LRUPs efforts has come from the lower-income Chicano; the middle-income Mexican American has been more difficult to mobilize. The financial and technical aid this group might potentially offer would be of enormous value to the party. Thus far, little headway has been made in recruiting this group in large numbers.

2. Demographic characteristics of the Mexican-American population may be changing so as to dilute the party's power. Obviously pulled by perceived greater economic opportunities in the cities of the northern part of the state and pushed by the ever-decreasing likelihood of finding agricultural work on mechanized farms, the Chicano may gradually shift the locus of his potential power. The diffusion of the Chicano population away from the fifty counties where he makes up some 25 percent or more of the population might not only break up a potentially forceful voting bloc but also make organizational activity much more difficult. It hardly seems a coincidence that all of LRUP's successes have been in small, rural, Chicano majority communities. The sheer tactics and costs of mobilization in a large urban setting may preclude large-scale organization.

3. A third factor involves the wisdom of the choice of the party to go statewide. With the severely limited amount of resources available, many have argued that a strategy that spreads those resources more thinly reduces the chances of success at the local level where the money and time might be better spent. The proponents of the move to statewide campaigns retort that by gaining greater visibility through statewide elections, resources will become available at a faster rate than before. Those who favor the statewide Raza Unida Party point out that if indeed it becomes evident that Chicanos cannot win statewide office, the alternative of "selling" the party's vote to the highest bidder not only at the state but also at the national level, is

20. Ibid.

still open to them. This, of course, requires a good deal of discipline and sophistication within the party's membership.

4. A fourth factor that may negatively affect the present and future of LRUP is the gradual ascendancy in Texas of a solid bloc of liberal Democrats. Moreover, it appears that this liberal faction will continue to make itself heard and felt in elections to come. The effect could be to cut deeply into the potential base of support that La Raza Unida Party is relying on.

5. A proposition that many Chicanos have discussed and that sounds tantalizingly attractive is a coalition of Chicanos and Blacks. Such a coalition has already been tried in some areas.[21] Although a coalition of this nature seems reasonable enough considering the similar economic and social conditions of the two groups, in fact it appears to be a long way off, due to the geographic dispersion and respective strength of party affiliation among both groups, and last but not least, the unwillingness to compromise. To what degree Chicanos and Blacks would be willing to engage in such negotiation and remain united is difficult to assess. Both groups have had much experience with compromise and have usually been the "givers" and seldom the "receivers."

6. A factor that may also be detrimental to the long-range party organizational efforts regards the possible national candidacy of Edward M. Kennedy in 1976. The effects of a 1976 candidacy are, however, difficult to ascertain. Most important would be the success La Raza Unida Party would enjoy in the intervening four years. Were it to develop a solid base of support strongly committed to it, the Democrats would probably have much difficulty cutting into LRUP's membership. If the membership drive of the party is slow, the 1976 candidacy of Kennedy might be fatal.

7. A final obstacle that La Raza Unida Party may have to contend with concerns the possible negative effects of identification with LRUP on incumbent Chicano politicians. This is illustrated by the experience of County Commissioner Albert Pena and Senator Joe Bernal, both of San Antonio. Both politicians have recently become identified with LRUP's efforts and openly denounced the Democratic Party's "benign neglect" of its Chicano constituency. Although identification with LRUP undoubtedly gave them strong support from Bexar County's substantial number of Mexican Americans, they had already enjoyed most of this support. The perception by many Whites and some middle-class Mexican Americans of La Raza Unida as an extremist, militant, radical organization probably brought out substantial numbers of people to vote against LRUP's candidates. Such a

21. Ibid.

"whitelash" did indeed prove fatal to Pena and Bernal, and La Raza Unida Party will surely be blamed by both Whites and Browns for having taken away a significant portion of the small voice Chicanos had in Texas government.

Conclusion

After the preceding discussion of the birth, infancy, and possible future of Texas' first third party aimed specifically at the some 2.5 million Mexican-American residents of the state, it should be apparent that the voice of the Chicano people is becoming much more unified than ever before. Although the past has seen continuous but scattered political action on the part of the Chicano, the present seems to indicate that La Raza Unida Party may be the unifying force so long needed.

Conceptually, however, what the discussion suggests is that the Chicano population of the state has changed. What is more, such changes have occurred throughout the history of the Chicano people. To think of Chicano culture as "traditional" and somehow static is absurd.[22] What we find upon close examination of the Mexican-American people is a continual adjustment to circumstances that are constantly changing. Thus, on the one hand, we have the adjustment of some who sought to deal with Whites who had taken land in the only way that seemed effective—through collective force. On the other hand, we find Chicanos creating their own institutions to meet the needs that White institutions would not or could not handle. An elaborate network of ethnic churches, welfare organizations, communication systems, and so forth are found throughout the Southwest. As needs increased, decreased, or merely changed, so did ethnic institutions arise, cease to be, or adjust.

The creation of the Chicanos' own political party seems to be another in a long history of ethnic adjustments to external and internal changes. Just as the other adjustments have had significant implications for the existence of Mexican Americans, so too does it appear that La Raza Unida Party will affect the future of Chicanos. The potential political power of the nation's second largest minority seems now to have found an avenue for actualization. Though the particular avenue of an ethnic political party has been nonexistent in the past, to say that Chicanos have "awakened" is a gross misrepresentation of historical facts. Instead, Chicanos have merely created another institu-

22. See Octavio I. Romano-V., "The Anthropology and Sociology of the Mexican Americans," in Octavio I. Romano-V., ed., *Voices: Readings from* El Grito (Berkeley, Cal.: Quinto Sol Publications, 1971), pp. 26–39.

tion geared to handle directly or indirectly the needs of today's Mexican American.

Perhaps as important as the mere development of La Raza Unida Party are the prospects for its survival. For the phenomenon of ethnic institutions is not new. Glazer and Moynihan, for example, repeatedly mention the tendency for immigrant groups to attempt to recreate the life of the "old country" as much as possible.[23] This attempt usually took the form of recreating the institutions that existed in the immigrants' land of origin. The authors go on to point out, however, that the recreated institutions eventually died out as the immigrants became assimilated into American life, and few new immigrants entered the U.S. to use them.

This pattern is not applicable to the Chicano. Not only is the rate of assimilation very slow but also the immigration rate from Mexico is astonishingly high. Between 1950 and 1960, for example, the number of *legal* immigrants to Texas alone was approximately 150,000.[24] Hence, just as the normal historical pattern of immigration to this country is not applicable to the Chicano, neither is the Glazer-Moynihan pattern of ethnic institutional death. It appears, then, that if the pattern of most Chicano institutions flourishing through the years holds, La Raza Unida Party's future may well be as bright as many of its organizers had originally hoped.

23. Nathan Glazer and Daniel P. Moynihan, *Beyond the Melting Pot* (Cambridge, Mass.: The MIT Press, 1963).
24. Browning and McLemore, *A Statistical Profile*, p. 9.

Patrick H. McNamara

Catholicism, Assimilation, and the Chicano Movement: Los Angeles as a Case Study

It is tempting to draw the conclusion that the Catholic Church has become largely irrelevant to the concerns of the Chicano movement in the Southwest. If one examines the vast journal literature dealing with Mexican Americans over the past few years, only two articles appear that focus on the religion at least nominally professed by over 90 percent of the Southwest's largest minority population.[1] A conclusion of irrelevance is probably premature, however. Elsewhere I have attempted to analyze recent structural and symbolic responses of the Roman Catholic Church vis-à-vis the Chicano Movement.[2] The appearance of PADRES, the organization of activist Chicano priests, and the appointment of Bishop Patrick Flores as auxiliary bishop of San Antonio may well augur a new role for the Church in the Chicano community, a role to which members of the Chicano movement will probably respond with favor.

In this paper, however, I would like to discuss briefly a thrust of involvement with the Mexican-American community on the part of the largest Catholic archdiocese in the Southwest—Los Angeles, California. I will suggest that the basic assimilationist ideology of this archdiocese has conditioned a negative image of the Church—an im-

Patrick H. McNamara, Department of Sociology, University of New Mexico. This paper was presented at the Workshop on Southwest Ethnic Groups: Sociopolitical Environment and Education, sponsored by The Cross-Cultural Southwest Ethnic Study Center at The University of Texas at El Paso, July 27–29, 1972.

1. Rev. Alberto Carrillo, "The Sociological Failure of the Catholic Church Towards the Chicano," *The Journal of Mexican American Studies*, 1 (Winter 1971), 75–83; and Cesar Chavez, "The Mexican American and the Church," *El Grito*, 1 (Summer 1968), 9–12.

2. "Catholicism and the Chicano: A Tentative Reassessment" (forthcoming).

age to which Chicanos have reacted at times with hostility insofar as they are rejecting the appropriateness of assimilation as a goal.

The Catholic Church as a vehicle of immigrant assimilation into the dominant society is a familiar working concept in American sociology. Warner and Srole pointed to three functions of ethnic school structures in Yankee City: transmission of an immigrant group's ancestral language, orientation to the Church's religious symbol system, and respect for the national heritage of the group's country of origin. However, they were quick to indicate that parochial schools "also function to orient the child to the American social system," and quoted a "prominent Catholic educator" who declared that the school "must be able to teach children 'good citizenship in the Republic and to prepare them for the eternal citizenship in the Kingdom of God.'" [3] In fact, they could say of the Irish Church in the late 1930s that it had "shifted in its national orientation until today it may be said to be an American Catholic Church rather than Irish Catholic." [4]

This is not to say, of course, that the Catholic Church promoted loss of ethnic identity; on the contrary, it continued to enhance ethnic self-consciousness by linking together religion and nationality as part of a process of American self-identification. As Andrew Greeley expresses it, "as the young person is socialized within his religio-ethnic group, he thinks of himself not so much as a Catholic, but as a Polish Catholic, Irish Catholic, Italian Catholic, French Catholic, thus distinguishing himself not only from Protestants but also from Catholics of other ethnic backgrounds." [5]

How has the Catholic Church affected assimilation of Mexican-American Catholics? I have previously argued that unique conditions in the American Southwest prevented the kind of involvement of institutional Catholicism with Spanish-speaking natives and, later, Mexican immigrants which was so familiar in the East and Midwest, an involvement promotive of assimilation in the case of the minority groups mentioned by Greeley.[6] The Southwest was the last territorial region to be explored and granted statehood, and only in recent decades have industrialization and urbanization made any considerable impact, particularly in the states of New Mexico, Arizona, and Texas. Consequences for the Catholic Church were perpetuation of its mis-

---

3. W. Lloyd Warner and Leo Srole, *The Social Systems of American Ethnic Groups* (New Haven: Yale University Press, 1945), pp. 236–38.

4. Ibid., p. 217.

5. Andrew M. Greeley, *The Denominational Society: A Sociological Approach to Religion in America* (Glenview, Ill.: Scott, Foresman, 1972), p. 125.

6. Patrick H. McNamara, "Dynamics of the Catholic Church: From Pastoral to Social Concern," in Leo Grebler, Joan W. Moore, and Ralph C. Guzman, eds., *The Mexican American People* (New York: Macmillan-Free Press, 1970), pp. 449–485.

sionary role—the padre on horseback is an appropriate symbol—and
the slow growth of precisely those institutions sponsored by the
Church which are promotive of assimilation: parochial schools, welfare bureaus, settlement houses, and so forth.

Los Angeles: A Special Case

Los Angeles, as the most rapidly industrialized city in the American
Southwest, presents an exception to the pattern stated above. In the
early decades of this century, both Protestant and Roman Catholic
clergy in Los Angeles established settlement houses and welfare institutions with an overtly assimilative philosophy. Caught up in the
"Americanization" movement sparked by World War I, church representatives instituted citizenship and language classes and sought in
other ways to help the increasing numbers of Mexican immigrants to
"adjust" as rapidly as possible to their new home. In the case of the
Catholic clergy, however, efforts to "Americanize" the Mexican immigrants were closely intertwined with defending them against Protestant missionary activities—which initiated a pattern of paternal "over-
lordship" that lasted until very recently. Protestants were not the ones
to make better citizens of Mexican immigrants; only Catholics could
do so, and in the process, protect immigrants against real dangers. A
Los Angeles Bureau of Charities Report in 1919 is striking in its language:

> The molesting hands of proselytizers who seek to tear out the heart of
> the foreigner the religion which he has and which alone will save him
> from becoming an anarchist, must not be tolerated. Too much harm has
> been done to our country by these zealots. The problem of Americaniza-
> tion would become easier if each tried to cooperate with the plans of the
> other instead of sowing seeds of discord and anarchy. The Bureau of
> Catholic Charities wishes to work hand in hand with every rightly dis-
> posed social worker and with all good citizens in an endeavor to solve the
> problems of poverty, delinquency, and citizenship, in making our country
> and our flag loved. We believe that in making Catholics better Catholics
> we shall make them better citizens.[7]

Eighteen years later, the same motif was discernible in a report on
youth clubs for Mexican teenagers in Los Angeles. The clubs, said the
priest director, were

> means to preserve the Catholic faith and life of the immigrants; to keep
> and foster the best of national traditions and customs; to instill the finest
> concept of Americanism and true patriotism; to develop leadership. In

7. First Annual Report of the Bureau of Catholic Charities, 1919 (Archives of the
Archdiocese of Los Angeles), p. 11.

fine, social action clubs strive towards the ideals of practical Catholicism and good citizenship.[8]

One could look far and wide to find more militant statements of the blend of patriotism and Catholicism that became the principal legitimating theme for the Catholic Church's involvement with its Mexican-American constituency in Los Angeles. To preserve Catholicism meant to encourage good citizenship, to create firm loyalty to a new mother country.

An important figure in the continuation of these motifs into the post–World War II decades was the Archbishop of Los Angeles, James Francis Cardinal McIntyre, installed as Archbishop in 1948. Until his retirement in 1969, he acted as one of the nation's most outspoken conservative Church prelates. In urging construction of parochial schools in East Los Angeles, the Cardinal continued the assimilation-protection themes stated above:

> The obvious to us is that the future citizens of this fair city and state will come in large numbers from the children of this eastern area of the city today. That they be safeguarded in their traditions and be preserved from an American brand of liberalism is our hope and prayer.[9]

In the decade of the 1960s, this patriotism-assimilation theme began to be combined with a new motif: respect for peaceful means of solving socioeconomic problems. In a feature article on a parish in East Los Angeles which sponsored a fairly elaborate War on Poverty program, *The Tidings* employed a sub-headline, "Eastsiders Disdain Loose Talk of Riot" and noted with approval that "the people have been able to make a *transition from poor to middle class over the years.*" The east side is "producing persons . . . responsible, qualified and able to chart means to solve eastside problems, men who see beyond demagogic self-interest." The pastor is quoted as saying, "People here are upset when they read that they are supposedly ready to riot because they are on the eastside. . . . I cannot understand this approach to problems. Do they expect instant perfection?" [10]

Conclusion

The Catholic Church in Los Angeles, claiming a membership in the 1960s of perhaps half a million Mexican-American Catholics, portrayed itself with striking consistency for almost fifty years as solidly backing

8. *The Tidings*, weekly newspaper of the Archdiocese of Los Angeles, November 26, 1937, p. 8.

9. Address to the Papal Knights, Los Angeles, June 3, 1948. Archives of the Archdiocese of Los Angeles.

10. *The Tidings*, February 18, 1966, p. 7 (emphasis added).

and inspiring whatever would support assimilation of Mexican Americans into mainstream American society. Accompanying this self-portrait was an insistence, particularly evident in the later 1960s, that this process need not be accomplished with "radical" protest or dramatic outbursts; in fact, the religious formation imparted by the Church should act to protect Mexican-American Catholics from these destructive forces.

Socialization into Catholicism, in this view, (1) aided Mexican Americans to become loyal, trustworthy, law-abiding American citizens; (2) protected them from the social evils of the day: Protestantism, Bolshevism, anarchism, Communism, delinquency, relativism in doctrine and morality; (3) equipped them with the means to move upwardly in the socioeconomic world of American society; and (4) motivated them to accomplish these goals without violence or social disturbance.

Assimilation and the Chicano Movement

An examination of recent writing on the Chicano movement leaves little doubt that assimilation, in the sense of upward mobility into middle-class American social and economic lifestyles, is rejected as a goal—or, at least, as a goal for all Chicanos. Alfredo Cuellar, in one of the first essays on the movement, indicates that suppression "of the common history, culture, and ethnic background of *la raza*" has been the price of striving for acceptance by the larger society; Chicano spokesmen "reject what they call the myth of American individualism." [11] Cultural nationalism, a later writer states, means that "the Chicano now seeks to establish political and economic hegemony over his communities in order to control them and perpetuate his existence as a distinct entity." More strongly, "many Chicanos want either a complete revision of the United States political and economic system or separation from it." [12] In a recent review of *The Mexican American People,* Charles Ornelas criticizes the study precisely for its assimilationist perspective: "Far from being apolitical, the book conveys a definite message—the only viable path for economic mobility is sociocultural assimilation along with political accommodation." [13] The antiassimilationist theme is even stronger in a currently popular critical perspective of Chicano scholars; namely, colonialism. "The Chi-

11. "Perspective on Politics," in Joan W. Moore, ed., *Mexican Americans* (Englewood Cliffs: Prentice-Hall, 1970), p. 153.

12. Y. R. Macias, "The Chicano Movement," in Wayne Moquin, ed., *A Documentary History of the Mexican Americans* (New York: Bantam, 1972), p. 500.

13. Book review of *The Mexican American People, El Grito,* IV, 4 (Summer 1971), 18.

cano largely remains unable to determine how things will be done in his own community. All the major institutions that directly affect the lives of the Chicano population remain in the hands of the colonizer." [14]

As core themes of the contemporary Chicano movement, anti-assimilationism and colonialism lie in direct opposition to the assimilationist policy of the largest and most financially stable of the southwestern Catholic dioceses, Los Angeles. I suggest that awareness, at times perhaps only implicit, of this opposition between the Chicano movement and the assimilationist ideology of Catholicism as represented in southern California, accounts in large part for the anger exhibited by Chicano activists with the Catholic Church. I have chronicled these expressions of dissent and outrage elsewhere: it is surely no accident that the major eruptions of strident protest against the Catholic Church have occurred in Los Angeles; i.e., the interruption of Midnight Mass at St. Basil's Church on Christmas Eve, 1969, in which five persons were arrested, and the subsequent "exposures" of Los Angeles archdiocesan property holdings in *La Raza,* the city's militant Chicano newspaper.[15] For a Church that displays a decades-long record of urging Mexican Americans to become loyal, law-abiding American citizens is highly unlikely to support Chicanos who organize high school walkouts and are subsequently arrested;[16] a Church that has assumed the mantle of protector from Communism, anarchism, and "liberalism" may be predicted to remain neutral concerning, if not to oppose outright a movement whose symbolic apparatus includes Castro-Che Guevara clothing, equipment (machetes, bandoleras and so forth), and revolutionary rhetoric. A Church that spent almost five million dollars constructing schools in east Los Angeles is bound to be uneasy in the face of protests against "the cultural suppression which so many Chicanos continued to face in schools. . . ." [17]

It would be a serious error, of course, to characterize all Church representatives, particularly on the contemporary scene, as antipathetic to the Chicano movement. Individual priests and members of the hierarchy, particularly Bishop Patrick Flores, have been deeply

14. Tomas Almaguer, "Toward the Study of Chicano Colonialism," *Aztlan,* 2 (Spring 1971), 18.

15. McNamara, "Catholicism and the Chicano: A Tentative Reassessment."

16. ". . . we asked for the Catholic Church to use its tremendous influence and wealth in the solution of poor education for the barrio Chicanito. As you remember, over one hundred high school Chicanos were beaten and arrested for merely demanding better education. Every single victim was Catholic, as were their families, yet when we went to St. Vibiana's Cathedral downtown, not one single priest would talk to the students." *La Raza,* 1, No. 2 (no date given), 53.

17. Ornelas, Book review in *El Grito,* p. 16.

involved with "la causa." (The presence of sympathetic priests with the Farm Worker Movement of Cesar Chavez is well known.) Most saliently, the new organization of Chicano priests, PADRES, promises to effect new ties of identification between southwestern Catholicism and both ideological and programmatic aspects of the Chicano movement. But the weight of tradition is not displaced completely in a matter of a few years. Assimilationist policies of the Los Angeles Archdiocese—policies, it may be speculated, which probably have had the support of the vast majority of Mexican Americans—have had the latent effect of reenforcing in the minds of Chicano activists a widely held image of the Church as an institution at best indifferent to the movement, and at worst, a reactionary opponent of its goals. To be sure, the Catholic Church "is really changing these days," in terms of the popular cliché, but the pace of change in a given region or diocese may not proceed rapidly enough to reverse the negative images and create those which match Catholicism's self-characterization as "the servant Church."

Stephen J. Herzog

Political Coalitions
among Ethnic Groups
in the Southwest

On Saturday, June 10, 1972, a caucus was held in Los Angeles of the delegates from California to the Democratic national convention in Miami Beach. The first item on the agenda of that meeting was the selection of thirty-three additional delegates and seventeen additional alternates to the convention. Senator George McGovern, who had won the California primary the previous Tuesday, had recommended a slate of seventeen delegates and six alternates, all of whom were accepted by the caucus that day. In addition, however, there were elections to be held for the remaining seats. The dynamics of that day involved a coalition between Chicanos and Blacks, which resulted in seats being obtained for all of their proposed nominees, with the exception of one Black.

This event, tied with the selection of a Black and a Chicano as co-chairpersons for the delegation from California, represents a concrete example of the success ethnic and racial groups can realize when they choose to work as coalition. This is not an isolated example of coalitions, but represents one of several attempts to combine the political strength of these groups to realize greater benefits for their people. This paper will attempt to identify not only other examples of coalitions that have been achieved but also where traditional coalitions appear to be breaking down, and more fundamentally, to investigate the factors that could lead to future decisions among racial and ethnic groups on whether or not to form coalitions.

Other coalitions that have appeared recently among these groups

Dr. Stephen J. Herzog, Urban Studies Institute Moorpark College. This paper was presented at the Workshop on Southwest Ethnic Groups: Sociopolitical Environment and Education, sponsored by The Cross-Cultural Southwest Ethnic Study Center at The University of Texas at El Paso, July 27–29, 1972.

include Black civil rights organizations and White groups, principally from the religious community, that supported the attempt by Cesar Chavez to establish a union for farm workers. During the grape strike, for example, civil rights, religious, and human relations groups all supported the farm worker effort to boycott the purchase of grapes.[1] When Chavez led a march from Delano to the state capitol in Sacramento during the spring of 1966, Black civil rights organizations provided equipment and personnel to insure that the marchers would maintain orderly progress and not violate the law.

Another demonstration of the increasing cooperation can be seen in the attempt by Chicano groups in New Mexico and Colorado to tie their desires for economic, political, and social improvement to similar desires on the part of Blacks and Indians. Indication of this is the increasing number of articles in the publication of the Tierra Amarillo cooperative, El Grito Del Norte, describing discrimination against these groups and activities to improve the lives of their people. In fact, the focus of the paper has been increasingly on the international movement of oppressed people.

In contrast, a coalition that has existed in the past, but that appears to be weakening, is that between the Jewish community and ethnic minorities. One characteristic of the early civil rights movement throughout the country was the support by Jews of Black groups through both financial backing and direct participation. Since Watts in 1965, however, support has been diminishing and there are serious questions about the future possibilities for coalitions between Jews and these other minorities. The present focus of the Jewish community on Israel and the treatment of Jews in Russia has led to a movement inward, which threatens the coalitions that existed in the past. This coalition also has been undermined by the antisemitism expressed by some members of Black militant organizations.

In evaluating the future possibilities for coalitions among ethnic groups, there are several variables that should be taken into account:

1. The particular goal the group is attempting to achieve,
2. The payoff for the members of ethnic groups from political action,[2]
3. The relative political strength of each group within the relevant political arena involved.

1. Stephen Herzog, Minority Group Politics (New York: Holt, Rinehart & Winston, 1971), p. 277.

2. The references to goals of members of the ethnic groups are based on the model of Edgar Littin, Ethnic Politics in America (Glenview, Ill.: Scott Foresman, 1970), pp. 20–37.

The goals the groups are attempting to realize play a major role in determining the extent to which coalition is desirable. When the objective is to secure common material goals, there are very definite tensions that test a coalition. For example, when the goal is better job opportunity, the competition for scarce rewards produces severe conflict. In the present economic situation, this pattern would certainly be typical, and is shown by the competition for funds for job-training programs. Similarly, in terms of educational benefits, serious conflict occurs over economic opportunity program funds, other forms of financial aid, and faculty and administrative positions, and we should not expect a change until a more adequate representation of ethnic group staff and students is assured. The same pattern appears in allocation of funds for participants in other programs, such as the Neighborhood Youth Corps, and often becomes a test of the political strength of each group. A factor that complicates this process of allocation of material rewards is the "more oppressed than thou" syndrome, where a group asserts a right to benefits based on a greater amount of past discrimination. It is usually possible to demonstrate that *each* group has been the victim of severe discrimination, and the central question then becomes the criteria for distributing the benefits.

The solution used to distribute these benefits, and others such as votes at the recent Democratic convention, has been to allocate the benefits on a percentage basis tied to the representation of each group in the population of the geographic unit affected. Thus, the appropriate number of Chicano teachers for the Ventura County Community College District was set by determining the percentage of the population of the county who were Chicano and multiplying the staff by that percentage. The number of Chicanos in the California delegation to Miami came from the percentage in the state times 271. The advantages of this method are: (1) the criterion is mathematical and objective, and thus exempt from criticism as being subjective (though the base for the computation—population—is the subject to challenge as far as the census not reflecting an accurate total of ethnic population); and (2) the basis for the measurement is value-neutral—numbers of people. Conversely, the major disadvantages are: (1) the process does not increase cooperation between the ethnic groups; instead, it has thus far increased competition for the limited resources available; and (2) there is no necessary correlation between merit and selection. This has been the most frequent criticism. It also makes the artificial character of the criterion that much clearer.

Tied to the desire for material rewards is the identification of the agency through which these benefits have been realized. For most of the groups, the political agent has been the Democratic Party, and the recent national convention served to reinforce these allegiances. The nomination process focused great attention on the role of the ethnic groups, even though all of their specific policy proposals were not adopted. Significantly, the first reference to the plight of the farm workers appears in the platform, and the only minority plank adopted on the floor of the convention was one dealing with Indians receiving first priority when surplus federal land is disposed of. At the same time, the growth of a separate political party in the Chicano comunity, La Raza Unida Party, is a demonstration of the frustration with the traditional parties. The success of the party in local elections in Texas, where it has supported successful candidates for offices in five counties, and in California, where it denied election to a state assemblyman, demonstrates that on at least a selective basis the ethnic groups can use their power to determine the electoral success of the traditional parties. Thus far, Blacks have shown an interest neither in forming a party to present candidates nor in joining the Chicanos in their efforts.

In other areas of social conflict such as education, housing, and law enforcement, there is little evidence of coalition formation. The current conflict over whether to support segregated or integrated education has not only divided the ethnic groups from the majority of society but has also caused divisions within the groups themselves. Although the traditional groups, such as the National Association for the Advancement of Colored People (NAACP), Mexican American Political Association (MAPA), and National Congress of American Indians (NCAI) have favored integration, the more radical groups, such as the Brown Berets and Black Panthers, which are also oriented toward the "Third World" and socialist ideology, favor separate systems of education. Cultural pride and ethnic studies become issues also at such schools as University of California at Santa Barbara and University of California at San Diego, where the emphasis on the "Third World" has produced a separatist orientation. Thus far, the Blacks, who have fought longest for integration and whose cultural ties are closest to the majority society, tend to favor desegragated education, and the Chicanos, Indians, and radical Blacks support separate education. Even within the "radical" groups, there is division. The supporters of the "Third World" orientation favor coalitions, while those favoring "cultural nationalism" are opposed to working with other ethnic groups, at least until they feel that they have built a strong cultural identification among the members of their own groups.

Conflict over which policy to support regarding education reflects a more fundamental question being faced by ethnic groups. That question is: Shall the groups attempt to maintain a separate cultural identity or integrate into the "American way of life"? The supporters of separate education are urging the maintenance of the separate culture and see schools as the vehicle for transmitting pride in culture. The other group appears more willing to become part of the majority society and not use the schools to transmit their specific ethnic traditions.

In the field of housing, there appears to be very little coordinated or cooperative effort. Almost exclusively, Blacks have pressed the issue of open housing and the need for more subsidized units. Although there are isolated drives for better housing for Chicanos, Blacks, and Indians (the support for fair housing legislation in the 1964 election in California is one example), no major coordinated drive exists on a national basis.

In law enforcement, the problem of competition for positions appears as a *potential* barrier to cooperation, although the current image of the policeman among ethnic groups is so low that changing the perception of the job is presently more critical than allocating positions among the groups. On the other hand, the potential is now greater for coalitions to challenge the methods of law enforcement in predominantly ethnic areas. The pattern of conflict between police and ethnic group members transcends the experience of any particular group, and publicity about the conflict between police and Blacks, for example, is now appearing in such Chicano newspapers as *El Grito Del Norte*.[3] Similar developments are appearing within penal institutions. At the Federal Correctional Institution at Lompoc, California, PUMA (United Mexican American Party) and the Afro-American Cultural society have worked out a relationship intended to reduce the conflict between Chicanos and Blacks, which previously had resulted in intergroup violence. Both see the prison staff as their common enemy, and feel that in the past they had been played off against each other. They are now alert to similar attempts, and they openly discuss their common needs.

One of the first payoffs for the groups is acquisition of influence in the decision-making process. The demand for greater representation of group members in elective and appointive office is currently heard more among Chicanos than other groups. Calling for more group members being selected within the established system is an indication that group "arriving" in traditional political terms.[4] The rise of more elected leaders will probaby follow, as it has with other groups. The Black caucus in Congress, Black mayors in several major cities, and other Blacks in appointive positions (such as Thurgood Marshall on

3. Vol. 4, No. 1 (June 27, 1972), 13, articles on Angela Davis and the San Quentin Six.

4. A recent survey showed that approximately 16% of the state's population has Spanish surnames, while Spanish-surnamed elected and appointed officials represented 1.9% of the total for governments of all labels in California. The fact that the survey was even done indicated the growing attention to this issue.

the U.S. Supreme Court) are examples of Blacks having achieved this result. No major efforts by ethnic groups to coalesce to gain positions for people representing their combined desires have yet appeared, although the La Raza Unida Party has endorsed some Blacks for office in Texas. Before that will happen, Chicanos and Indians will probably have to feel that enough members of their own groups have achieved such positions that their specific objectives have been accomplished. The only major coalition, if it can be called such, is the one that supported the McGovern nomination, and that seemed to produce some genuine feelings of cooperation among the various groups.[5]

Another aspect of the drive for office is the issue of apportionment of voters and the ability of groups to select group members for office. Chicanos are currently concerned about ending the ethnic gerrymandering that has resulted in the use of their votes to elect Democrats, but at the same time have left them so divided as to preclude the election of Chicanos. Because it was a case of ethnic gerrymandering against Blacks in Tuskeegee Alabama that led to the reapportionment decisions of the 1960s, it seems appropriate that Chicanos would now attack the same technique for diluting their political voice.[6] To date, Blacks have benefited more from reapportionment than have Chicanos. Thus, the additional congressional seats allocated to California included a "safe" Black seat in Los Angeles, but none for Chicanos.

Ultimately, the groups will have to assess whether their goals can be better achieved by going it alone or in conjunction with others. Where the objective is the psychic need for recognition of the group or acceptance of its place in the society, the tendency will likely be to go it alone, if nothing else, to maximize the feeling of victory. This can be seen in:

1. The desire for "showcase" members on boards, commissions, and other appointive positions,
2. The rejection of whites as members of the Student Nonviolent Coordinating Committee when its leader, Stokeley Carmichael, attempted to show the strength of the slogan "Black Power,"
3. The rejection of whites as "blue-eyed devils" by the Black Muslims and Malcolm X in his earlier years.

Where the objective is material success for one group only, the growing sophistication of ethnic groups and the increasing emphasis on

5. It appeared that the late Robert Kennedy was creating this coalition in 1968 in his campaign for president, but with his death, that effort ended.

6. *Gomillian N. Lighfoot*, 364 U.S. 399 (1961) .

economic restructuring should produce more coalitions. This can be seen in:

1. Blacks and Chicanos accepting Saul Alinsky as an organizer because of his ability to produce change,
2. Cesar Chavez working with Black and Anglo groups in the farm labor effort,
3. A Coalition of Indian tribes working with Blacks and Whites in the Washington fish-ins.[7]

However, where the issue is more localized and the prospect for change in personnel and policy is more likely, the test of coalitions will be the hardest. Thus, the willingness to share power will be put to the test when the groups can expect to place their members in office. The failure of Blacks to build a coalition with Chicanos behind Tom Bradley in his race for mayor of Los Angeles in 1969 contributed heavily to his defeat, and proposals to expand the membership of the Los Angeles County Board of Supervisors from five to seven has been held up by Black and Chicanos claims to the additional seats. In Los Angeles, an added factor is the relative equality of voting power of the two groups. Both are strong and appear to be trying for power for their own people. In Ventura County, on the other hand, the Chicanos make up 22 percent of the population, and the Blacks only 2 percent. As a result, the Blacks are more receptive to a coalition, while the Chicanos are opposed. The impact of government boundaries also affects the chance for coalitions. Because of the multitude of cities and counties in Southern California, the groups are so fragmented that their ability to vote as a bloc in local elections is undermined. This, combined with the ethnic gerrymandering mentioned above, further reduces the potential both for the formation of coalitions and their subsequent use. Conversely, the chance for coalition will be greater at the state and national levels. For example, a meeting of an Emergency Summit Conference of Asian, Black, Brown, Puerto Rican, and Red people was held June 3–4, 1972, to discuss national and international issues. At the level of condemning U.S. policy in Vietnam, and broad principles regarding "the fight for freedom and justice, the fight against hunger and disease, . . . "[8] there was consensus. Whether this consensus will be reflected in voting for, say, the next mayor of Los Angeles, remains problematic.

This factor raises the additional question of how the groups will

7. Herzog, *Minority Group Politics*, p. 281. The fish-ins were also one of the few coalitions among Indians themselves.
8. *El Grito Del Norte*. Vol. 4, No. 1 (June 27, 1972), 13.

react as they confront the possibility of electoral success. As long as they have had no expectation that their efforts would lead to victory in a concrete form, they could assert a commonality of interests. As they approach the possibility of having personnel in positions of authority, the tendency to favor their own group members over others reappears. This problem was revealed very clearly in the California delegation to the Democratic convention where Willy Brown, one co-chairperson, favored Blacks, and Dolores Huerta, another, favored Chicanos in allocating delegate, alternative, and guest pass privileges.

In conclusion, there are indications of growing possibilities for coalitions between ethnic groups as the level of political sophistication and involvement increases, and the groups conclude that they share the same problems.[9] There are many barriers to be overcome, however, including attitudinal divisions within each group about methods of achieving change and the type of change desired, and the differing levels of sophistication between Blacks on the one hand, and Chicanos and Indians on the other.

9. Current legislation sponsored by Assemblyman Brown of California to eliminate group IQ tests would benefit not only his fellow Blacks, but Chicanos and Indians also.

II. POLITICAL OUTPUTS AND FEEDBACK

Response of the System to Chicanos and Native Americans

It has become fashionable for political scientists to analyze the American political system within a pluralistic framework. This approach contends that public policy is formulated in response to interest group pressures, and because all individuals are free to organize into groups and approach decision makers, public policy necessarily must take all groups into account and, to a greater or lesser degree, will benefit all segments of society. To many political scientists this analysis has become an article of faith, an ideological statement rather than an empirical statement to be verified or rejected.

Other analysts challenge the validity of the pluralistic model and contend that public policy is in fact shaped in response to the wishes of a select few, of a "power elite." Ethnic militants have modified the power elite argument and insist that, however narrow or broad the decision-making circle is, American pluralism becomes monolithic on issues of race. Whatever their view, all analysts must ultimately concede that Chicanos and Native Americans do not make policy at a national level, and with but a few exceptions seldom make policy even at local levels. Moreover, President Nixon's dismantling of the Office of Economic Opportunity in the face of massive minority group opposition should convince even the die-hard believer of the inadequacy of the pluralistic model to explain political decision-making in the United States.

Although neither Chicanos nor Native Americans serve as policy-makers, there is a major difference in the relationship each has with governmental institutions. Native Americans are and have long been considered wards of the federal government. As such, the federal government has been forced to develop policies explicitly for Native-American tribes. As is well known, however, these policies have been formulated without the benefit of input from nor much interest in the wishes of the Native-American people. Chicanos, on the other hand, have been virtually ignored by policymakers. Thus both groups suffer under policies which they did not formulate, to which they did not contribute in any meaningful way, and which they often oppose.

The negative effects of that "power game" have been great and deep. The education sector provides perhaps the most dramatic example of the devastating impact the reigning cultural superiority paradigm has had upon Native Americans and Chicanos of this country. Before turning to the specific perspectives and viewpoints of the various contributors, it is appropriate to note that education as a field of inquiry in a total systems sense has been sadly neglected by social scientists. As David Easton has pointed out, in the past when political scientists have concerned themselves with education, they too narrowly confined their attention to the uses of education in the competition for power and to political philosophical discussions of ways and means to use the education system in promoting someone's conception of the "best" social scheme in a particular society. Easton goes on to suggest that increased specialization of scholarly disciplines and research, in the study of relationships between education and the polity, has also contributed to this neglect.[1]

In addition, we can note that education traditionally in this country has been regarded as something to be treated "apart and separate" from politics. A norm that continues to prevail, as part of the conventional wisdom in education, is the "need to keep politics, like religion, out of our American schools." A related point is that relationships between political and education systems have been considered as matters primarily of local concern because U.S. education has been decentralized structurally since its inception. This, coupled with an exaggerated macroorientation of U.S. political scientists, has tended to further insulate the field of education from systematic scrutiny and study by political scientists.

Education, as a general field of social scientific study, thus has been left to the educator. And educators traditionally have concerned themselves primarily with operational matters from a closed-system perspective. Their principal concern has usually been with the development of improved programs, procedures, and the introduction of reforms in educational processes. They have been reluctant and slow to study the educational system as a part of the national social and political structure. Until recently, there have been only meager efforts to examine the links between education and the polity, the economy, and the total society.

---

1. "The Function of Formal Education in a Political System," *School Review*, 65 (1957), 304–306.

It is small wonder then that such a dearth of serious efforts exists in the area we call ethnic politics and education. In fact, there exists a great gap to fill in the whole general area of education and the polity of which ethnic political studies form a part. The chapters presented here may be considered a beginning toward filling this gap. This section then can be considered a serious attempt to begin systematic inquiry into the interrelated impacts of cultural superiority policy in this country as manifested in a variety of policy areas including manpower training and education.

Several programs the government has initiated for Chicanos and Native Americans in the manpower training area were chosen to open this section. Professor Rankin's study describes the process by which a Chicano-oriented program was developed, and documents the resistance of President Nixon, legislators, and other governmental agencies to the participation of Chicanos in the formulation and implementation of this and similar programs. The selection by Stauss and Clinton similarly analyzes the Bureau of Indian Affairs adult vocational training programs and suggests the need to reconsider the total impact of these programs. Although they find that this program does in fact provide participants with needed job skills and employment, they question whether it can be considered successful without first considering how the loss of highly motivated individuals affects tribal self-determination, an often-cited objective of government policy. The authors raise this and other questions that must be answered before the BIAs Adult Vocational Training Program can be considered a bona fide "success." Perhaps the most lucid example of the policy-making impotence of Chicanos and Native Americans can be found in the formulation of educational policy-making.

In turning to the formal structure of the education system, we can see that the specific factors and modern developments that have given strong recent impetus to the study of relationships between ethnic political variables and education are several. For years the role of the educational system in this country has been viewed as a culture-preserving and culture-transmitting one. In a macro-sense, three traditional functions of the education system were to (1) provide the skilled human resources needed to run the economic system, (2) furnish the ways and means to inculcate in the general populace a common set of cultural norms and values, and (3) assure in the general populace a general acceptance of the existing authority and law-making national structure. Particularly significant is the point that the educational system's acceptance of the functional mandate to promote a "common set of cultural norms and values," among Chicano and Native-American groups, inevitably required a remaking of the minority youngster in the image of the white middle-class child. Schools accepted this challenge to Americanize this divergent clientele with alacrity and a missionary zeal based on a "white man's burden" rationale. The resentment of these groups toward that dehumanization effect is summarized most succinctly by Armando Rendon:

> The United States has been anything but a melting pot, because the gringo has purposely segregated, separated and relegated the non-Anglo to an inferior and degraded status. Melting pot has meant surrender of one's past and culture to something euphemistically called American society and culture.[2]

Recent minority demands and militancy together with the dawning of a post-industrial era have begun to change that traditional view of education. The result has been a general acknowledgment today that changes in the education system are necessary prerequisites to the improvement of social conditions for the minorities of this country.

Two major developments of the past decade account for this dramatic shift in perspective and this new valuation of education. First, minority groups recognized that education is an important determinant of lasting improvements. Importantly, Chicanos and Native Americans have made educational reform a major political issue and were quick to place the educational system as a primary institution to be changed. Across the nation black, brown, and red minorities have mounted continuing attacks on all levels of education institutions.

Second, there has been a concomitant agreement and growing realization on the part of national decision-makers that future technological advances and development in a post-industrial era are linked directly to the improvement in socioeconomic position of the lower strata of U.S. society. This was the rationale undergirding the war on poverty manpower programs previously described. Chicanos and Native Americans thus have become key target groups in national strategies. Although the resultant national response to this felt linkage between education and the improvement of the socioeconomic status of minority groups can hardly be termed adequate (especially when viewed from the minority perspective), there does appear to be a growing acceptance of the importance of educational reform for improving the situation of Chicanos and Native Americans.

These shifts in emphasis have had dramatic impact on the field of education, for they have thrust educational systems center-stage. From the typical public educators' viewpoint, increased national focus has brought welcomed new inputs of financial support, but it has brought also *not* so welcome new involvements in local educational matters by federal agencies. The sudden new valuation has carried unanticipated

2. *Chicano Manifesto* (New York: Collier Books, 1972). This has become a popular quotation—see, for example, *Maryknoll Catholic Publication*, March 1973.

consequences as numerous educational programs, products, and organizational pattern alternatives (all designed to improve existing educational practices for disadvantaged minority clients) have been pressed upon local school districts across the country. Public educators were at the outset, and continue to be ill-prepared and worse, ill-disposed to cope with the nature and quality of the feedback generated about the negative effects of their schools on minority youngsters.

With rare exceptions, the public educational system response to the new pressures has been discouragingly conservative. In general, public educators have chosen to retrench and resist these efforts toward the equalization of educational opportunities with predictable results on Chicanos and Native Americans. Unfortunately, educators have proven dramatically effective in marshalling the middle-class support necessary to resist change and to maintain their traditional systems and the status quo. The tragedy in this sad state of affairs is that everyone loses rather than gains from this generally myopic view of public education. The dimensions and implications for educational policy development of that tendency are analyzed by Uranga, Arciniega, and Lynch in the final chapter.

Susan Navarro Uranga, one of the principal investigators on the U.S. Commision on Civil Rights Mexican American Education Study, summarizes the dismal record of public education in meeting the needs of Chicano pupils in our schools. As she points out, the Mexican American Education Study constitutes a massive indictment of Southwest public school approaches to the education of the culturally different and documents clearly the urgent need to change educational conditions and practices.

Arciniega analyzes the changing concept of equal educational opportunity. He predicts that the demand for equal educational opportunity will become the most serious domestic issue to be faced in this country in the coming decade. He contends that, given the present state of U.S. "logic, legislation, and lethargy," there is no technical or politically feasible nonexplosive solution to this national issue.

Lynch examines the organizational issue of goal dissonance in the operation of Native-American school systems in this country. He traces the colonialistic ideology and the resultant educational rationale by which the white Anglo-directed Bureau of Indian Affairs in this country has (1) determined all goals for all Indian schools, (2) developed educational programs and schools to "Americanize the heathen," and (3) systematically kept them "unique." The need for self-determination and native-controlled and operated schools, according to Lynch, provides the only viable alternative to the dysfunctional present BIA system.

As a closing note, it is important to point out that we purposefully have chosen not to mention any of the actual proposals for redirective change or new directions advanced by the authors of this final section. We did not want to spoil the following "mindongo pedagógico" for you.*

* The phrase is borrowed from the title of an unpublished paper written by our good friend and colleague, Arturo Cabrera, "Chicano Educational Priorities: Mindongo, Hash, or Potpourri," University of Colorado, Boulder, delivered at The Cross-Cultural Southwest Ethnic Study Center Workshop on Southwest Ethnic Groups: Sociopolitical Environment and Education held at The University of Texas at El Paso, July 27–29, 1972.

Jerry Rankin

Mexican Americans
and National Policy-Making:
An Aborted Relationship

Policymakers in Congress in executive agencies and at state and local levels have been virtually ignorant of the unique problems and needs of the Mexican-American people, and there has been almost no policy designed specifically to serve the Mexican-American community. This study, through a case-study description of the Department of Labor's Manpower Program, attempts to indicate why governmental agencies have ignored and continue to ignore the demands and needs of Mexican Americans

Gaining governmental recognition as a disadvantaged minority proved one of the most frustrating obstacles to full citizenship ever facing Mexican Americans. Few Congressmen even seemed to know they were "out there" until the *barrios* almost threatened to blow as high as the ghettos had a few years before. Perhaps the most telling instance of governmental ignorance about problems among Mexican Americans (and other Spanish-speaking people in the U.S.) occurred when Congress was supposed to enact the bill that eventually created

Jerry Rankin, Department of Political Science, Bradley University. This paper was presented at the Workshop on Southwest Ethnic Groups: Sociopolitical Environment and Education, sponsored by The Cross-Cultural Southwest Ethnic Study Center at The University of Texas at El Paso, July 27–29, 1972.

Adapted in part from a manuscript in preparation for publication by University of Arizona Press, originating as a Ph.D. dissertation, University of Arizona, 1971, and funded by the Ford Foundation (grant number 700-0550). Bradley University provided support for work on the manuscript between May 1972 and May 1973. I acknowledge appreciatively the assistance of informants in congressional and administrative offices whom I visited in Washington during December 1969, September–December 1970, and December 1972; though I mention none of their names except for Rep. Edward R. Roybal (D Ca.) who told me the story below about the "lost" bill.

the Cabinet Committee on Opportunities for Spanish-Speaking People.[1] The bill carried the title, "Establish an Inter-Agency Committee on *Mexican American* Affairs" (my emphasis).

Senator Joseph Montoya (D N.M.) introduced the bill on January 28, 1969, and the Senate Government Operations Subcommittee on Executive Reorganization held hearings in June to consider the need for an agency to coordinate government efforts to assure extension of domestic assistance services to Mexican Americans.[2] Representative Frank Thompson (D N.J.) introduced a companion bill in the House of Representatives on September 29, and Speaker of House John Mc-Cormack (D Ma.) referred it to committee. Some two months later, Rep. Thompson and his colleague, Rep. Edward Roybel (D Ca.) wanted to move on the bill before the session ended. They contacted the chairman of the House Government Operations Committee, but he knew nothing of the bill. The two sponsors scouted about, and eventually found it languishing in the Foreign Affairs Committee; "Mexican American Affairs" obviously meant international relations between Mexico and the United States to Speaker McCormack! More dimensions than just the geographic separate the Northeast and the Southwest, and the hearings seemed not to have improved appreciably congressional perception of Mexican Americans' problems. The same kind of difficulties plagued those who were trying to advance the interests of Mexican Americans in the Labor Department's Manpower Administration.

Bureaucrats respond to political demands the same as elected officials, though interests must have political access to administrative officials just as they must have access to Congressmen in order to accomplish anything. Mexican-American employment interests find it difficult to affect favorable administrative decisions in the Labor De-

1. President Johnson, indebted for the "Viva Johnson" support from Mexican Americans in the 1964 election, established the Inter-Agency Committee on Mexican American Affairs (IACMAA) by executive order in June of 1967 to (1) hear solutions to Mexican Americans' problems, (2) assure that federal programs reach Mexican Americans and provide the assistance they need, and (3) devise new programs as necessary for resolving the problems unique to the Mexican-American community; see *Weekly Compilation of Presidential Papers*, 3 (June 12, 1967). The IACMAA held hearings the following October; see *A New Focus on Opportunity* (Washington: Government Printing Office, 1968).

2. Ira Sharkansky, in *Public Administration: Policy Making in Government Agencies*, 2nd ed. (Chicago: Markham, 1972), p. 11, emphasizes the importance of bureaucrats in policy-making. Francis E. Rourke, in *Bureaucracy, Politics, and Public Policy* (Boston: Little, Brown, 1969), pp. 13–24 and 64–69, notes that administrators have constituencies the same as elected officials. Frederick C. Mosher, in *Democracy and the Public Service* (New York: Oxford University Press, 1968), pp. 10–14 and 91–95, discusses the bureaucrats' representational role, as does Louis C. Mainzer, in *Political Bureaucracy* (Glenview, Ill.: Scott, Foresman, 1973), pp. 126–51.

partment. A Mexican American who served as Special Counsel to the
Senate Committee on Labor and Public Welfare in 1970 observed from
his relations with the Manpower administration, "*chicanos* have no
muscle in the Department of Labor. It is imbued with eastern mono-
linguals." Many such Easterners still think of Mexican Americans as
quaint strangers in a foreign, rural Southwest rather than as an urban minority with many of the same problems usually associated with
Black Americans—plus a few others. In late 1972, however, Malcom
Lovell, Assistant Secretary of Labor for Manpower boasted, "it can be
safely said that the Department of Labor has a mature awareness of the
unique needs of the Spanish-speaking and it is making an increasing
effort to meet the needs." [3] This awareness developed slowly.

By 1972, the Manpower Program as such had been in existence and
developing for some ten years. Lovell recalled that it took until the
mid-sixties for Manpower policymakers to comprehend that they
should divert their efforts from the "technologically displaced to the
chronically displaced and the working poor." [4] After Manpower policymakers achieved a better grasp of the nature of unemployment as a
social and economic problem, Lovell noted also that "it took time to
learn the nature of the differences among the various groups compris-
ing the disadvantaged." Though Black Americans claimed the lion's
portion of emphasis among minorities in work-training in 1965, the
Manpower administration accommodated the Mexican-American employment interest by funding Operation SER, a self-help organization
working in the area of employment.[5] Mexican Americans became part
of the Manpower administration's constituency; and Manpower programs began recognizing, at least in some measure, the factors that
make problems among Mexican Americans and other Spanish-speaking citizens unique: "A language barrier, a sense of ethnic isolation,
and a cultural heritage alien not only to mainstream Anglos but also

3. Malcolm R. Lovell, Jr., "Progress Report: The Quest for Equity," *Manpower*, 4
(September 1972), 2–6.

4. Ibid., p. 2.

5. Operation SER originated as a modest volunteer effort in Houston to find jobs
for Mexican Americans around Houston in 1965. The League of United Latin
American Citizens (LULAC), the American G.I. Forum, and eventually the Community Service Organization supplied the encouragement and leadership for the
Houston group to expand its efforts to other equally needy areas across the Southwest. Recognizing the employment needs of Mexican Americans and potential effectiveness of the organization, the Labor Department and the Office of Economic
Opportunity jointly funded Jobs for Progress, or Operation SER, for the first time
in 1966. See *Operation SER: Final Report, 1970* (Santa Monica: Jobs for Progress,
Inc., 1970), and *Manpower Report of the President, 1967*, p. 67. By 1972, Operation
SER had offices in twenty-nine cities, aiding in training and job placements as well
as monitoring and evaluating local training projects, according to Patricia Marshall,
"A Chance to Be," *Manpower, 4* (September 1972), 16–22.

to other disadvantaged people." Finally, these developments attracted attention in Congress.

By the end of the sixties, there existed a working relationship among certain officials in the Manpower administration who were sympathetic to Spanish speaking interests and appropriate committees in Congress.[6] Development of this relationship indicated gradual clarification in congressional minds as to who the Spanish-speaking are and what their problems are like. Though slow to come to terms with specialized problems among the Spanish-speaking, Congress finally adopted on December 10, 1970 a comprehensive Manpower bill, the Employment and Training Opportunities Act of 1970, which included categorical programs for dealing with the difficulties peculiar to Mexican Americans —adult basic education, bilingual training, and instruction in English as a second language. President Nixon vetoed the bill on December 16.

President Nixon opposed further categorization of programs. He wanted to reform training programs, gearing them to his proposed changes in the welfare system which emphasized work incentives, consolidation of programs to eliminate duplications with a radical decentralization of authority over remaining programs, and returning a share of federal revenues to the state and municipal levels of government. The Administration named the combined proposals the New Federalism.

The Nixon Administration throughout its first term continued refining the revenue-sharing scheme to consolidate authority for planning and administering the programs at the state and local levels. The Administration concentrated its argument for the proposal on the waste and inefficiency of centralized federal assistance programs as they had evolved since the New Deal, and insisted that needs for assistance should be accounted for by "the levels of government nearest the people."[7] Although the president repeatedly asked Congress for authority to "simplify the federal system and make the delivery of goods and services at the regional, state, and local level more effective,"[8] he invoked executive authority and proceeded with the decentralization plan. The plan attracted little public attention during the president's first term, probably because of the national preoccupation with the war in Vietnam. When the U.S. involvement in the war ended in late January 1973, the New Federalism became a highly visible issue.

6. Specifically, the House Committee on Education and Labor and its Select Committee on Labor, as well as the Senate Committee on Labor and Public Welfare, especially the Subcommittee on Employment, Manpower and Poverty.

7. Michael D. Reagan, in *The New Federalism* (New York: Oxford University Press, 1972), describes the origin and development of the plan and evaluates its potential.

8. *Congressional Quarterly Almanac,* 27 (1971), V 8A.

The New Federalism, as it materialized in early 1973, contained all the worst elements feared by Mexican Americans who had found some promise in existing federal assistance programs. In other words, about the time Mexican Americans learned a strategy to realize some of the material benefits of United States citizenship, the rules of the game threatened to change. Though the president spoke of "curbing waste" in federal assistance programs, he took steps to end the Community Action Program (CAP) of the War on Poverty. Community Action Agencies (CAAs), the local components of the War on Poverty, provided for neighborhood-based organizations capable of acting independently of state and local governments. That is, the Community Action Program enabled CAAs to contract directly with OEO for services like day care, work-training, health care, and the like without going through state and municipal officials who often had reputations for discriminating against the minority poor. With such a possibility available, spokesmen for employment interests among Mexican Americans who worked to get unemployed and unemployable Mexican Americans into Manpower training projects adapted their plans to the community approach. For example, Ricardo Ontiveros, who had experience with both OEO and manpower programs, proposed in 1971, ". . . contract programs for the Spanish-speaking to Spanish-speaking organizations. What we have been proposing is that the Manpower Administration give funding and technical assistance to Spanish-speaking manpower organizations which will enable them to develop relevant programming. Then manpower programs will operate more efficiently and meet the real needs of our people." [9] Ontiveros thus proposed to skirt state and local officials, and the Nixon Administration meant to close this avenue.

From the beginning of CAP in the sixties, community action workers provoked resentment from state and local officials in vocational education, the federal employment service, and other programs. Community action workers often used unorthodox techniques which established agencies disapproved of, and they often taunted the older agencies for using outmoded methods. More important, CAAs received many federal dollars which might have gone through the established agencies if there were no Community Action Program. Most important of all, CAAs sometimes promoted political activities among the poor against established local authorities. Resentment of these various activities resulted in a series of steps to bridle the CAAs. The steps began with restrictive amendments to the Economic Opportunity Act in 1967. The steps culminated in the New Federalism, which called for the complete demise of OEO and the Community Action Program.[10]

9. "A Piece of the Action," *Manpower*, 3 (September 1971), 11.

10. See James L. Sundquist, *Politics and Policy* (Washington: Brookings Institute,

The advocacy rule of community action workers was common knowledge, as was the Nixon Administration's plan to curb their activities as soon as the second term was a reality. Nobody imagined, however, that the Administration would act so quickly or so ruthlessly. On November 9, *The New York Times* carried a front page "rumor" that OEO was in trouble, and right after the inauguration *The Washington Post* reported on January 24, 1973, that "the Nixon Administration plans to dismantle the Office of Economic Opportunity and distribute its components among other agencies." By February 17, *The Washington Post* reported that the "dismantling" was practically an accomplished fact.

Although the dismantling of OEO turned into a wrecking job so spectacular as to draw front page coverage in *The Washington Post* practically every day in the month of February, no one who has experienced or observed the relationship between the government and Mexican Americans should have been surprised that Mexican Americans received no public mention in speculation about the consequences of ending the War on Poverty. No relationship had existed until the late 1960s. During the sixties, sympathetic bureaucrats, mostly in manpower training and other antipoverty projects, recognized special problems among Mexican Americans. By the fall of 1970, even the Nixon Administration began patronizing the Spanish-speaking community with a highly touted sixteen-point program to bring more Mexican American and other Spanish-speaking administrators into the federal bureaucracy.[11] One *chicano* in the federal bureaucracy thought his own appointment represented tokenism, and said, "*chicanos* are just one more pain in the ass to the Administration—one more concession to make." There appeared little cause to disagree with that assessment, especially considering that Mexican Americans simply added to the list of groups with particularized problems who were seeking more categorical programs in the War on Poverty while the president wanted fewer, or none.

Ending the Community Action Program, with its remarkable flexibility in tailoring projects to accommodate demands for particularized

1968), pp. 148–49n; and Robert A. Levine, *The Poor Ye Need not Have With You* (Cambridge: M.I.T. Press, 1970), pp. 63–82, esp. pp. 66 and 76, on the 1967 amendments.

11. He also gave the Cabinet Committee of Opportunity for Spanish-Speaking People a 42 percent increase in their budget for 1972, according to the Cabinet Committee newsletter, *HOY*, I (March 1972), 8. Cabinet Committee personnel reportedly spend a great deal of time in the field during the 1972 presidential campaign. The president received an unprecedented vote for any Republican among Mexican Americans, too. Ironically, rumors circulating in Washington by the end of February 1973 indicated that CCOSSP might be junked with the rest of any executive machinery that was tainted by political advocacy.

solutions to problems, surely worked to the disadvantage of poor Mexican Americans who had been receiving encouragement in improving their own material condition. Dividing services under OEO among other Cabinet departments like Labor and HEW placed Mexican Americans in the position of having to deal with agencies that had not been just indifferent to their advancement but sometimes hostile to it. As early as 1970, Mexican Americans testifying in congressional hearings on legislation to modify the manpower program showed apprehension over enhancing the authority of state and local officials in manpower training and other welfare services.[12] Nobody seemed to be listening.

Observing the policy-making process from the Mexican Americans' perspective, therefore it seems that the process is exceedingly quick in making moves contrary to their interests and ponderously slow in making moves that advance their interests. Actually, there exists no deliberate effort among policymakers to depreciate the importance of problems affecting over ten million Spanish-speaking citizens, half of whom are Mexican Americans. Most policymakers could hardly be so cavalier. Nonetheless, the political recognition Mexican Americans achieved through bureaucratic channels during the sixties slipped away in the early seventies as more prominent interests attracted policymakers' attention in the new era of policymaking—and unmaking—

12. As early as 1970, Mexican Americans testifying in *Hearings, Manpower Development and Training Legislation, 1970*, Pts. I–IV, 91st Cong., 1st and 2nd sess. (1969–70), pp. 421–22 and 558–63, before Senate Labor and Public Welfare Committee's Subcommittee on Employment, Manpower, and Poverty showed apprehension over enhancing the authority of state and local officials in manpower training and other welfare services. For example, Dr. Hector García, national chairman of the American G.I. Forum, said, referring to Texas: "It is idle and useless to expect the state governor or state establishment to administer any program for the benefit of minority groups, the poor, the unemployed, or underemployed. . . . The state, through its various agencies and their almost inherent biases, has caused many of the problems we have today." Moreover, Esteban Torres, Executive Director of the East Los Angeles Community Union, told why many Mexican Americans seemed apprehensive of the president's plan: the New Federalism "is remiss in a most crucial area, and this is participation of community groups. Community organizations . . . will cease to function in the manpower programs of the poor if state employment services take over that function. Organizations working in the ghetto and the *barrio* have been most effective . . . in reaching and communicating with persons who for various reasons, have lost confidence . . . in government- or employer-oriented agencies."

Both García and Torres, in short, wanted to avoid stipulations for control of poor peoples' programs by state and local officials. Finally, Carlos Guerra from an Operation SER project in Texas suggested, "I think we might look into control of these programs straight from . . . the Labor Department . . . [like under CAP]. . . . We shouldn't have to go through local power brokers." (By the end of February 1973, however, *The Washington Post* reported that even Operation SER received notice that its funding would depend on local resources in the future.)

which was inaugurated along with President Nixon. Mexican Americans have yet to make themselves a political force with which to reckon. Yet the accelerating *chicano* movement could change that. If the Great Society did nothing else for Mexican Americans, it brought a few *chicanos* into government—at least briefly—and encouraged formation of an informal, nationwide communication network among people committed to the advancement of *la raza*. They work elsewhere now, but they stay in touch and their efforts are designed to breathe new life into the now moribund relationship that exists between governmental agencies and the Mexican-American people.

Joseph H. Stauss / Lawrence Clinton

The Bureau of Indian Affairs, Adult Vocational Training Program: Success, by Whose Criteria?

The Indian Migration

The migration of the American Indian from the reservation to the city has continued now for over a decade, yet only in very recent years have the American people become aware of this population shift. The "Red Power" movements highlighted by such events as the seizure of federal property (Alcatraz and Fort Lawton, for example) and fish-ins by groups of Indians from different tribes have brought national attention to the now popularized "modern-day plight of the Indian."

The Indian has not always come to the city by choice. More to the point, he has been forced to migrate to avoid the disastrous economic conditions of the reservation. A minority among the many minority groups in the United States, the Indian finds himself at the bottom of the social, political, and economic totem pole. The present state of poverty on the reservation is illustrated by any social statistic you investigate. Indian life expectancy is only two-thirds the national expectancy, one-third of all adult Indians are illiterate, and the unemployment rate is over 60 percent on most reservations.[1]

Joseph H. Stauss, Department of Sociology, University of Arizona and Lawrence Clinton, East Texas State University. The research reported in this paper is a contributing project of Regional Project W-113, Western Experiment Stations, "Improvement of Employment Opportunities and Earnings for Disadvantaged People in Non-Metropolitan Areas," and was conducted as Project 0078, Department of Rural Sociology, Washington State University. Principal Investigators were Howard M. Bahr and Bruce A. Chadwick. This article is based upon an earlier draft which was Scientific Paper 3796, Agriculture Research Center, College of Agriculture, Washington State University. The cooperation of the Employment Assistance Office of the Bureau of Indian Affairs in Portland, Oregon, is acknowledged with thanks.

1. William Brophy and Sophie D. Aberle, *The Indian: America's Unfinished Business* (Norman: University of Oklahoma Press, 1966); and Howard M. Bahr, Bruce A.

In an attempt to improve such conditions in 1956, the Employment Assistance Program was created by the Bureau of Indian Affairs. This program, along with other factors such as the increasing level of education of the Indian, the rapid growth of reservation populations, and the military experience of World War II and the Korean War have lead to a dramatic shift in the Indian population from the reservation to the city.

Since this shift in population has taken place, a number of studies have been made focusing on the process of adjustment of the Indian in the city. Data has been gathered from Indians that migrated to the city, both with and without the assistance of the Bureau of Indian Affairs.[2] This study focuses only on Indians relocated by the Bureau's Adult Vocational Training Program.

The Adult Vocational Training Program

Public Law 959, passed by the 84th Congress on August 3, 1956, established a program of Employment Assistance for Indian people. This Employment Assistance Act provided for three major programs—the Vocational Training Program (AVT), the Direct Employment Program (DEP), and On-the-Job Training Program (OJT)—as well as twenty smaller programs.

These programs have had two general effects. They have assisted over 100,000 Indians to migrate from the reservation to the city, and they have trained a sizeable proportion of these migrants in skills that they need to obtain jobs in the city.[3]

In order to enroll in the AVT program, an applicant must meet several requirements. He must be at least one-quarter Indian, be between the ages of 18 and 35, and reside on an Indian reservation or on trust or restricted lands under the jurisdiction of the BIA. Employment Assistance field offices are located on most reservations to

Chadwick, and Robert C. Day, *Native Americans Today: Sociological Perspectives* (New York: Harper & Row, 1971).

2. Harry W. Martin, "Correlates of Adjustment Among American Indians in an Urban Environment," *Human Organization,* 23 (1964), 290–95; Joan Ablon, "Relocated American Indians in the San Francisco Bay Area: Social Interaction and Indian Identity," *Human Organization,* 23 (1964), 302; and "American Indian Relocation: Problem of Dependency and Management in the City," *Phylon,* 26 (1965), 365; Theodore E. Graves, "Alternative Models for the Study of Urban Migration," *Human Organization,* 25 (1966), 295; John Price, "The Migration and Adaptation of American Indians to Los Angeles," *Human Organization,* 27 (1968), 168; and Bernard E. Anderson and Donald Harvey, "American Indian Labor Mobility: A Problem of Cross-Cultural Adjustment," Mimeograph, 1970.

3. Alan L. Sorkin, "Some Aspects of American Migration," *Social Forces,* 48 (1969), 243–70, and *American Indians and Federal Aid* (Washington, D.C.: The Brookings Institution, 1971).

enroll potential trainees. These trained personnel recruit for the program and take applications for AVT services.

After the application forms are filled out, interviews conducted, and aptitude tests completed at the field office, applications are sent to the appropriate area office for approval. If approved, the applicant is notified and a tentative date is set for his arrival in the particular city where BIA-approved courses are given. The applicant's expenses and those of his family are paid by the BIA. Funds are available for medical examinations before training, transportation to the site of training, payment of major medical needs while in training, cost of tuition, books, and other supplies. There is a monthly stipend for food and shelter.

Course selection is left up to the applicant provided he meets the requirements for acceptance in that specific course. However, both the Bureau and the institution that provides the course must approve the applicant's course of study. This will not be done unless both the Bureau and the school feel the individual can complete the course of study. The length of courses varies from 4 to 22 months. After completion of a course, job placement services are provided by the Bureau, and there are periodic checks on a trainee's adjustment to his new job.

Previous Evaluations

There has been only one large evaluation of the BIA relocation and employment assistance programs. This was a descriptive and evaluative study entitled "A Follow-up Study of 1963 Recipients of the Services of the Employment Assistance Program, Bureau of Indian Affairs," commonly designated the "TOB" study by the BIA officials. The study was conducted by the BIA itself, and revealed that the completion rate for a national sample of the participants in the program in 1963 was 65 percent. The final report stated that "the relocation of Indian people and their adjustment to new and different situations is a complex problem in human behavior and should be carefully assessed and evaluated periodically." [4] Despite this recognition of the need for continued evaluative research, no subsequent study of a new sample has been initiated or reported by the BIA or other research group.

Sorkin analyzed the data from the TOB study and concluded that the process of migration was educationally selective, with the better educated more apt to migrate. He also concluded that three years after participating in the Employment Assistance Program in 1963, the participants had doubled their average annual earnings and

4. TOB, "Follow-Up Study of 1963 Recipients of the Services of the Employment Assistance Program, Bureau of Indian Affairs," Mimeograph, 1966.

showed a decline in antisocial behavior. He recommended that these programs be operated on a larger scale to accommodate all potential applicants.[5]

Objective and Procedures

The major purpose of the present study was to evaluate personnel records of the AVT program in the Portland BIA Area (which includes the states of Idaho, Washington, Oregon, and Alaska) to evaluate the program's success. "Success" was measured in several ways. First, the number of participants who completed their program of study was compared to the number who dropped out of the program. Second, the AVT program was compared to other programs that sponsor vocational training for the disadvantaged. Third, an assessment was made to determine whether or not the participants were employed in jobs related to their training. Finally, comparisons of the amount of income before and after training revealed the impact of the training in terms of wages.

This study is limited to those participants, 245 of 316, in the AVT program in the Portland BIA Area for the fiscal years 1964 to 1966 for whom complete records were available. During the fiscal years 1964, 1965, and 1966, 316 Indian people entered the adult vocational training program in the Portland BIA Area. Three of every four trainees were men. Most were young—71 percent were under 24—and most were more than half Indian. Sixty-nine percent of the trainees had been rated "high" on the General Aptitude Test Battery administered during their intake into the program, and over half (51 percent) had high school diplomas. Six of every ten were not married, and the same proportion had never been arrested. They came from 42 different tribes and were enrolled in 35 different courses of vocational instruction.

Of these 316 participants, 223 (71 percent) completed their program of study and 93 (29 percent) either were terminated by the BIA or the training institution or else dropped out of the program for personal reasons; thus, the completion rates for all participants and for the sample are the same.

Measures of Success

In order to assess the success of the AVT program, it is important to compare it to similar programs serving similar populations. But comparable federal training programs are difficult to find because of

5. Sorkin, "Follow-Up Study" and *American Indians.*

the unique characteristics of the target population of the Bureau's AVT program. The American Indian suffers from the same handicaps that effect other poor, undereducated, technologically displaced, racially disadvantaged populations. Add to this the Indian's historical isolation, his cultural heritage which is incompatible with the clock-oriented, white-dominated economy, and his adjustment to problems when he migrates to the city, and the difficulties in finding suitable comparison populations are magnified. Two federal programs that are somewhat similar and yet, in crucial ways, different, are the Manpower Development Training Program (MDTA) and the Job Corps.

Manpower Development Training Program (MDTA)

In the early years of MDTA the main goal was "to retrain experienced adult family heads displaced from established jobs by technological and economic change." As the employment picture brightened, the emphasis was readjusted to youth, then to the disadvantaged.[6] In the first four years (1962–66) of the MDTA institutional training program, over 80 percent of the participants' incomes were above the poverty level *before* they entered the training program. Apparently, the most disadvantaged people were not the major users of the program. Therefore, comparisons between these two federal programs (AVT and MDTA) which focus on two quite different populations would be expected to favor MDTA. After all, MDTA trainees had already established themselves as part of the working community before taking their training. Also, MDTA trainees did not have to relocate to enter training. A major similarity is that both programs are federally sponsored vocational training programs.

Evaluations of MDTA programs have consistently shown that approximately two-thirds of the trainees complete their educational program.[7] Despite the higher age and educational status and higher proportion of married participants—all factors positively linked to completion of training—in the MDTA program the Bureau's AVT Program manifested a higher completion rate (71 percent).

Job Corps

Job Corps was created as part of the Economic Opportunity Act in 1964. Its main target group was youths between 16 and 21 years of age. The goal of Job Corps was to prepare youths for citizenship and to improve their employability by training them in some type of skill. Unlike the MDTA program, the Job Corps did not attract the

6. Sar A. Levitan and Garth L. Mangum, *Federal Training and Work Programs in the Sixties* (Ann Arbor, Mich.: Institute of Labor and Industrial Relations, 1969).

7. Earl D. Main, "A Nationwide Evaluation of M.D.T.A. Institutional Job Training," *The Journal of Human Resources* 3 (1968), 159–70.

"cream" of the unemployed or underemployed youths. At the beginning of the program, over 40 percent of the participants had completed less than nine years of schooling. Since Job Corps' inception, the definition of success (or completion) has changed from completion of two years of training to a completion of a six-month period of training. Six months have come to represent the crucial minimal involvement, although most of the programs are nine months in length. According to a study done by Louis Harris and Associates, the longer a corpman stayed in the program, the greater his chances of being employed after training. In the fiscal year 1967, only 44 percent of the Job Corps' trainees lasted six months or longer.[8]

The basic difference between the Job Corps and AVT is that Job Corps trained a younger group of participants, mostly white. An important similarity is the fact that in both programs, participants left home to receive training. The 70 percent rate of completion of the AVT is significantly higher than the 44 percent for Job Corps. Furthermore, mean length of stay in the Corps for fiscal 1967 was 5.3 months;[9] for the AVT participants in the Portland BIA Area the mean length of stay was 10.6 months.

Comparisons with these two programs illustrate the achievement of the AVT. If one considers the target group of the AVT program—rural reservation Indians with little working experience in the white community—and the social science literature concerning the adjustment problems of Indians in the cities, the high comparative success rate of the AVT program is an achievement.

The third method of measuring success and a very important feature of the AVT program is that at least 91 percent of the trainees that completed their program of study were able to obtain employment in an occupation directly related to the training they had received. It should also be noted that in almost all of the remaining cases, information about employment was not available. This should not be interpreted to mean that the remaining trainees had not obtained a job, but simply that the information about their employment was not included in their case record. Thus, the number obtaining relevant employment is probably higher than 91 percent. The 1966 TOB data revealed that three years after beginning the program, "61 percent of the recipients were actively employed in positions directly related to the training taken."[10]

The fourth method of evaluating the success of the program was to compare income before training to income after participation in

8. Levitan, *Antipoverty Work and Training Efforts: Goals and Reality* (Washington, D.C.: National Manpower Policy Task Force, 1967).

9. Ibid.

10. TOB, "Follow-Up Study."

the AVT Program for the 175 participants who had completed their program of study. Information was available in only 159 cases, however. In the year before training, the average annual income for single individuals was $1,360; after training, the average starting salary was $438 per month, for a projected annual income of $5,256. For married participants the average annual income before training was $2,270; after training the starting income was $538 per month or $6,456 per year. Both initial income figures fall below the poverty line ($3,000 for a married couple and $1,500 for a single individual per year) as defined by the Council of Economic Advisors in 1964.[11] After completion of the program, the average projected income was considerably above the poverty line for both married and single participants.

Discussion

It may be unfortunate that there is manifested by many Indians a generalized belief that *all* programs associated with the BIA are detrimental to their way of life. The BIA, as the working arm of the government, certainly has not been aided in its mission by many of the federal policies it has had to administer. The general disrepute of the BIA must be added to the already tremendous handicaps the AVT Program faces in working with its unique clientele. The 71 percent completion rate, favorable comparison to other federal programs, and increased income of trainees are direct evidence of the merits of this program.

However, it must be stressed that there are many questions associated with complacently accepting the AVT "success" rate. It becomes apparent from reviewing the records of applicants accepted into the program that the "cream of the crop" are selected. A very good screening process is used to weed out those individuals who stand little chance of completing a given program. These individuals who applied but were rejected are left to lead a poverty existence on the reservation unless some other "program" picks them up.

An equally important question is raised from the individual Indian's standpoint concerning the need to leave the reservation for training. There would seem to be involved here a basic contradiction to the stated objectives of many government officials (see, for example, the president's State of the Union Address, July, 1970) to foster Indian self-determination. If in fact training programs were provided on the reservations and then a corollary attempt were made to provide meaningful and steady employment in those areas, it would seem that the objective of Indian self-determination would be better served. It is

11. Paul B. Horton and Gerald R. Leslie, *The Sociology of Social Problems*, 4th ed. (New York: Appleton-Century Crofts, 1970).

a standard joke in Indian country that the BIA has created more welders to build ships than the Navajo reservation currently has need for. It would seem that the Navajo nation has a very small navy.

Our findings on increased income speak more directly to the questions raised of the effects of training an individual in a given vocational area which forces him to seek a living in an urban area. Any attentive reader of our study would have to be impressed by the substantial increase in income (or potential income) manifested by the participants of the AVT Program. Putting aside the psychological consequences of forcing a separation from the land and kin group of a people whose very existence has historically been so closely tied to those relationships, the practical economic aspects of being forced to live in an urban area raise numerous questions. The Indian who leaves the reservation loses his U.S. Public Health service benefits (medical and dental care), his relatively inexpensive housing and transportation, and the food, clothing, or other essentials that may have been produced at home. He instead enters the urban area where all of the expenses must now be met by his increased income. The projected annual incomes of $5,256 for a single person and $6,456 for married participants must be put into perspective with the added information of a study just taken based on a random sample of the urban Indian and white population in Seattle, Washington. The report states that "the average Seattle Indian income for 1970–71 was $3,100 (below the poverty line) while the average white income was $4,326." [12] If statistics like these are any indication of the condition of urban Indians nationwide, one wonders where the over 100,000 "highly trained" and "well paid" recipients of the BIA, AVT program are located.

The process of BIA relocation and its long-range effects on Indian people and continuation of their cultural needs continued examination. The report by Sorkin that 61 percent of the recipients of AVT were three years later still employed in positions directly related to their training demands further exploration. The continued relationship with the reservation they left of Indians who have gone through this training and relocation process is a fertile area of research for the Native-American scholar. Continued research bearing directly on such questions as we have raised concerning the "success" rate of the BIA, AVT program are badly needed in the Native-American literature today.

12. Bruce A. Chadwick, Howard M. Bahr, and Joseph H. Stauss, Unpublished project memorandum from "Antecedents and Correlates of Racial Discrimination and Responses to Discrimination," National Science Foundation (GS-3248), 1972, p. 2.

Susan Navarro Uranga

The Study of Mexican-American Education in the Southwest: Implications of Research by the Civil Rights Commission*

The U.S. Commission on Civil Rights has been involved in the study of Chicano education in the Southwest[1] since 1968. The study undertaken by the Commission was one of the first comprehensive examinations of the Chicano student in the public elementary and secondary schools of the Southwest.[2] It compiled information on (1) conditions in the schools attended by Chicanos, (2) educational practices in these schools, and (3) educational achievement of Mexican-American students in these districts.

Susan Navarro Uranga, Mexican American Education Study, U.S. Commission on Civil Rights. This paper was presented at the Workshop on Southwest Ethnic Groups: Sociopolitical Environment and Education, sponsored by The Cross-Cultural Southwest Ethnic Study Center at The University of Texas at El Paso, July 27–29, 1972.

* The information in this paper is taken from the reports of the Civil Rights Commission, Mexican American Education Study; however, the views expressed are those of this author and not necessarily of the Commission.

1. For purposes of this study, the Southwest includes the following states: Arizona, California, Colorado, New Mexico, and Texas.

2. Previous research has oeen confined to single issues such as reading achievement, or to limited geographic areas such as studies on a single city or state.

    James S. Coleman, in *Equality of Educational Opportunity,* U.S. Department of Health, Education and Welfare, Office of Education, Washington, D.C., 1966, examined the effect of the school and its condition and practices on the performance of children. This study, though it provides some very useful data on Mexican Americans, does not provide information by state, ethnic density of school or district, or on programs and policies of special interest to bilingual children.

Methodology

Data on districts and schools were compiled in three phases. The first phase involved analysis of data taken from a stratified random sample of all school districts in the United States, which included all districts with a student population of 3,000 or more. The study encompassed 93 percent of Chicano pupils and 94 percent of all pupils in the Southwest.

The second phase of the data collection involved the Commission's own mail survey of 538 districts and 1,166 schools throughout the Southwest to principals and superintendents, which elicited information about the types of programs and policies within districts and schools, staffing patterns, and achievement levels.[3]

Finally, a field study was conducted in which Commission staff interviewed principals and counselors to collect information that could not be collected by mail. The field study was limited to 52 schools in California, New Mexico, and Texas.[4] It included rural, urban, and suburban schools in each state selected. In Texas, San Antonio and Corpus Christi and the area between these two cities were selected. In New Mexico, Albuquerque and areas in the southern part of the state were surveyed. Finally, in California, the Santa Clara County including the city of San Jose was selected.

A total of 494 classrooms were systematically observed by Commission staff for physical, administrative, instructional, social, and emotional aspects of the school environment. These components were systematically observed through the use of interview schedule and pupil-teacher interaction recording techniques.[5]

Publications

To date, the Mexican American Education Study has published five reports. The first, *Ethnic Isolation of Mexican Americans in the Public Schools of the Southwest,* identifies demographic characteristics and the degree to which Chicano students and teachers are segregated in Southwestern Schools. Three basic findings stem from Report I:

3. Those districts which did not respond to the Commission's survey are Kingsburg and Lucia Mar in California, Norte Conejor in California, Silver City in New Mexico, and Houston and Edcouch-Elsa in Texas.

4. Ninety percent of all Chicano students in the Southwest attend public school in California, New Mexico, and Texas.

5. The interview schedules and school and classroom protocol forms were developed by Dr. Monroe K. Rowland. The two forms used to record classroom interaction are the Flanders Interaction Analysis, developed by Dr. Ned Flanders, and the Observation Schedule and Record, devised by Dr. Donald M. Medley and Dr. Harry E. Mitzel.

(1) Mexican-American public school pupils are severely isolated by districts and schools within individual districts; (2) for the most part, Chicanos are underrepresented on school and district professional staffs and on boards of education; and (3) the majority of Mexican-American staff and school board members are found in predominantly Mexican-American schools or districts.

Mexican-American students comprise approximately 20 percent of the total number of pupils in the Southwest. In 1968, when figures for this study were compiled, there were 1.4 million Chicano students in Arizona, California, Colorado, New Mexico, and Texas. The vast majority of these are in California and Texas, where 82 percent of all Chicano students in the Southwest are found. However, Mexican Americans constitute the highest proportion of enrollment (38 percent) in New Mexico. Over 50 percent of all Chicano students in the Southwest attend school in large urban districts with enrollments of 10,000 or more.

Although Mexican-American pupils are unevenly distributed among the states and concentrated in specific geographic areas within each state, they are also concentrated or isolated in districts and schools of the Southwest. About 404, 000 Mexican-American pupils, or 30 percent of this ethnic group's enrollment in the Southwest, attend schools in approximately 200 predominantly Mexican-American districts.[6]

The largest number of predominantly Mexican-American districts (50 percent or more) is in Texas. Ninety-four Mexican-American districts, almost all of which are located in southern Texas, contain nearly 60 percent of the state's total Mexican-American enrollment. About 20 percent of Texas' Mexican-American students attend school in districts which are nearly all Mexican American.

Most of the other predominantly Mexican-American districts are in California and New Mexico. Together, these states contain as many Mexican-American districts as Texas [about 90]; however, the total Mexican-American school population of these districts is much smaller. They include only about 94,000 Mexican-American pupils, while the 94 Texas districts include 291,000 pupils.

A major aspect of the Commission investigation was aimed at ascertaining the extent to which the Mexican-American composition of schools does not resemble that of the districts in which they are located. The Commission found that 30 percent of Chicano students in the Southwest attend these imbalanced schools. Although the extent of ethnic imbalance does differ sharply among the five states, four large urban school districts—Los Angeles, Denver, Albuquerque, and Tucson—account for a significant percentage of Mexican-American

6. Predominantly Mexican-American districts indicate those districts in which 50 percent or more of the student population is Mexican American.

students who are in schools with a disproportionately high Chicano enrollment.[7]

The Commission's report also examines the representation and school assignment of Mexican Americans holding staff and service positions in the schools.[8] Except for those persons employed as custodians or teacher's aides, Mexican Americans comprise substantially less of school staff than they do of enrollment. Mexican Americans are grossly underrepresented among teachers. Of approximately 325,000 teachers in the Southwest, only about 12,000, or 4 percent, are Mexican American, while about 17 percent of the enrollment is Mexican American. Black teachers, although they are also underrepresented, outnumber Mexican-American teachers by almost two to one. Texas and California employ three-fourths of all Mexican-American teachers. Most of the other Mexican-American teachers (15 percent) are found in New Mexico.

Mexican-American teachers are, to a greater extent than pupils, found in predominantly Mexican-American schools. One-third of the teachers are in schools whose enrollments are 80 percent or more Mexican American. Although the larger number of Mexican-American teachers are assigned to predominantly Mexican-American schools, they still constitute a very low percentage of teachers in these schools, mainly because so few members of this ethnic group are employed as teachers.

Mexican Americans are also underrepresented on local boards of education. Of approximately 4,600 school board members in the Commission's survey area, only about 10 percent are Mexican American.

Report II of the series, *The Unfinished Education,* examines five measures of school controlled educational outcomes: school holding power, reading achievement, grade repetition, overageness, and participation in extracurricular activities.

School holding power is measured by the percentage of students entering first grade who continue in school. The proportion of minority students who remain in school through the twelfth grade is significantly lower than that of Anglo students. Mexican Americans demonstrate the most severe rate of attrition. The Commission estimates that out of every 100 Mexican-American youngsters who enter first grade in the survey area, only 60 graduate from high school;

7. Two-thirds of Chicano pupils in Texas and New Mexico attend predominantly Mexican-American schools which are not considered ethnically imbalanced because of the large number of predominantly Chicano districts.
8. These staff include classroom teachers, school principals, assistant or vice principals, counselors, librarians, other professional nonteaching school staff, secretaries, custodians, and teacher's aides.

only 67 of every 100 Black first graders graduate from high school. In contrast, 86 of every 100 Anglos receive high school diplomas.

For Mexican Americans, there are sharp differences in school holding power among the five states. Of the two states with the largest Mexican-American school enrollment—California and Texas—holding power is significantly greater in California, where an estimated 64 percent of the Mexican-American youngsters graduate. Texas demonstrates the poorest record of any of the states. By the end of the eighth grade, Chicanos in the survey area have already lost 14 percent of their peers—almost as many as Anglos will lose by the twelfth grade. Before the end of the twelfth grade, 47 percent of the Mexican-American pupils will have left school.

Throughout the survey area, a disproportionately large number of Chicanos and other minority youngsters lack reading skills commensurate with age and grade level. At the fourth, eighth, and twelfth grades, the proportion of Mexican-American and Black students reading below grade level is generally twice that of Anglos reading below grade level. For the total Southwest survey area, the percentage of minority students deficient in reading reaches as high as 63 percent for Chicanos and 70 percent for Blacks in the 12th grade. In the eighth grade, the Chicano youngster is 2.3 times as likely as the Anglo to be reading below level, while the Black student is 2.1 times as likely.

Reading achievement drops greatly for children of all ethnic groups as they advance in age and grade. For minority children, however, the drop is more severe. At the fourth grade, 51 percent of the Mexican Americans and 56 percent of the Blacks, compared with 25 percent of the Anglos, are reading below level. By the eighth grade, corresponding figures are 64 percent for Mexican Americans and 58 percent for Blacks. Further deterioration occurs by the twelfth grade despite the fact that many of the poorest achievers have already left school. At this stage, 63 percent of the Mexican Americans are reading below level, as are 70 percent of the Blacks and 34 percent of the Anglos.

The Commission found that grade repetition rates for Mexican Americans are significantly higher than for Anglos. Some 16 percent of Mexican-American students repeat the first grade, compared to 6 percent of the Anglos. Although the disparity between Mexican Americans and Anglos at the fourth grade is not as wide as in the first grade, Mexican-American pupils are still twice as likely as Anglos to repeat this grade.

Overageness is another measure of achievement related to grade repetition. The Commission found that Mexican Americans are as much as seven times as likely to be overage as Anglos. In the eighth grade, more than 9 percent of the Mexican-American pupils are over-age, compared to a little more than 1 percent of the Anglo students.

Again comparing the two largest states, the difference is impressive. More than 16 percent of Chicano eighth-graders are overage in Texas. In California only about 2 percent are.

Extracurricular activities make the school experience more mean-ingful and enhance school holding power. The Commission found, however, that Mexican-American students are underrepresented in extracurricular activities, regardless of whether they are a majority or a minority in a school.

The Commission concludes that under these five measures of school achievement, the public schools of the Southwest are failing to educate Chicano children. Part of this failure is explained in Report III, *The Excluded Student,* which examines the exclusion of the language, culture, and community of the Chicano from the public schools of the Southwest.

The suppression of the Spanish language is the most overt area of cultural exclusion. Schools have repressed languages other than English, regarding them as an educational handicap and a deterrent to Americanization. Nearly 50 percent of the Mexican-American first-graders do not speak English as well as the average Anglo first-grader. These children are often compelled, however, to not only learn a new language but also to learn course material in this language. One-third of the schools surveyed by the Commission admitted discouraging Spanish in the classroom. Methods of enforcing the "No Spanish Rule" vary from simple discouragement to strict discipline.

There are various programs schools may use to meet these language difficulties. The three most important programs are Bilingual Educa-tion, English as a Second Language, and Remedial Reading.

Bilingual Education, which utilizes both the linguistic and cultural aspects of children, is the only program that modifies the traditional school curriculum. Although Bilingual Education holds great promise for both Mexican-American and Anglo students, it is seldom used. Only 6.5 percent of the Southwest's schools have bilingual programs, and these are reaching only 2.7 percent of the Mexican-American school population—only one student out of nearly 40.

English as a Second Language (ESL) Programs are much more limited than Bilingual Education and thus less effective. The sole objective of ESL is to make non-English speakers more competent in English. No effort is made to present related cultural material. Unlike Bilingual Education, ESL requires no modification of the school cur-riculum. An estimated 5.5 percent of the Mexican-American students in the Southwest receive some kind of instruction in English as a Second Language.

Of the three programs discussed, Remedial Reading is the most limited. It requires no change in the school curriculum and little teacher training. Using a strictly monolingual approach, Remedial Reading has been much more accepted than either Bilingual Education or ESL. However, this program deals with only a symptom of the broader problem of language exclusion in the schools. More than half of the Southwest's schools offer Remedial Reading courses, yet only 10.7 percent of Chicano students are enrolled in these classes.

A second exclusionary practice is the omission of Mexican-American history, heritage, and folklore from the classrooms. The heritage of the Mexican American is excluded in textbooks, and by the lack of relevant courses and activities. The Commission found that the curricula in most schools fail to inform either Anglos or Mexican Americans of the substantial contributions of the Indo-Hispanic culture to the historical development of the Southwest. Only 4.3 percent of the elementary and 7.3 percent of the secondary schools surveyed have a course in Mexican-American history.

In addition to course content, heritage is also excluded in the cultural selectivity of schools. School and classroom activities, whenever they deal with Mexican-American culture, tend to stress only the superficial and exotic elements—the "fantasy heritage" of the Southwest. This reinforces existing stereotypes and denies the Mexican-American student a full awareness and pride in his culture.

The exclusion of the Mexican-American community is the third area examined in the Commission's study. To determine the extent of community involvement, four specific areas were examined: contacts with parents, community advisory boards, community relations specialists, and consultants on Mexican-American education.

Teachers and administrators utilize notices sent home and PTA meetings most frequently as methods of communicating with parents. Although an estimated 4,000,000 persons in the Southwest identify Spanish as their mother tongue, only 25 percent of the elementary and 11 percent of the secondary schools send notices in Spanish to Spanish-speaking parents; 91.7 percent of the Southwest's elementary schools and 98.5 percent of its secondary schools do not use Spanish as well as English in conducting their PTA meetings.

Contacts with parents and community advisory boards are methods by which the schools can communicate directly with the Mexican-American parents and community. However, only one district in four actually has a community advisory board on Mexican-American educational affairs. When these methods prove unsuccessful in the establishment of free communication, a community relations specialist may be called in to serve as a link between the people and the power structure. Schools often rely heavily on this individual to bridge the communication gap with the linguistically and culturally different community. The study demonstrated that 84 percent of surveyed districts did not use community relations specialists at all. Thus, in spite of the need, most school systems have not established this type of liaison with the barrio.

The data concerning the use of Mexican-American educational consultants are similar; school districts are not availing themselves of experts who can help them determine and resolve their failures in educating Mexican Americans.

Report IV examines the effects of the Texas school financing system on Chicano education in this state. Specifically, it looks at disparities in:

1. State aid to local school districts, in particular the Minimum Foundation Program, which provides more than 90 percent of state education funds,
2. Property valuations within districts,
3. Property tax effort, or the rate at which property is taxed in each school district, and
4. The economic burden of property taxes on Mexican-American and Anglo citizens.

A companion report that discusses the state of the law relative to school finance has also been prepared.

Suggestions for remedies of the Texas school finance system are now being considered by the Texas State Committee of the Commission. The State Committee is an advisory body to the Commission and is composed of about twenty-five prominent citizens in Texas. The Committee's recommendations, along with the Commission's report on Texas school finance and the role of law in school finance, were released in September 1972.

> The basic conclusion of this report is that Mexican Americans are not receiving a financial return commensurate with the drain on their pocketbook. Per pupil expenditures are substantially lower in Chicano than in Anglo districts. Expenditures range from a high of $484 per pupil in districts 20 to 30 percent Chicano to a low of $296, or about three-fifths that amount, in districts 80 percent or more Mexican American.
>
> The state of Texas has devised a system of school finance by which expenditures on education are strongly tied to the property wealth of the district and the personal income of district residents. Although the state Minimum Foundation Program may have been intended to correct fiscal inequities, it has proved far from successful in practice. The Texas Minimum Foundation Program can perhaps best be described as a repressive jumble of provisions and conditions that do not adequately reduce financial disparities between Anglo and Mexican-American districts and insure that

significantly less is spent to educate Chicano children than their Anglo counterparts.[9]

Subsequent Reports

The Commission's fifth report on Mexican-American education examines differences in teacher-pupil interaction between classes of varying Mexican American and Anglo composition as well as differences in verbal behaviorial interaction for Chicano and Anglo students within individual classrooms. This report was published in April 1973.

Data for this report were derived from field studies conducted in 52 schools in California, New Mexico, and Texas in the fall and winter of the 1970–71 school year.[10]

The sixth report of the Mexican American Education Study will examine the effect that school practices and conditions have on the educational outcomes of Chicano students and will also outline the Commission's recommendations for remedies. Most of the data for analysis will be taken from the principals' questionnaire used in the spring 1969 mail survey. The analysis will determine how school factors such as staffing characteristics, language programs, facilities, grouping and tracking, Mexican-American composition of school enrollment, and the socioeconomic status of pupils relate to student outcomes. The most important outcome to be studied will be the reading levels of Chicano students. However, four other outcomes—dropout rates, overageness, college-going rates, and participation in extracurricular activities—will also be analyzed.

This paper has presented a summary of the Commission's findings on Mexican-American education in the Southwest. During four years of research, we have attempted to find and document those policies and practices which tend to impinge upon the educational opportunities of Mexican-American children. The Commission is aware of, and has examined, other areas of research and program development not included in this series. There still exist, however, crucial areas that have not yet been examined, some of which are outlined here.

Federal elementary and secondary educational programs, authorized primarily through the Office of Education (HEW), have been funded

9. U.S. Commission on Civil Rights, *Mexican American Education in Texas: A Function of Wealth* (Washington, D.C.: U.S. Government Printing Office, August 1972), p. 29.
10. A detailed discussion of the sampling procedures employed in selecting these 52 schools is contained in our report on methodology which has recently been made available to the public.

in excess of $2 billion for fiscal 1973 programs. These programs range from massive expenditures through Title I of the Elementary and Secondary Education Act to the Education Professions Development Act and Dropout Prevention. Although few major programs are directed exclusively to Mexican Americans, all can and should encompass areas of inquiry into the special concerns of this group. Little is known, however, of the actual number of projects in any specific area directed to and by Chicanos, or of the number of Chicano students benefitting from these. An overall analysis of these programs is vital in determining whether or not Chicanos are being reached.

It is also particularly critical to evaluate the effectiveness of programs that do reach the Mexican-American child. Though the funding continues and interest in the recipients of the allocations magnifies yearly, there is little indication that the so-called "compensatory education programs" are developing successful methods of teaching. Although there are a myriad of programs designed to upgrade the level of the minority child's achievement, the programs themselves have not been evaluated in terms of effectiveness. This is not an indictment of these programs, but a question of direction. The major emphasis is placed on the input of funds and the numbers of children served rather than on the outcome or effectiveness of these innovative efforts.

Title I of the Elementary and Secondary Education Act is the primary national education program for economically disadvantaged children and represents the single largest allocation of grant funds to elementary and secondary education. Of the $1.5 billion appropriated through Title I in fiscal 1972, $260,000,000 were granted to Arizona, California, Colorado, New Mexico, and Texas, where a large percentage of those children in schools receiving Title I funds are Chicano. Criteria, regulations, and guidelines for approval of applications for Title I grants include meeting the special educational and supportive needs of economically and educationally deprived children in areas of high concentration of low-income families. Evaluation on a project-by-project basis is also required; however, no provision is made for standardized evaluation of all projects so as to permit comparison of projects or the sharing of information in specified areas. Of greatest concern to many observers is the fact that there is little evidence nationwide that programs funded under Title I have made a significant impact, educationally or otherwise, on children being served. A recently published study of Title I [11] indicates that though some isolated state and local projects have been successful, most have failed to provide participating children those educational and, to a

11. Michael J. Wargo et al., *ESEA Title I: A Reanalysis and Synthesis of Evaluation Data from Fiscal Year 1965 Through 1970,* American Institute for Research in the Behavioral Sciences, Palo Alto, California, March 1972.

lesser degree, supportive services which were outlined in the structure of Title I. Further, the study found that state and local education agencies have failed to comply with Office of Education guidelines and regulations in implementing their programs. Of special importance to Chicano communities is that these guidelines specify that the needs of non–English-speaking and bilingual children can and should be met through Title I funds.

The Bilingual Education Program, funded since 1969, now covers 125 projects and 60,000 children in the Southwest. Though this bilingual-bicultural education is widely thought to be the most promising for Chicano children, no systematic evaluation of the projects has been done. Research of this concept as a teaching method and isolated evaluations of each of the projects funded under Title VII have been done. However, no standard criteria have been established to judge the efficacy of all such programs in the Southwest. Further, there has been no systematic study of the effectiveness of the bilingual-bicultural programs in raising either the achievement levels or self-concept of the Chicano children. Also, no major study of the various types of bilingual education has been done to establish the grouping of components most likely to produce a successful project. If bilingual education is to continue to meet the needs of Chicano children in the Southwest, an analysis of programs now in effect is essential.

Professional teacher training is clearly of great importance in the educational process. In addition to shaping what and how children learn, the teachers' attitudes and perceptions of a student's ability can affect the child's total achievement in school. For the minority child, the teacher assumes the vital role of a link toward a meaningful self-image and the ability to perform in the first nonfamilial environment. It is unfortunate that despite the research on teacher training in the Southwest, few training methods have been developed that have enabled teachers to deal with the Chicano child's "different-ness" or sensitivity in accepting him as he comes to school. In making meaningful changes in teacher training in the Southwest, large-scale standardized evaluation and experimentation of schools and teachers must be made so as to point out major weaknesses in the teaching of Chicano children and those new techniques most successful in modifying these weaknesses.

Research on the financing of elementary and secondary schools is of major importance in determining the actual educational expenditure for minority children. Though much research on differences in expenditures between districts has been done, information on spending levels between schools within districts is sparse. It is strongly suggested that extreme variations in per pupil expenditures exist between Chicano and Anglo pupils in schools within districts in the

Southwest. However, no survey has been done which shows that such a pattern exists.

What we have presented here must not be seen as solely a castigation of Southwestern public schools but rather as an indication of the vital need for change. The series the Commission is presenting is only a first step toward breaking the wall between what is known about the Chicano child in the public school system and what remains unknown. Our concern toward a positive and viable reorientation of our educational systems must be linked with research that points toward a new and better form of education for Chicano children in the Southwest.

Tomás A. Arciniega

The Myth of the
Compensatory Education Model
in Education of Chicanos

If there is no struggle, there is no progress. Those who profess to favor freedom and yet depreciate agitation are men who want crops without plowing the ground. They want rain without thunder and lightning. They want the ocean without the roar of its many waters. This struggle may be a moral one; or it may be both moral and physical; but it must be a struggle. Power concedes nothing without demand. It never did and it never will. Men may not get what they pay for but they must certainly pay for all they get.

Frederick Douglas

This paper deals with a specific goal: the attainment of equal educational opportunity in the United States. As I ponder recent developments—the "where" and "how" we are going with our research, development, and training efforts in education—I am convinced that we are on a rollercoasting Juggernaut heading for the *big showdown*. I predict that the demand for attainment of equal educational opportunity in this country will become the most serious domestic issue to be faced in the coming decade.

Let me make my thesis even more explicit. Given the present state of our logic, legislation, and lethargy in this area, efforts by Chicanos, Blacks, and Indians to secure an equitable share of the benefits derived from education is a goal that does not appear to have a technical or politically feasible solution. At the same time presently rising levels of frustrations, expectations, and dissatisfactions among minority mem-

Tomás A. Arciniega, Dean, School of Education, California State University, San Diego. This paper was presented at the Workshop on Southwest Ethnic Groups: Sociopolitical Environment and Education, sponsored by The Cross-Cultural Southwest Ethnic Study Center at The University of Texas at El Paso, July 27-29, 1972.

bers indicate too that it is a goal which politically will be impossible for this nation to avoid. It is in this somber context then that I wish to discuss what I here have labeled the Myth of the Compensatory Education Model and the implications of that public educational response.

That the attainment of equal educational opportunity is increasingly becoming an explosive national issue should not be surprising, given the fact of modern technological existence where distribution levels and benefits of education are so closely linked to "utility" factors such as income levels, occupational structures, socioeconomic status, and titular trappings and to volatile social problem issues such as segregation, job discrimination, residential patterns, and so forth. Unpleasant as many educators may find the thought, there is no denying that the educational system performs a manifest social function in determining the future stratification system of society. Schools and universities have become primary allocators of privilege and status. This allocation of privilege function and its implications for social policy is often either intentionally overlooked and played down or at best it is slighted in the usual discussions of educational problems faced by the "disadvantaged." It is central, however, to the following analysis of the concept of equal educational opportunity.

The Concept of Equal Educational Opportunity

Review of recent research and development efforts and ongoing educational programs targeting on the minorities of this country reveals two differing views of what constitutes equality.

The equal access to schooling view is the more traditional. This view contends that equal educational opportunity is said to be attained when it can be demonstrated that different segments of the population have a roughly equal opportunity to compete for the benefits of the educational system. Minimum conditions of this view are summed up by Green as follows:

> that there be provided for every person within the society some school with approximately comparable curricula, facilities, staff, and management. If there are children for whom no school at all exists, then those children do not have equal educational opportunity. Moreover, if the schools available for some are significantly deficient, then the children who attend those schools do not have equal educational opportunity." [1]

This view focuses primarily on inputs to the educational system. In short, the principal qualifying conditions to the achievement of equal

1. Thomas Green, "Educational Planning in Perspective," Futures Inc., IPC Science and Technology Press Limited, IPC House, 32 High Street, Guildford, Surrey, England. 1971, p. 27.

educational opportunity are (1) equal access to school for all who wish to attend and (2) that all schools be roughly equal as regards quality of staff, instructional materials, and school plant facilities.

Proponents of this view would argue that the decision to secure what the school has to offer—to benefit from the system—is a simple matter of personal choice. The individual chooses to benefit or not to do so. Once he decides, it would be his personal intellectual capacity, drive, and ambition that would determine the results of that choice. Equal educational opportunity is said to have been provided, although persons may not equally take advantage of or secure the opportunities open to them. Thus, according to this view, the fact that Chicanos (in the case at hand) do not benefit equally from the present educational system has nothing to do with the existence or nonexistence of equal opportunity, but rather is a matter of personal choice and talent or lack of it on the part of Chicanos.

The equal benefits view focuses on the distribution of the results or benefits derived from the system. Equality of opportunity exists only if you have an equal benefits situation and not merely equal access. The burden of responsibility for insuring the type of education where all segments of the population benefit equally lies squarely on the school systems involved. Conversely unacceptable inequalities are said to exist when the educational institutions involved can be shown to be excluding a given group from obtaining equal benefits from those institutions.

Although there is insufficient space here to detail a complete comparative analysis, let me anticipate and respond to the two most common rebuttals which inevitably arise in discussions of the equal benefit view. First, the equal benefits view as described here does not mean *all* students are to achieve at the same level. (Although, I feel that stand could be argued rather successfully too if one took Bloom's Learning for Mastery[2] theoretical position.) However, the point here is that the range of achievement should be approximately the same for the various groups being served by the educational system. Second, regarding the distribution of inputs or resources, it may well be that a commitment to achieve equal educational opportunity will necessitate unequal allocations of resources as well as *substantial* increases in accessibility in order to achieve that goal. Recent federal legislative and program guidelines justify disproportionate funding on that basis.

Although hindsight enables us to present the differing concepts of equal educational opportunity, as I have done, in full contrast it is important to recognize the evolving nature of their development and

2. Benjamin Bloom, "Administrator's Notebook," (Pamphlet) University of Chicago Press, Midwest Administrative Center, 1971.

to trace a few salient historical points. The notion of educational opportunity came into being with the birth of tax-supported public education in the nineteenth century. Public education arose as a result of the basic transformations in society wrought by the industrial revolution and the demand for trained specialists. Public education was charged early with the task of providing equal education to all except the rich who attended private schools, the poor who did not attend, and the minorities who were excluded. As Coleman points out, equality of educational opportunity for those served contained four conditions: (1) common curiculum, (2) free education, (3) access to some school by children of diverse backgrounds, and (4) equal facilities within given locales.[3]

In addition to the obvious exclusions, several dubious assumptions can be noted in this early conception of equal educational opportunity. As Coleman points out, the notion of free education assumes the nonexistence of inequalities in opportunities because of low economic status and ignores the problem of the poor staying in school beyond the age of employment, especially when staying in school did not significantly affect the positions they filled anyway. Second, it was assumed that somehow through simple exposure to the common curriculum, equal opportunity was provided. The school was placed in the passive role of being responsible simply to make available the opportunity to learn. The task of benefitting from the opportunity was left to the child.[4]

Next, the assumption of common curricula was challenged by the recognition that not all children were college-bound. It was successfully argued that to expose all children to a college-bound common curriculum was to deny some the equality of educational opportunity, because their time could be better used in vocational preparation. Equality of educational opportunity came to mean differing curricula for different types of students.[5]

The third condition in the original definition, the right of children of diverse backgrounds to attend the same school, was successfully challenged in the *Plessey vs. Ferguson* case of 1896. The Supreme Court ruled that "separate but equal" facilities were not unconstitutional and segregation was legalized. This decision was reversed in the *Brown vs. Board of Education of Topeka* case of 1954. The court ruled that racial separation was inherently unequal in its effects on children. By focusing on the effects of schools on children, the Supreme Court introduced

3. James S. Coleman, "The Concept of Equal Educational Opportunity," U.S. Office of Education, Washington, D.C., U.S. Govt. Printing Press. 1966.

4. Ibid.

5. Ibid.

a new assumption; *equal educational opportunity depended upon the results or benefits derived from school attendance.*[6]

Since that case, U.S. public schools have been faced with the legal mandate to desegregate and to provide equal opportunities to students of different racial groups. Although the Supreme Court has not ruled directly on the case of the Mexican American, it is implicit in the equal protection clause of the U.S. Constitution that the principles outlined in *Brown vs. Board* case apply to other minority groups. This was the ruling in the recent landmark case *Cisneros vs. Corpus Christi Independent School District.* The court ruled that Mexican Americans were an identifiable minority which had been subjected to discrimination as such and were entitled to protection under the *Brown vs. Board* decision.[7]

Extension of protection under the *Brown vs. Board* decision was granted further in the celebrated Serrano and Rodriguez cases in California and Texas, respectively. In both cases, the courts ruled that the present basis for financing public education through property taxation was discriminatory. And recently, in the San Felipe Del Rio School Consolidation case, the U.S. District Court extended the ruling to include curriculum and staff development. The school district was ordered to insure equal educational opportunity for Mexican-American children by including bicultural education as an integral part of the school district curriculum and to recruit Mexican-American teachers and administrators.[8]

Full emergence, on a nationally recognized basis, of the equal benefits view did not come until publication of the following studies:

1. Racial Isolation in the Public Schools (1966) [9]
2. U.S. Office of Education Study on Equality of Educational Opportunity (Coleman Report–1966) [10]
3. Mexican American Education Study[11]

6. James S. Coleman, "The Concept of Equal Educational Opportunity," in *Harvard Educational Review, Equal Educational Opportunity* (Cambridge, Mass.: Harvard University Press, 1969), pp. 9–24.
7. Civil Rights Digest, U.S. Government Printing Office, Washington, D.C. (16), 1971.
8. Civil Action No. 5281, The U.S. vs. State of Texas, "A Comprehensive Educational Plan for the San Felipe Del Rio Consolidated Independent School District," August 13, 1971.
9. Racial Isolation in the Public Schools, Vol. 1, U.S. Commission on Civil Rights, U.S. Government Printing Office, Washington, D.C., 1967.
10. Coleman, "The Concept of Equal Educational Opportunity."
11. Mexican American Education Study, U.S. Commission on Civil Rights, U.S. Government Printing Office, Washington, D.C.; #1 Ethnic Isolation of Mexican Americans in the Public Schools of the Southwest, April 1971. #2 The Unfinished Education: Outcomes for Minorities in the Five Southwestern States, October 1971.

In assessing the lack of equality of educational opportunity among racial and minority groups, these reports (particularly the Coleman Study) focused not only on the idea of equality of inputs (finances, facilities, curriculum, teacher quality, and so forth) but also upon equality of output in terms of student achievements. Although the Coleman report evoked considerable controversy and many criticized the predictors used to measure school outcomes, there was ready acknowledgment that the survey had successfully challenged the simplistic equal access view and that a new dimension had been added to the evolving concept of equal educational opportunity.

These studies evoked great consternation and national debate about how best to achieve equality of results. Coleman leaves the impression that efforts to focus on input are doomed to failure because they have little relation to output. He concluded that

> schools bring little influence to bear on a child's achievement that is independent of his background and general social context; and thus this very lack of an independent effect means that the inequalities imposed on children by their home, neighborhood, and peer environment are carried along to become the inequalities with which they confront adult life at the end of school." [12]

These findings can lead to at least two different interpretations of how best to achieve equality of results for minority group children. One is that equal benefits from schooling can best be achieved by successfully overcoming the negative effects of their deprived environments. Steps must be taken to remedy the deleterious influences on the child of his home, neighborhood, and peer group. This is essentially the rationale for the "compensatory education" approach of recent years. Programs were developed to *compensate* for deprivations stemming from home, peers, and neighborhood and to acculturate the child into middle-class values and behavior.

A second view is that equality of results can best be achieved by shifting the focus to the school environment. The task is to create school systems that accept and capitalize on the strengths of cultural difference. The promotion of cultural differences is recognized as a valid and legitimate educational goal and is utilized in developing the full potentialities of the minority child. Thus, equal benefits from the system are to be achieved *not* by transforming the Chicano or Black child in order to make him over in the image of the dominant group

---

#3 The Excluded Student, Educational Practices Affecting Mexican Americans in the Southwest, May 1972. #4 Mexican American Education in Texas: A Function of Wealth, August 1972. #5 Teachers and Students: Differences in Teacher Interaction with Mexican American and Anglo Students, March 1973.

12. Coleman, "The Concept of Equal Educational Opportunity."

but by reforming the school he attends along cultural pluralistic lines. The two basic strategies derived from the initial decision to move toward national achievement of equal education opportunity are depicted schematically in Figure 9.

FIGURE 9. SCHEMATIC OF ALTERNATIVE RESPONSES
TO THE EQUAL BENEFITS VIEW

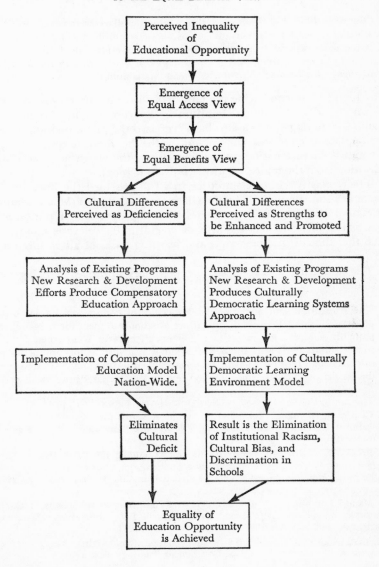

The Myth of Compensatory Education

Compensatory education has been the more prevalent of the two approaches. It has provided the model for the development of programs aimed at minority populations in recent years. The growing rejection of this premise is perhaps best summarized by Ivan Illich:

> "Between 1965 and 1968 over three billion dollars were spent in U.S. schools to offset the disadvantages of about six million children. . . . It is the most expensive compensatory program ever attempted anywhere in education, *yet no significant improvement can be detected in the learning of these "disadvantaged" children.*[13] (Emphasis mine)

The literature documenting the failure of the compensatory model has grown rapidly. Gordon, Hamilton[14], Brischetto and Arciniega[15], Ramirez[16], to name only a few, have criticized the preoccupation of the compensatory education movement, with the identification of dysfunctional characteristics of the deprived and the view that almost any deviation from the majority culture is dysfunctional.

The Texas Advisory Committee in 1970, provided the impetus for the policy statement made by the Office for Civil Rights (Memorandum to School Districts 1970) which reflected the operational philosophy that school districts should provide a culturally relevant education such that the culture, language, and learning styles of all children are recognized and valued.[17]

The mounting failure of the compensatory approach is being met with dismay.

> The frustration and anger of the lay critics of "education for minority-poverty children" because of the failure of schools to meet the demands for palpable evidence of success on any or all criteria is matched by the concern and despair of those professionals responsible for producing results. Rationalizations used in past years that the programs were too new, the funding too weak, the staffs too few and unprepared, the social prob-

13. Ivan Illich, *Deschooling Society* (New York: Harper & Row, 1971), pp. 4–5.

14. Charles V. Hamilton, "Race and Education, A Search for Legitimacy," *Harvard Educational Review, Equal Educational Opportunity* (Cambridge, Mass.: Harvard University Press, 1969), pp. 187–202.

15. Robert Brischetto and Tomás Arciniega, "Examining the Examiners: A Look at Educators' Perspectives on the Chicano Student," unpublished paper presented at the Rocky Mountain Social Science Assn., Salt Lake City, Utah, April 27–29, 1972. (See p. 23.)

16. Manuel Ramirez III, "Culturally Democratic Learning Environments: A Cognitive Styles Approach," Systems and Evaluations in Education, Multi-Lingual Assessment Project, P.O. Box 1567, Riverside, California, 1972.

17. "Civil Rights in Texas," U.S. Commission on Civil Rights, *Texas Advisory Committee,* Washington, D.C., U.S. Government Printing Office, 1970.

lems too pervasive, are no longer acceptable to the community supporting the schools.[18]

The urgent need to move vigorously toward redirective change in the public educational system is clear. It is clear too that at this point we are not talking about small incremental changes in the institutional setting of the school, but rather redirective efforts must be dramatic and broad-gauged. The challenge is clear; the times demand that we organize and use our schools to promote the type of society America "ought to be" and less a reflection of "what is."

The educational system that is suggested in accordance with this view should have as a basic organizational goal—the promotion of cultural pluralism. Schools and universities would be structured to provide Chicano students with the basic knowledge, skills, and political awareness to work effectively within the societal institutions while at the same time to promote positive institutional changes in the opportunity structure for the benefit of minority members.

Bicultural schools with bicultural curricula would be essential basic elements of this type of school system. Both English and Spanish would be utilized at all levels as media of instruction, with the specific intent to develop functional proficiency in both languages. Chicano culture would be reinforced along with the majority cultural system. Ideally, Chicanos and Anglos alike would complete their schooling able to function adequately in both languages and both cultural systems.

The focus of redirective efforts would be on changing the educational system to meet the needs of culturally different students. Changing the structure, curriculum, and normative "set" of the school system is seen as a more viable approach to educating *all* students than changing the child to "fit" the school.

Schools would be representative of the communities they served in the ratio of minority administrators, teachers, and counselors. Special emphasis would be placed on developing schools as microcosms of the "ideal pluralistic" society.

The Redirective Challenge

The mounting of an alternative, more humanistic paradigm to the compensatory view will be far from easy. It will require first a dedicated and substantial commitment on the part of federal, state, and local agents and more importantly, from people like ourselves. The

18. Adelaide Jablonsky, "Status Report on Compensatory Education," Information Retrieval Center on the Disadvantaged, *Disadvantaged Bulletin*, Horace Mann-Lincoln Institute, Teachers College, Columbia, N.Y., 7, Nos, 1 & 2 (Winter–Spring 1971), 1.

road to travel is difficult and poorly illuminated in all too many cases, but we can be encouraged also that significant work has been going on despite our national overcommitment to the compensatory model.

Second, we will need to develop a clear statement of rationale to include core assumptions and concepts. Some of the basic assumptions on which this new paradigm should be built include:

1. The roots of the educational problems of the Chicano are not culturally based.
2. The chief impediments to success by Chicanos in school cannot be attributed to deficient home or peer environments but to the various external restraint systems imposed on the group by virtue of its subordinate position in society.
3. The focus of research instruments should be shifted from the students' ethnic subculture to the structure of the educational and other societal institutions.
4. Educational systems must be restructured to reflect what "should be" and less "what is" in American society.
5. To be effective, changes in the educational system must be accompanied by changes in the political and economic sphere so that wealth and power are more equally distributed in society.[19]

Third, we will need to carefully and systematically chart where we are in relation to where we need to go. Once established then, the process of committing funds to stimulate needed development in priority areas can begin. The attached matrix (Figure 10) is a first attempt at providing a mechanism for charting the state of the art in the area of Education for Cultural Pluralism. Once all programs have been identified and classified as per our 16-cell scheme, it will be necessary to develop evaluative criteria for each category program. The organization and coordination of the research and development framework being suggested above is a massive undertaking that can best be accomplished by the new National Institute for Education.

Next, a framework for early and timely dissemination of products, knowledge, and management systems will need to be developed nation wide. This will require at the minimum the involvement and commitment of state departments of education, community, and universities as well as the actual public school systems using the products.

Fourth, academicians from a variety of disciplines will need to be involved. The problem of eradicating institutional racism, cultural bias, and discrimination in education is an interrelated part of the total societal system. There is little to be gained from "tinkering" with schools without directing attention to the total milieu. Thus the need

19. Brischetto and Arciniega, "Examining the Examiners," p. 23.

FIGURE 10.   MATRIX FOR CLASSIFYING DEVELOPMENT EFFORTS IN THE
EDUCATION FOR CULTURAL PLURALISM AREA

	Collection of Basic Information & Data	Basic Research: Development of Relevant Theories	Development of Bicultural Education Problems	Development of Bicultural Training and Operation Systems
Early Childhood & Primary Education				
Intermediate & Secondary Education				
Community College & University Education				
Alternatives to Formal Education				

for interdisciplinary effort on a "cell by cell" basis as noted above is essential.

Last, in moving to effect these needed changes, we need to remember, particularly in working with schools and minority communities, that the process of involvement is equally as important as the product we are trying to "push." Joint genuine involvement of school and Chicano grassroots leadership is essential both from the standpoint of the expertise all can provide and because only this approach will create the required receptivity and commitment.

Patrick D. Lynch

Professionals and Clients: Goal Dissonance in Native-American Schools

One of the greatest problems of our time is the lack of response in organizations to clients. It is expressed in many ways: too much centralization in Washington, too much power given to government, too much money taken in taxes for too few services, credibility gaps between government and the public.

Organizations become increasingly bureaucratized with their development of new specializations, rules for relating to clients, limitation of competence, selectivity of professionals and clients, and structural arrangements designed to limit decision-making. Schools are bureaucracies, professional organizations are bureaucracies, churches become bureaucratic with time, so do voluntary organizations like the Red Cross, YMCA, Boy Scouts, United Fund, and health-care organizations. The advance of professionalism can be equated as well with the increase in bureaucracies as with the application of scientific knowledge. Medicine is now perhaps the most highly professionalized, most scientific, and most bureaucratized "voluntary" organization to be found. As it became more professional, medicine became by its own definition more selective of clients and less responsive to them, and more self-contained. Medicine exists now by its own ethos as much to advance its own science, as it defines that science, as to help clients.

Goode has proposed seven characteristics affecting the acceptance of an occupation as a profession:

1. Codification of knowledge and skills into a body of principles.
2. Applicability of that knowledge to concrete problems of living.

Patrick D. Lynch, College of Education, The Pennsylvania State University.

3. People of the society must believe that the knowledge has the capacity of solving the problems.

4. Members of the society must believe that it is proper that the occupational group solve the problems with the knowledge available.

5. The profession itself should help to create, organize, and transmit the knowledge.

6. The profession should be accepted as the final arbiter in any disputes over the validity of any technical solution lying within its areas of supposed competence.

7. Members of the society should view the profession as having a kind of mystery that ordinary men cannot acquire by their own efforts or even with help.[1]

Command of knowledge escalates into a mystery. The occupation becomes a priesthood of a cult perceived as necessary for taking care of certain problems. An exchange takes place as knowledge extends and society perceives a need for service based upon that knowledge. The occupation provides the service and in return is rewarded with a mystique. The mystique deepens as the occupation relates more knowledge to its service and sanctifies its practice with appropriately complex terminology.

As mystique and social distance grow, the occupation is granted more autonomy, translated into freedom to practice its complex science. Particularistic and affective relationships with clients are replaced as the older occupational members yield to the new norm creators of the profession. The new professionals hold universalistic and affectively neutral values. The more autonomous the professionals the freer supposedly to provide better services to clients. The more autonomous the professionals become, the less they can be influenced by lay control.

Until the 1970s in the Bureau of Indian Affairs, for example, the professionals were among the most independent group in American education. In fact, the Bureau constitutes a classic case of the process outlined above. The system they fashioned, however, is now undergoing extensive change. The occupation of the late Fall 1972 is symbolic of how the Bureau has changed. It is interesting to study the system as it existed and to observe the process of how autonomous professionals built this educational system.

Schools for the Native Americans (Aleuts, Eskimos, Indians) have long been run by the Bureau of Indian Affairs of the U.S. Department of the Interior. It is the purpose of this paper to discuss the nature of the Indian education system as an example of educational bureaucracy,

1. William J. Goode, "The Theoretical Limits of Professionalization," in Amitai Etzioni, *The Semi-Professions and Their Organization* (New York: The Free Press, Macmillan, 1969).

and to discuss goal-setting in that context. As the only governmental agency to govern a school system run specifically for a minority group by the federal government, the BIA has existed supposedly to serve the interests of Native peoples for well over a century. The Department of War at one time administered Indian affairs, but it finally dawned on someone that it was probably a conflict of interest that the agency dedicated to destroying a people should also administer their welfare. Hence, in 1832, the Bureau of Indian Affairs was formed.

How does a government agency determine goals for a minority group in America? Does it dissolve the group into the melting pot, protect its members as a unique part of Americana—as a museum piece —does it "modernize" but not "acculturate" them, does it turn them over to the churches, or does it let them make the great decisions about their goals and destiny? The Bureau of Indian Affairs has done all but the latter at various times in its history. There has never been a consistent policy however, that has lasted longer than thirty years. The last policy—that of self-determination—is really just beginning.

In spite of self-determination, let no one be fooled that every day is in every way better for the tribes and urban groups numbering between 800,000 and 1,000,000 by 1970 U.S. census estimates.* Land holdings and water resources of tribes have dwindled faster in the past five years than at any previous time since the days of allotment which took away two-thirds of the tribal holdings between 1887 and 1928. By 1980, it is estimated that two-thirds of the Native children will be attending urban public schools, if the flight from reservations continues. That event will leave an even smaller proportion of Native people to be the concern of the federal government. Increasingly state and public school systems will have to be made cognizant of their responsibility toward Native children; so far, states have been remarkably indifferent to their fate.

Colonial systems of Western powers, once freed and given responsibilities to enlarge their purposes, have not been notable for expanding educational opportunity at a high-quality level for the masses. Typically, they have continued to resemble the parent system far more than they have appeared to create "peoples' schools." Several African nations, for example, still have their secondary examinations graded in Paris, Cambridge, or Oxford. These systems typically have concentrated on preparing elites for the civil service (often too many for the positions available) and a limited number of professionals. Seldom have they attempted to develop the technical manpower needed by a modernizing

---

* It is important to regard U.S. census figures as estimates because of the difficulty of gathering accurate information from a people scattered among a large society, and the application of criteria of Indian membership. Native people are very likely undercounted in the decennial census.

nation. Once a nation clearly changes social directions by ending foreign economic and cultural domination, it invariably begins the task of reconstruction by attempting to change its educational system; witness Mexico, Cuba, North Vietnam, and China.

The BIA system can be said to be emerging from a long colonialist phase. With President Nixon's charge in 1970 to the Native Americans to determine their own future, goal-setting for schools (it is hoped) will increasingly become the responsibility of the Native peoples. If one views the BIA school system as a colonial system, as one prototype of other public systems in the United States run for minorities, it is possible to define it as a system in which the progressive retardation phenomenon is evident; the higher the grade, the farther the Indian children fall behind grade norms.[2] Similar findings have been established for other minority groups. In Mosteller and Moynihan we read:

> In terms of grade levels, by grade 3 the middle [class] black child is half a year behind, a year and a half by grade 6, and three by grade 12. In other words, half these children finish the 12th grade with less than the equivalent of a 9th grade education. For 12th grade Negro students throughout the nation, only 16 percent were at or above grade level. Similar results hold for Puerto Ricans, Mexican Americans, and American Indians. And this, of course, is the compelling, undisputed finding of the EEOR [*Equality of Educational Opportunity* report]. This is a central fact of American Society. It having been established, it would seem impossible for that society to ignore it.[3]

Studies made by Anderson in 1953[4] and Coombs in 1958[5] both reported lower scores for Indian children than for white children when measured by standardized achievement tests. It appears that this condition has not changed.

The Southwest Cooperative Educational Laboratory conducted a study of achievement of Native students in high schools in 1967–68. A total of 1,928 students were given pre- and post-tests in the fall and spring of that school year. The authors state:

> Again it is evident that academic achievement is progressive from grade 9 through grade 12 but not comparable with national norms. For example,

2. Philleo Nash, "An Historical Perspective: A Selective and Critical Education of Earlier Research Efforts on American Indian Education," in Herbert Aurbach, *Proceedings of the National Research Conference American Indian Education*, Kalamazoo, Michigan, Society for the Study of Social Problems, 1967.

3. Frederick Mosteller and Daniel P. Moynihan, *On Equality of Educational Opportunity* (New York: Random House, 1972), p. 24.

4. Kenneth Anderson et al., *Educational Achievement of Indian Children* (Washington, D.C.: BIA, U.S. Department of the Interior, 1953).

5. L. Madison Coombs, et al., *The Indian Child Goes to School* (Washington, D.C.: BIA, U.S. Department of the Interior, 1958).

Indian students are about one year retarded academically, as measured by the total battery score, when they enter ninth grade, but are about two and one-half years retarded when about to graduate from high school. Again as in 1967, the highest ranking is in language and the lowest is in mathematics.[6]

Bass in 1969 reported a study of Indian high school graduates of the class of 1962 from Southwestern U.S. high schools, both public and federal. Some of the findings reported were:

1. A majority of those who did not continue their education after high school were dissatisfied with their course of action. Nearly 90 percent of those who expressed discontent said they wished they had continued their education or training beyond high school so as to be qualified for more interesting and more remunerative employment.
2. Among those who continued their education after high school and those who did not, the greatest percentage stated that the most encouragement to continue their education came from parents. Non-school people such as relatives and friends, along with parents, were identified by a majority as offering most encouragement. Teachers and counselors were not cited nearly as often as those sources of encouragement.[7]

What accounts for the same progressive retardation phenomenon reported so frequently over a twenty-year period? Schools for Indian children include public schools and in those schools, too, the progressive retardation phenomenon appears. Tests may themselves be such an artifact of Anglo-American culture that they are constructed to measure "cultural growth," in which of course a child in a non-Anglo culture would usually be deficient. Norming techniques themselves may be one variable. Another explanation I would suggest is a "colonization hypothesis." Stated as simply as possible, it is that teachers of a society treating a minority as a nonparticipating force in that society will view schooling mainly as a socializing and acculturating experience rather than a cognitive experience for the children of that minority.

If the society views Indian people as a cultural island to be assimilated, the professionals in such a school system are more apt to place greater emphasis upon acculturation than upon skill-learning. Becoming able to "live in" becomes more important than learning. The silent pupil, one of the great marks of the BIA system, is viewed with satisfaction because he is soaking up the life-ways of the society,

6. Willard P. Bass, *An Analysis of Academic Achievement of Indian High School Students in Federal and Public Schools*, Albuquerque, New Mexico, A Progress Report, SWCEL (May 1969), p. 15.
7. Ibid., pp. 51–52.

and not troubling himself too much with skill-learning. BIA schools can be seen as a model of American Colonialist schools for minorities. Those minorities, when viewed as potential labor sources, can best be served not by post–high school preparation, which is the only kind of preparation that affords American children learning skills at grade-level by grade 12, but by some kind of socialization-acculturation agenda. This process during the sixties was called "motivation training." Thus, learning rules, picking up "motivation," and internalizing obedience to the system are good preparation for the kinds of jobs minority members are to be prepared to hold. Such jobs are those which Anglos have disdained and so are in constant demand for filling, but have few applicants. Those who learn skills at too high a level are no good for those kinds of jobs.

The goal displacement of acculturation for cognitive skills is hardly a surprising or unique phenomenon in American schools. A school of educational philosophy has held this position quite consistently for some fifty years. Present-day educational reformers are casting the same position into a rhetoric of despair over the schools' mission. That thinking goes something like this: Based on information from sources such as the Coleman report of 1966, it seems that schools really don't make a difference, but economic class and family circumstances account for the greatest variability in achievement. So let the schools simply perform custodial or socialization functions, and let the society, or family, or "learning networks" (if they ever materialize) take over the job of teaching skills.

To argue this is to presume that Indian schools have attempted what in fact they have not attempted. The apparent goal-lessness in this area of the Bureau schools has been striking. The agenda of socialization was arrived at by professional consensus, but not made explicit in Bureau memoranda or rules. The effect was however as powerful. Parents may have desired an emphasis on skills. The Bureau schools, however, did not stress skill-learning, and certainly did not stress post–high school preparation as their aim. They stated no aims, but by agreement of the reluctant "everyone" concerned, the Bureau schools' aim was to acculturate, and for an elite, to teach skills—an entirely rational goal structure for a colonialist system, by which the occupiers gradually bring around the natives to the system.

Changes in goal-setting have occurred only recently, as Native groups have begun to ask questions about the explicit goals of their schools. Once questions are asked, it becomes difficult to state, much less defend colonialist aims; impossible to admit frankly that socialization-acculturation has been more important than skill-learning. With increased inputs of clients' opinions into the goal setting structures, these schools will be forced to continue to move toward skill-learning and toward post–high school preparation. Skill-learning is better training for job preparation than socialization-acculturation, so in their wisdom the Indian parents and students are in fact proving better decision-makers than the professionals have been. If only we could bring such a Jeffersonian approach into medical care! The revision of organizational aims can only be made effective through more client decision-making, not less. This is where the professions in America have made their greatest social error—they have presumed that what is best for the growth of their profession (in the professionals' eyes) is best for the client. It hasn't been so in the Bureau schools, and it hasn't been so in health care, government, agriculture, economics, or welfare. The BIA offers the best example of the education profession working undisturbed by clients' influence. It is worth serious study for that reason alone. It is a study of the kind of system professionals build, left to their own devices.

Goals for American schools have been inferred from societal norms and aims. Local value structures have had little impact upon cognitive goal structures of American schools but considerable impact upon their noncognitive goals. Waller describes community norms as affecting the roles played by teachers and students; these roles are mainly outside the concerns for cognitive growth.[8] In schools for Native Americans (Aleuts, Eskimos, Indians), goals have been those of the society, not of the community being served. This paper examines that dissonance in the goal structure of schools for Native Americans.

In order to examine goal-setting it is necessary first to examine the structure of schools for Native Americans. Native children attend public schools, federal schools, private and mission schools. In 1971–72 about two-thirds of Native children attended public schools, one-fourth attended federal schools, which are administered by the Bureau of Indian Affairs, and one-twentieth attended mission and private schools. The percentage attending public schools has been increasing while the percentage attending BIA schools and private or mission schools has been declining. The mission schools are rapidly dwindling in consequence, but the private school, including the Indian owned and run school, may become a very important type.

American educators are less well-acquainted with the Native-American school system than they are with foreign systems. The Indian schools, included in the term Native-American schools, have long been insulated from the influence of professional organizations, parents, and tribal cultural influences.

The school system run by the Bureau of Indian Affairs historically consisted of boarding schools in which children as young as five years

8. Willard Waller, *The Sociology of Teaching* (New York: John Wiley Science Editions, 1965).

of age entered to begin a life in a "total" environment, relieved only by visits from parents or friends, or visits to home and family. Recently, boarding schools have relaxed visiting hour regulations and permitted students to visit homes sometimes every week. As recently as 1969, such frequent visits home were discouraged or forbidden in many boarding schools because it was feared that the students would not come back. The boarding school described here is the kind of institution that alumni remember with such vividness—Haskell, Chemawa, Ft. Sill, Phoenix Indian School, Riverside, Intermountain, Albuquerque Indian School—all are examples of institutions in which an Indian boy or girl often spent as much as twelve years.

The boarding school as a total environment in some cases, like Chemawa, Intermountain, Riverside (California), and Wahpeton, is far removed from the living area of its clients. Visits home and from home are difficult. Students come long distances to schools by bus, airplane, or train in the Fall. Many students return home only in the Spring. One can distinguish boarding schools as organizations by the characteristics of autonomy of staff, psychological insulation from the culture, rigidity of organizational processes, and extreme specialization of functions. All four are hallmarks of an educational bureaucracy.

Great distances from client populations lent autonomy to the staff of the boarding school. There was no need to be concerned about parental visits or board "inspections." Boards are new to Native boarding schools and are still officially classified as "advisory." This means that legally they have had no power to dispose of resources, appoint staff, or influence curriculum. However, advisory boards increasingly are exercising a more legitimate kind of power conferred by tribal authority over their children and by virtue of informal agreements with the BIA administration. Autonomy is beginning to erode as advisory boards exercise increasing influence and power.

Autonomy of staff was assured also by virtue of the great distance from Washington as well as from the client populations. Contrary to the mythology created by educational bureaucrats at the local and area levels, administrators at those levels had great power. Decision-making over curriculum and allocation of resources was delegated to area and agency levels.* Centralization in education in fact is still not possible because of unique arrangements which provide that the chief education officer of the BIA in Washington often has no line authority over officials in the field. It is only through the manipulation of the

* The Bureau of Indian Affairs has area offices at Juneau; Sacramento; Portland; Billings; Minneapolis; Aberdeen; Phoenix; Albuquerque; Window Rock, Arizona; Muskogee, Oklahoma; Anadarko, Oklahoma, and for the Western and Southeastern U.S. tribes at Washington, D.C. Each area is divided into agencies, and schools come under agency authorities.

budget that the chief education officer can have any significant power.

Among the other consequences of great autonomy for units in the field is the lack of an information base in the central office. There has been no collection of test scores, dropout data, placement data after graduation, per pupil unit costs by area, agency, or school in the central office in Washington. In 1972 the central office staff finally began the planning of an information retrieval system that will furnish some of these data to the Washington office. Traditionally, it has been assumed that such data are needed only at the area level. Area offices and schools vary widely in the kind of data they collect and the frequency with which they collect the data.

The nature of the boarding schools' organizational structure is remarkably similar whether in Alaska or Oklahoma. Autonomy at the area and school level did not breed variety, but a remarkable similarity. Goals were seldom stated but were obvious and evident as in any colonialist system. In one study, one set of goals seen by staff appeared to be to socialize the Native child to "American" society. The students meanwhile saw preparation for post–high school education as the main function of the school—a goal seen as highly unrealistic by the staff.[9]

Autonomy provided the school administrator the means to resist inspection from above and from without. It was a powerful protection against accountability to the budget-makers and the clients. The game simply was to keep enrollments up so that staff could be maintained or increased, and other resources could be gathered as opportunities provided. Witness the disparity in per pupil expenditures reported in the Abt Associates study. A low of $282 at the Tuba City, Arizona boarding school, which was an elementary school, and a high of $555 was reported for the Loneman Day School, an elementary school in the Aberdeen area.[10] While costs are difficult to compare because of the mix of boarding and day students, high school and elementary schools, it is clear that competition among administrators accounts for the success of one area over another. "Indian politics" has been played by administrators in efforts to bring into focus tribal needs and priorities at various times. Competition among units results in another phenomenon, that of inconsistency in allocative priority. Today's outstanding school, heavily funded, may become tomorrow's forgotten unit. The success of tribal authorities in working with administrators to obtain resources from Washington accounts for the waxing or waning of a school's relative resource position. Administrators who can work with tribal authorities and the state's congressional delegation can wield the clout needed to bring home the resources.

9. *Systems Analysis of Indian Education in BIA Schools*, Abt Associates, Inc., 55 Wheeler St., Cambridge, Massachusetts, 1969, pp. 46–52.
10. Ibid., pp. 17–20.

A state's congressional delegation plays a powerful role in obtaining resources for a BIA boarding school. Boarding schools, with their large professional and nonprofessional staffs and local purchasing power, are a boon to a local economy. Intermountain School at Brigham City, Utah, is a case in point. There is no logic behind the location of a boarding school which at one time housed well over 2,000 Navajo students, and still houses over 1,000 students, some 300 air miles north of the edge of the Navajo reservation. Such a school is clearly a "smoke-less industry" for the town.

Another example of how the location of Indian schools is viewed by many communities comes to mind. In the Fall of 1971 a private college in a Southwestern community closed for lack of funds. Many citizens had spent their savings on bonds to build the college's build-ings. In desperation, the community went to the state for help, which refused it on the grounds that there were already too many state-sup-ported colleges clamoring for funds. After the state's refusal, the com-munity made an effort to bring an Indian school onto the vacated premises from a large city over 200 miles away. The Indian student population would have been enrolled hundreds of miles from home, but the only point of significance to that community was that its build-ings needed to be filled and its economic plight alleviated. The Indian community did not desire the transfer so it did not occur, but a decade earlier that outcome might have been different.

Congressional representatives are close to resource decisions in the BIA because of the relative importance such resources assume in states such as South Dakota, Alaska, New Mexico, and Arizona. An interac-tion between BIA administrators, tribal representatives, and the state's congressional delegation frequently affects resource allocations. Tribal representatives are now becoming more powerful in this interaction, but the participants are similar, the congressmen now are apt to be more conscious of direct tribal representation rather than assuming that the BIA administrators have the "last word."

Goal determination at a school level is increasingly becoming possi-ble because of the tradition of autonomy, especially as school boards be-gin to wield a new kind of legitimate but nonstatutory power. Those advisory boards now seen as clearly representing clients can exercise power over appointments and transfers of professional and non-professional staff. Boards are exercising veto power over selection of professionals and power to recommend positively certain nonprofes-sional staff. It is difficult for an administrator of a BIA school in 1973 to be able to hold his position in the face of outright opposition from board members.

Instructional goals are not yet being set by advisory boards, but it is clear that they may soon be doing this. Many board members have been "trained" to act as public school board members even though their legal position is much different. Congress could empower the advisory school boards to act as legally constituted federal boards, of course, and with such power, they could become de facto governing boards. It is possible that there will emerge a power struggle between local advisory boards and the national advisory council for Indian education or other boards created by Congress or the executive branch for Indian education. In that event, goal-setting will become a process of interaction between national and local bodies much like the state and local school boards interact to set goals for public schools.

Autonomy of the professionals in the BIA has meant isolation from professional organizations. Professionals within the BIA were inducted quickly and thoroughly into the bureaucratic norms—workshops and training sessions abounded. However, the BIA was poorly represented, if at all, in such national organizations as American Association of School Administrators, Association for Supervision and Curriculum Development, American Educational Research Association, American Psychological Association, National Association of Secondary School Principals, or National Association of Elementary School Principals. The isolation even extended to state education associations. Few teachers were released to attend the state or national meetings. It is not surprising then that so few professionals know much about the BIA system. Isolation maintains ignorance by outsiders who might otherwise become curious and interested. Acquiring the language of the insiders was difficult unless one interacted with those in the system, and without the special terminology, an outsider quickly betrayed his ignorance of the intricacies of the system.

A second organizational feature of the boarding school has been the isolation of the institution from the client's culture. A radical culture break is demanded of the child entering into the boarding school for the first time. The difficulty of access by parents to the school, the historic antipathy of the BIA schools to children's using their tribal language, the remoteness of location from the child's home, and the immersion of the child into a strange new "total environment" called for a break with the past not unlike that involved with a prison or a mental institution. The child divorced from his culture was forced to become totally dependent upon the system, its rewards, and its objectives. A student entered a closed system and had to surrender completely to its ways or get out. Leon states that separation of children five to eight years old can produce serious effects and that there is no doubt such children are unhappy in boarding school.[11]

11. Robert L. Leon, "Mental Health Considerations in the Indian Boarding School Program," as reported in Special Subcommittee on Indian Education, *Indian Education,* Part 5 (Washington: U.S. Government Printing Office, 1969), p. 2205.

Apart from the question of whether children suffer emotional harm, which is a most serious problem for boarding schools to consider, it is apparent that a subculture created by students and staff is evolved. It is a boarding school subculture, perhaps neither Indian nor Anglo, but with elements of both cultures. It has not yet been described in a scholarly work. It has been lamented or praised depending upon the commentator's experience, but there is unquestionably an alumni segment of the boarding schools with a special set of experiences who have had a powerful impact upon modern Indian life. As in all total institutions, the subculture thus created has a life and rationale of its own. It has little apparent connection with tribal life and customs. It is doubtful that it "prepares" the participants for anything other than more institutional life—perhaps graduates of boarding school do well in the military because of their prior training.

In the past the dominant role in the lives of students in the boarding school has been played by the nonprofessional, or nonacademic staff. These staff are mainly Native people who run the dormitories. They hold high custodial values. Their main purpose has been to control students and keep the system running with meals, sleeping, recreation, and orderly behavior. The outward appearances of this living system are no more Indian than Anglo, even though the employees administering their part of the system are Indian. The relationship of the living portion of the student's day to his culture can only be seen occasionally as a boy or girl displays something from home in his room or above his bed. There have been few attempts to bring tribal customs into the dormitory life. It is seen as no more "Indian" or "Native" than the classrooms with their picture of Pilgrim fathers marching to church, guns in hand. So that portion of the total environment which might have been related to the student's culture has been no more like "home" than the classroom or laboratory. The entire environment, then, has been designed as an alien climate for the student. Cultural insularity has bred its own subculture with its own norms and cues to the child. The child learns a new life in a setting unlike either his own culture or the great society enveloping it.

The sudden rise of student militance and the dawning of "due process" for student expression has shocked the system to its foundations. The student subculture has become in the last few years powerful enough to challenge the system from within. The boarding schools are now facing a crisis of major proportions as students conscious of their tribal relationships and their power to embarrass the administration are creating demands for freedom unheard of three years ago. The school subculture rests on a student compliance that is rapidly withering, and the system as yet has not found ways to cope with student resistance to authority. Insulated as the boarding school is from tribal authority or community, the administration is helpless to call upon community or tribal authority to resolve its dilemma. In a public school close to its community, the parents and staff together would propose solutions to problems posed by student power, but the boarding school is still spiked on the hitherto great advantage of insularity. In order to resolve its dilemma, the system must surrender its insularity and autonomy in order to gain assistance from its clients—the Indian tribal organizations.

A rationale offered by the system for its insularity in some cases has been that its clientele came from diverse tribal origins. In order to avoid mediating and negotiating with such a diverse community, the boarding schools chose to invent their own culture. As Native Americans build their own secondary structures, however, and rely less and less on their primary structures such as tribe, clan, and family, this will offer less of an excuse to the boarding school and force it to deal with more formal structures with specialized interests and concerns.

As intertribal relations become more extensive, negotiations among tribal groups for setting educational goals might be predicted, even after early conflict over such goals. As tribes compare goal expectations, they will become more experienced at setting goals for Bureau schools. It has become obvious to tribal groups that as they postulate goals, alternatives other than BIA schools have become obvious, hence the creative surge beginning in 1968 of alternative schools such as contract schools, tribal schools, tribal community colleges with open enrollment, and tribal adult education programs.

The goal-setting mechanisms have been set in motion, and the creative force of the Native-American communities will continue to create opportunities for entire tribes. The products of such imaginative tribal pedagogy is a frontier for schooling undreamed of by those Cassandras, the Illichs and Jenckses; they lean away from such despair of man's ability to change his institutions.

A third characteristic of the BIA boarding school is its organizational rigidity. The bureaucratic powers of the civil servant and of the professional educator have combined to invent a system atrophied at a certain point of development. That point in time for the classroom seems to have been somewhere in the 1930s. The dormitory system appears to have been perfected earlier, perhaps in the 1920s when its military and moralistic regimen were routinized much as it was at least until about 1969.[12]

The inflexibility of organization is due in great part to the civil servant who administers all aspects of the Bureau but the educational

12. The Meriam Report describes dormitory life as it existed almost unchanged until 1969 in Lewis Meriam et al., *The Problem of Indian Administration* (Baltimore: The Johns Hopkins Press, 1928).

program. Buildings, grounds, payroll, personnel, materials and equipment purchasing all must be negotiated by the educator with the non-
educator civil servant whose one function is to maintain the system.
The nonacademic functions are so rigidly controlled that processes
relatively simple in a public school system such as obtaining travel
orders and payment, promotion, and building modifications are extremely time-consuming and difficult. The BIA education system consists only of the academic and dormitory personnel. All other operational personnel and administrative personnel are responsible to
officials other than educators. Professionals must justify the rearrange-
ment of classroom walls to functionaries who have only building construction and maintenance responsibility for educational decision-
making. These functionaries have less contact with the clients than the
educators, and so feel little compulsion to modify the system or even
to make it work efficiently. Rules for relationships between the educational and maintenance functions of the system are numerous. If en-
forced literally, they limit normal work activity and almost prohibit
decision-making. It is easy to prevent action in such a system but difficult to get work done within it. It is miraculous that any really innovative or flexible structural arrangements can be made in the BIA under
these conditions.

Finally, an organizational characteristic of the boarding school is
extreme specialization. The boarding school is divided into academic
and dormitory areas. The former is staffed by professional personnel
who have little or nothing to do with the living characteristics of the
system. The professionals teach and administer the academic program.
There is little interaction between academic staff and students outside
of school hours. The dormitory personnel have control of the students
during all the remaining hours, which constitute by far the larger portion of the day.

The dormitory staff, referred to as "guidance personnel" in many
schools, include mainly nonprofessional staff who are Natives. Dormitory personnel are sub-professional, have lower civil service grades than
professional personnel, and are not paid as well. The dormitory positions historically have been the entry into the educational system for
the Indian people. The higher-grade and remunerated professional
ranks are largely filled by non-Native people, so there exists a graded
structure, the base of which consists of Native sub-professionals, and
the top of which is occupied by non-Native professionals.

The dormitory, or "guidance" personnel have the main custodial responsibilities for the student. They must wrestle with the alcohol, glue-
sniffing, absenteeism, and other behavior problems of students. It is not
surprising that their concern is primarily more the control of students.
Faced with increasing student restiveness over strict rules, the dormi-

tory personnel have had to bend the rules or face student reaction which they might not be able to handle. The academic staff have been largely uninvolved in solving these "dormitory" problems. The students might be reacting against both academic and dormitory features of the system but the academic staff are insulated from the protests of the students. The dormitory staff and administration are the most involved with protest groups. The administrators, at least locally, are vulnerable.

The nature of the two roles is not as important in this discussion as the rigid separation of roles and extreme specializations. Civil service rules are partly responsible for this phenomenon of exclusivity, but the boarding school itself has created a rigid interpretation of what is academic and what is living area or dormitory. In order to use the living or dormitory time of students for programmed academic or study functions, a breakdown of the separation of function is required which is not easy to accomplish.

In addition to boarding schools, the BIA education system includes day schools, which are attended by students living at home, and peripheral dormitories in which students live and from which they attend public schools. Day schools do not exhibit the characteristics of psychological or cultural separation from clients to the degree that boarding schools do. Indeed, some day schools (such as those in the Hopi area) have more community involvement than do most public schools. The peripheral dormitories exhibit the characteristic of insulation quite as much as do boarding schools. The peripheral dorm does not have an academic staff. Relationships between dormitory staffs of those institutions and the faculty of the public schools attended by the Indian students are rare and fleeting. The peripheral or "bordertown" dormitory originated in an effort to bring as many Indian children into the public school system as possible. It is also a great resource for public school systems which receive large amounts of money from the BIA for those students attending the school.

The emergence of the contract school such as the Ramah school in New Mexico has created a new kind of institution in Indian education. Funded by the BIA, the school is not operated by the BIA. A board exercises real control. Accountability for program to the community is evident. Fiscal accountability exists toward the federal funding authority. Accountability for programs in BIA-operated schools, if it exists at all, is upward. Fiscal accountability in the BIA is more important and is upward, not toward the community, which does not control funding.

The autonomy of the area and local units of the BIA-operated system did not make program accountability necessary. Data on outputs of the schools were not gathered consistently nor were they reported upward. Fiscal controls were exerted from above, but not according to program.

This system, then, is complex and highly resistive to change. Bureaucratic processes are slow and only extreme crises appear to generate anything other than the most sluggish operation of the system. Faced with such extreme rigidity in a rule-oriented, highly specialized organization with diverse sources of decision-making power compartmentalized and encapsulated, confronting the system became necessary for clients desirous of change.

Several stimuli caused reorientation of goals and subsequent movement in the system. One major stimulus was the creation of Office of Economic Opportunity (OEO) and its Indian desk in the mid-1960s. With OEO funds, Native people had the opportunity to practice leadership in erecting new organizations and relating them to the older tribal structures. OEO funds enabled Indian leaders to meet one another, create new communication systems, and to attack Native problems at a national level. Native leaders were drawn into national policy discussions as well as discussions about local needs. Both sets of needs began to be defined by a wider leadership cadre defining and involving larger numbers of clients.

Having funds and control over Head Start, Neighborhood Youth Corps programs and a few contract operations provided experience to emergent professionals who gained experimental knowledge. It was but a step from experimenting with Head Start to thinking experimentally about the Bureau system. In the Rough Rock demonstration school, OEO and BIA funds were combined to create a pilot system with undreamed-of consequences for Indian education.

With President Nixon's statement concerning self-determination and the appointment of Indian leaders in the BIA, it was possible for ideas to be translated into action. Contract schools have become possible for many tribes. A tribe contracting BIA operations as the Zuni began to do in 1969 now is promised for the Navajo Nation. Contracted operations are an interesting functional equivalent because they keep the bureaucracy from growing. The personnel of contracted schools are not necessarily civil service personnel, hence a built-in method of reducing the bureaucracy is possible. Contract operations are more flexible because they do not require use of the old rules. They give boards direct, not advisory control.

Goals can be used to determine outputs of schools. Goals can be used to direct programs toward accomplishing goals and can provide a rationale for the use of resources. Involving clients in the goal-setting of organizations can provide a self-adjusting mechanism that will make bureaucracies attentive to their main purpose, which is that of serving clients. Goal statements cannot be easily constructed without data gathered and provided to clients on prior performance. The knowledge Native peoples have now of their school system comes more from personal experiences of family members and friends dropping out of school, or being forced out, feeling the frustration of inadequate college preparation, or suffering rejection in the job market for lack of proper preparation. These powerful personal experiences are common among Native-American families. The data concerning achievement of the Indian child are not easy to find because they have not been systematically collected, and when collected have not been disseminated to tribal groups.

Processing of information concerning students by parents and students themselves is a feedback mechanism that professional educators have been fearful of. Yet we know of no better regulating mechanism for the student to observe and change his learning patterns, or for the organization to modify its teaching function, according to what we know of individual and group behavior.

The emergence of functionally equivalent educational institutions controlled by Native Americans is bringing educational accountability. Native groups will have to be able to use the information developed by the system to make intelligent decisions regarding system goals and objectives, and decisions regarding their own behavior vis-à-vis the system. To keep hands on the system, the clients and their representatives will need to be able to monitor the system's performance. Without that the system will find a new excuse for socialization, and plenty are available. We in the education profession must explore the alternatives and when necessary call the goals of "living in" or "socialization" by their right names and be honest about their consequences.

Predicting the future of education is like predicting the ecclesiastical future. One is tempted to foretell more of the same—linear forecasting. One hopes for qualitative changes, however, of the kind that began to ventilate the church after John XXIII. Changes in structure are predictive to some extent, and a very limited extent, of the output changes in education. The top structure of governments and education ministries in French- and English-speaking Africa changed, but so far greatly different output changes have not occurred. The colonialist model is hard to change because it breeds products who think of it in existing normative terms. A colonialist system does not exist to change its society, but to perpetuate it with minimum discontent and dislocation.

Changes are not bred by the education system, or within it. Great changes only come from without, in response to great societal pressures. Colonialist education systems remain intact for centuries—witness Latin America, where only Cuba's system has been changed, and where the Chilean system will change further only under greater societal duress. America's education system has responded only under the most severe pressures. Brown vs. Board of Education in 1954, Sputnik, Tinker vs. Des Moines Ocean Hill-Brownsville, Title I of ESEA, Head Start, and

Serrano vs. Priest are examples of society's forcing goal changes upon the system. True, the final reaction to each of these events will not be catalogued for a generation, at least, but the point is that these events were stimulated from without, not from within the educational system. There existed no body of literature written by professional educators calling for an end to segregated black and white schools prior to 1954. Professionals were not emphasizing reform in science and foreign languages prior to Sputnik's stimulus. Educational administrators were not leading their systems for more recognition of students' rights prior to the Des Moines decision of 1969. Dorothy Day, James Agee, and Michael Harrington wrote about poverty before 1961; the voice of conscience was not professional. School finance experts called mainly for ever more complex state aid formulas, but none called into question the very nature of the property-tax-supported system prior to Serrano vs. Priest. Education has had prophets of philosophy and methodology; we glory in our Dewey and Counts, but where was our Myrdal?

Professionalism in education has not served as prophecy, but as very conventional wisdom. The future is not built by professionals who predict shinier "nows" given mountains of new money. It is built by the politicians and jurists whom we decry and lament. Those who say no to our conventionality (usually in their greater people's wisdom) have other goals in mind. The control of education by future-oriented board members and legislators is what will ultimately move and change the system, its goals, and its outputs. Those who say "teach the boards to allow the professionals to have their way" are saying "hang on to the present." Professionalism in medicine declares that woman's life span must exceed man's by ten years—that's how it is. Professional engineers concentrate on building more highways and ignore the mass transit possibilities. Agricultural economists can't see how we can have small farms and small towns. Professionals like to "train" school boards—and there are legions who would like to train Indian school boards to behave just like public school boards in the conventional wisdom of system processes. The creative movements in the education of Native Americans haven't come as a result of any paraprofessional training given to school boards. School boards can give direction to professionals by choosing goals and making choices from among program possibilities. Professionals, left to themselves, don't set goals, but know only how to run a system to benefit certain kinds of children. A fine hierarchy of objectives thus subtly comes into being when professionals are allowed complete latitude in direction by lay boards. Quietly, the system selects certain students, prepares certain students for certain occupations, and disposes of others. The rationale for all of this is mystifying.

Schools have power. They have power over children and over communities. They have power over the professionals and nonprofessionals in the system. Checks and balances create a healthy distribution of power and place limits on the accretion of power within the system. The danger of assigning the power in the school system to the professionals results in a distorted view of the community held by the school. The community diminishes and the school assumes its own reason for being. The school becomes almost a thing in itself, like art for the sake of art, with no relationship to the world around it. Like the mysterious goings-on at Los Alamos prior to 1945, it seems to consume endless resources, but passes along nothing. The American Society is now rebuilding its educational framework. This framework is necessarily political, as the network of power distribution might better be called. Redistribution of power appears to include the program accountability by professionals to laymen at a local level, and by professionals at a local level to professionals and political bodies at state and federal levels. As this redistribution occurs, there is an opportunity for Native-American communities to build their own accountability structures at local, tribal, and national levels. Such a system need not parallel or resemble the public school system as it is restructured. The distribution of power in the Native system can be unique. Professionals, it appears, will no longer have an autonomous role in whatever system is created by Native Americans, so the professional will be more responsive to the community whether it be local or larger in scope. The boards created by the Native Americans may be overlapping or conflicting. They need not be neatly compartmentalized and may be competitive between local and tribal levels or between tribal and national levels. It may be more healthy to have unclarified zones of power between levels of boards so that negotiation can work out the necessary power allocations. The public school boards are constantly testing their powers against state school boards, and both are allied against federal encroachments. It would be presumptuous for observers to expect the Native communities to do that which public school systems have never been able to do in stabilizing power arrangements. Indeed, there are powerful arguments against too stable arrangements. Local public school boards for too long ignored social needs and state school boards appeared too helpless or too indifferent to intervene and correct inequities at either local or state levels. In this time of restructuring, Native communities have an opportunity to experiment with many different kinds of structural arrangements. Public school systems could benefit by having some new models to observe.

If the BIA system diminishes in importance and, as now seems likely, a much larger proportion of Native students attend public schools, some novel structural alternatives may be called for. As the function of operating schools declines, the BIA's advocacy role may have to be increased. As power is turned over to the Native communities, new kinds of boards at national, tribal, and local levels may be called for. Boards may exist with power over federal funds or over certain programs. Advocacy boards without funds and program control would lack power. Boards could be formed to interact with public school boards and state school boards, for example, with the power of monitoring programs and funds for Native children. The federal responsibility to educate Native children could be delegated to such boards. Whatever form the power arrangements take, the structures should be created by Native people. These can and should become models for all educational systems. This society needs more diversity in education, and when we begin to reconstruct the educational system we may be able to tolerate some structural alternatives among states and communities. The direction of the school in preparing students for occupations and post–high school education can best be set by boards. A multiplicity of choices for students can be guaranteed by a complex control system. Diversity of structure and distribution of power among boards can be a stimulus to guarantee differential function and output. Tolerance of diversity within the society and within educational frameworks is not incompatible with excellence of professional effort.

An analysis of the system of education built by professionals, especially the boarding school, provides a case in which the professionals worked without client interference. The model was neither adaptive to clients nor innovative. It combined the conventional public school classroom with a military dormitory life. Professionals without client intervention did not necessarily build the best educational world. The new school models constructed by Native professionals and lay people are adaptive and creative. They are structurally different, have different programs, and are adaptive to clients. And they appear to have goals.

American education needs the diversity of these models. We can learn from the discussions of goals between the community members of such schools and their professionals. Models are hard to invent; professionals are now straining for innovation. Rough Rock, Rock Point, and Ramah are innovative, but their greatest innovativeness is their relevance to their community. They didn't pay $100,000 a year to a certain teacher, they don't leave the lights on at night, and they aren't built on slogans like "every kid a winner." Professionals and lay people are playing genuinely new roles in these schools. The danger to professionals lies not in having to work with the community in designing model schools but in having to explain to communities what poor schools are doing.

Postscript to Anglo America

Have you learned lessons only of those who admired you, and were
  tender with you, and stood aside for you?
Have you not learned great lessons from those who reject you, and
  brace themselves against you?
or who treat you with contempt, or dispute the passage with you?

Walt Whitman